MW01167075

DIRECTORY of PROFESSIONAL RESUME WRITERS

How to Find and Work with a Pro to Accelerate Your Job Search

Louise Kursmark

Directory of Professional Resume Writers

© 2008 by Louise Kursmark

Published by JIST Works, an imprint of JIST Publishing
7321 Shadeland Station, Suite 200
Indianapolis, IN 46256-3923
Phone: 800-648-JIST Fax: 877-454-7839 E-mail: info@jist.com

Visit our Web site at **www.jist.com** for information on JIST, free job search tips, tables of contents and sample pages, and ordering instructions for our many products!

See the back of this book for additional JIST titles and ordering information. Quantity discounts are available for JIST books. Have future editions of JIST books automatically delivered to you on publication through our convenient standing order program. Please call our Sales Department at 800-648-5478 for a free catalog and more information.

Trade Product Manager: Lori Cates Hand
Copy Editor: Susan Dunn
Cover Designer: Katy Bodenmiller
Cover Photo: Veer Images
Interior Designer and Page Layout: Toi Davis
Proofreaders: Linda Seifert, Jeanne Clark
Indexer: Joy Dean Lee

Printed in the United States of America
12 11 10 09 08 07 9 8 7 6 5 4 3 2 1

Library of Congress Cataloging-in-Publication Data
Kursmark, Louise.
Directory of professional résumé writers : how to find and work with a pro to accelerate your job search / Louise Kursmark.
p. cm.
Includes index.
ISBN-13: 978-1-59357-519-9 (alk. paper)
1. Résumé writers--Directories. 2. Résumés (Employment) 3. Job hunting. 4. Career development. I. Title.
HF5383.K868 2008
650.14'2029--dc22
2007044966

All rights reserved. No part of this book may be reproduced in any form or by any means, or stored in a database or retrieval system, without prior written permission of the publisher except in the case of brief quotations embodied in articles or reviews. Making copies of any part of this book for any purpose other than your own personal use is a violation of United States copyright laws. For permission requests, please contact the Copyright Clearance Center at www.copyright.com or (978) 750-8400.

We have been careful to provide accurate information in this book, but it is possible that errors and omissions have been introduced. Please consider this in making any career plans or other important decisions. Trust your own judgment above all else and in all things.

Trademarks: All brand names and product names used in this book are trade names, service marks, trademarks, or registered trademarks of their respective owners.

ISBN 978-1-59357-519-9

CONTENTS

INTRODUCTION

Changing jobs is a high-stress, high-stakes event. After all, your career choices have enormous impact on your life. The job you get (or don't get) influences your income and lifestyle, your daily routine, perhaps your relationships with loved ones, and ultimately your personal happiness! And each job you take affects the next job and thus alters your career path in some way.

With so much riding on the outcome, it's no surprise that the things you need to do to get that new job often feel daunting and stressful. Writing a resume, contacting employers, going on interviews, and negotiating salary are all essential parts of the process, but they're probably not your favorite activities or your greatest skills.

Luckily, there are professionals who can help you—people who are experts in the art and science of resume writing and all aspects of job search and career management.

The Expanding Career Services Industry

No one knows precisely how many professional resume writers there are in the English-speaking world. The five major resume-writing associations whose members were invited to contribute to this book together contain nearly 1,700 members, but this is just the tip of the iceberg. Facts like these make it difficult to establish firm numbers:

- The majority of professional resume writers are sole proprietors of small practices and thus might be overlooked in industry analyses.
- Some resume writers work part-time while pursuing full-time careers in other fields.
- Larger resume-writing firms typically employ resume writers as on-call contractors, enabling the firms to adjust their staffing as demand ebbs and flows. The majority of these contractors run their own private practices as well.
- Although not their primary line of business, resume writing and editing services are also provided by many others in the career field—people such as career coaches, career counselors, outplacement consultants, college and university career center professionals, military career transition specialists, and even recruiters.

Numbers may be hard to pin down, but there is no doubt that the career services field is growing. In fact, the Bureau of Labor Statistics reports that "Employment

Services" will be one of the fastest-growing industries in the U.S. during the coming decade. And when you think about it, this vigorous growth makes a lot of sense. It simply mirrors the dramatic changes that have taken place in the world of work over the last generation.

The New World of Work

Thirty or forty years ago, it was common for new workers to emerge from high school, college, apprenticeship, or another training program and start to work at a company that would remain their employer until they retired. As you might imagine, there wasn't much demand for professional resume writers or career coaches!

Now, of course, the entire scenario has changed, and "work history" is a much less stable, more fluid concept than it was for our parents or grandparents. Workers move freely from job to job and employer to employer. Periods of self-employment might mix with temporary, contract, consulting, or interim assignments. Job tenure and employer tenure have grown short, as shown by these data published in 2006 by the Bureau of Labor Statistics:

- The median tenure with current employers is only 4 years—and for employees between the ages of 25 and 34, it is only 2.9 years.
- The average "Young Baby Boomer" (born between 1957 and 1964) held an average of 10.5 jobs from ages 18 to 40.

Not only do people change jobs and employers more than they did in the past, but also the entire method of looking for a job changed permanently with the advent of the Internet. In the past, job seekers would scan their local newspapers and mail in a resume, or perhaps show up at their target employer and fill out an application. Given the relatively small number of candidates, recruiters and employers would carefully peruse every resume and application.

Now, job seekers can zap out a resume in response to literally thousands of jobs they can find every day in just a few minutes on the Internet. Employers can post their jobs on dozens of sites and plug in the precise keywords for the qualifications they are seeking. In theory, it's a great system. But in practice, employers are awash in resumes and simply don't have the time to carefully consider each candidate's qualifications. In today's fast-growing economy, the volume is high and the pace is quick, and it's easy for resumes (and candidates) to get lost in the system.

An entire industry has sprung up to meet the challenges of this volatile environment, as more and more people are recognizing the value of enlisting an expert to help them stand out in a very large crowd and manage repeated career transitions.

Who Are These Experts?

Career services professionals include resume writers, coaches, consultants, counselors, and people who work at state one-stop/workforce development agencies, college and university career centers, and military transition centers. Many work as independent practitioners or as contractors to larger firms—and sometimes they do both!

These experts came about their expertise in a variety of ways. People who use the title *counselor* are usually state-licensed and have advanced degrees in a counseling discipline. Others who call themselves *coaches* or *consultants* might have a background in business or human resources along with some coach training; they might or might not require licensing by the state. There is no college major or licensing requirement for *resume writers,* but there are numerous training programs, credentialing bodies, and professional associations through which resume writers can learn the fundamental skills, tools, and trends of their profession.

Headhunters Are Not Career Services Providers

It's a common belief that job seekers can enlist the services of a recruiter, or headhunter, to find a job. Before you put all of your eggs in the recruiter basket, consider the reality of recruiter relationships:

- Recruiters don't work for you; they work for the companies that pay their fees. Thus, they have no intrinsic loyalty to individual job seekers. Their loyalty lies in meeting the employer's request by finding the right candidate for a specific search. They are not concerned whether or not you are that candidate.
- Recruiters will not look for a job for you. They will attempt to match you up to jobs they are currently recruiting for. If you're not a perfect match, they have no motivation to spend any time or effort on your job search.

This might sound like a harsh assessment of the recruiting industry, but once you understand their priorities and loyalties, you can stop expecting them to do unrealistic things—like finding a job for you—and rely on them to be your advocate and ally only when you are a prime candidate for one of their searches. In that instance, they will be extremely helpful and valuable!

This book will help you navigate through the sea of professionals who can help you with your resume and your career. Drawing upon my own experience as a professional resume writer and career consultant for more than 15 years, I help you understand what a resume writer can—and *can't*—do for you. I give you some guidelines to help you evaluate the expertise, experience, qualifications, and approach of various writers and select the one who is the very best fit for your specific needs. And finally, I provide a directory of professional resume writers, sorted into areas of expertise, to give you a starting point for selecting the right expert for you.

How This Book Is Organized

In part 1, you'll find in-depth discussions of how to find your resume writer, beginning with an overview of what your writer can and can't do for you (chapter 1), followed by factors for evaluating resume writers and specific questions to ask (chapter 2), then a description of the various steps involved in developing your new resume (chapter 3). Not to be overlooked, chapter 3 also includes a review of the various strategies and activities you should pursue as you put your new resume to work.

Part 2 is the actual Directory of Professional Resume Writers, sorted into various subsets. Chapter 4 groups the writers according to specialty areas, while chapter 5 breaks them down geographically. Chapter 6 is the alphabetical listing, containing full contact information for each writer, including in most cases the writer's Web site. There is also a short personal statement that will give you insight into each writer's approach and personality.

Part 3 is a bonus section—a collection of 46 sample resumes, contributed by the featured resume writers. These will help you appreciate what goes into a good resume. As you browse the selection, you'll find that the work of some writers just feels right to you. Be sure to check out these samples as you are considering hiring a writer for your own resume.

Lifetime Benefits

Given the statistics for job and company tenure, it's highly unlikely that your current transition will be your last! The benefits you receive from working with an expert will have a long-lasting impact as you manage your career for the remainder of your working life. I look forward to helping you choose the right partner for your career success.

PART 1

How to Find and Work with a Professional Resume Writer

CHAPTER 1

How a Professional Resume Writer Can Help You

For many, the first step in the job search process is writing a resume. The task is usually accompanied by feelings of stress, uncertainty, doubt, and discomfort. How do you know what an employer is looking for? How can you prove that you have it? And how can you stand out in a sea of other well-qualified candidates?

So the resume-writing task begins under stress and is connected to highly important life decisions. Yet there are no hard-and-fast rules, no A-to-Z process that you can follow when creating your resume. Every book on the subject offers a slightly different slant. Every person you speak to has somewhat different advice. Given the difficulty of the task, the importance of your career, and the vast array of available opinions and advice, it's not surprising that you might be confused, discouraged, or disappointed with your own attempt at writing a resume.

If that's the case, you might be contemplating finding a professional resume writer to come to your rescue, to help you sort all of this out and give you the best shot at the job you want. This chapter examines how a professional resume writer can help you—and what a professional *can't* do for you.

The Benefits of Working with a Professional Resume Writer

A professional resume writer can provide benefits like these.

An Objective Assessment of Your Career and Capabilities

Simply because they are so important, it's difficult to be objective about such things as your resume and your career. Perhaps you are being overly optimistic about the jobs you're qualified for—or underestimating your value. As well, you might not be up-to-date with the kinds of information employers will be looking for.

A resume professional knows

- How to position you for the jobs you're seeking—as effectively as possible within the reality of your experience and qualifications
- How to showcase highly desired skills, experiences, and qualifications so that they will catch the attention of employers
- How to select the most important information from the vast amount of data you could possibly include about your past jobs, education, and other activities
- What to eliminate and downplay so that your resume does not harm your chances of getting the job you want or screen you out from your target companies

An Understanding of Employer Needs

Professional resume writers have helped thousands of people get jobs. Because of their exposure to so many different job seekers and employers, they are knowledgeable about the qualifications for a wide array of jobs, and they know what information will catch the attention of employers.

When you have questions—"should I include this experience, that knowledge, these credentials, those details?"—your resume writer will filter all of the issues through this deep knowledge of what employers care about and make sure your resume focuses on relevant information that "speaks" to hiring authorities.

The Ability to Draw Out Details and Experiences That Will Make Your Resume Powerful and Unique

How eloquent are you? How well do you tell the stories of your career? And do you know what those most compelling stories are?

When you work with a resume expert, you will be asked insightful questions about your career and your achievements. Professional resume writers are skilled at asking these important questions in a variety of ways to dig out the "good stuff" from people with a wide range of communication styles. When you don't know what to say or how to say it, your writer instigates, guides, and encourages you to produce the material needed to create a powerful resume.

Professional Writing and Formatting Skills

Let's face it: Not everyone is a good writer. Nor is every job seeker highly skilled at document design and formatting. You might think that what really matters is the content of your resume, not its appearance. But in fact recruiters, HR professionals, and hiring managers are strongly influenced by what your resume looks like, how easy it is to find the information they need, and the overall impression the document conveys.

A resume expert knows how to

- Design an attractive and professional-looking page
- Choose the right font and font enhancements to strengthen the impact of the document
- Organize the material so that readers focus on the most important information and skim over what is less critical
- Use powerful words, phrases, and sentences to convey meaning with high impact and strong relevance
- Paint a "word picture" of who you are, one that attracts employers and emphasizes your value
- Disguise awkward situations (such as short job tenure, lack of a college degree, or lack of accomplishments in a specific job) so that they don't stand out as red flags to employers

In short, a resume writer uses a variety of professional skills to create a winning document for your specific circumstances.

Knowledge of Effective Job Search Methods

When your resume is complete, do you know what to do with it? Beyond responding to online postings, are you prepared to conduct an effective job search that stimulates interest from the right audiences at your target companies?

Finding a job is a complex process. Given the immense number and vast diversity of online options such as job sites, resume-posting sites, and corporate employment sites, it should be incredibly easy to find out about jobs and apply for them. You might be surprised to learn that the Internet is one of the least effective methods for actually landing a job. If you are unaccustomed to looking for a job, you could easily spend days, weeks, even months being very busy but very unproductive.

Professional resume writers are knowledgeable about how to conduct an effective search. In fact, many writers are also professional career coaches, consultants, or counselors who can provide additional services, beyond resume writing, to help you navigate the maze of options and help you choose and pursue the methods that are best for you.

Will I Get a Good ROI (Return on Investment) from a Professional Writer?

It can be difficult to quantify the return on your investment in career services. After all, you can never directly compare "before" activity with "after" activity because so many factors come into play. Did the job market open up? Did one of your prior contacts pay off? Did working on your resume give you greater clarity that translated to more effective interviewing?

Plus, once the resume is complete, what you do with it has an enormous impact on your success. Are you conducting a broad and integrated job search (see chapter 3 for details) or relying on Internet postings? Are you working your plan aggressively or half-heartedly?

Still, consider the cost of ineffective career management—the cost of being unemployed, underemployed, and underpaid. It translates to losses not just today, but long-term. Consider these points in calculating how you will benefit from your investment:

- If your work with a professional resume writer results in a job just one week sooner than on your own—you've already earned your payback.
- If you negotiate a 10 percent higher salary through the help of your career coach, think what that will translate to in higher salaries each year as you move forward in your career.
- If your resume writer's help leads you to your dream job, you'll benefit every day in increased job satisfaction and personal fulfillment. And who can put a dollar figure on that?

And don't forget, you might be able to deduct the cost of resume writing and other career services on your tax return. Check with your tax advisor for details... but do save the receipts, just in case!

What a Resume Writer *Can't* Do for You

Obviously, as a professional resume writer myself, I am enthusiastic about the value and benefits of working with a professional to manage your career and job transition. But it's also important to be realistic about what a resume writer can and can't do for you. After all, it's your career, your life; the ultimate responsibility for finding a job and managing your career rests with you. Your writer is a partner and expert resource who will help you succeed. Your writer is not a miracle worker or a magician!

A professional resume writer can't and won't do the following:

- **Find a job for you.** No matter what promises you might hear from anyone connected with your job search, don't buy into the myth that someone (anyone) will do all of the work for you—assess your skills, match them with available jobs, screen you into the interview, and "sell" you for that position. In fact, if you hear this promise, beat a quick retreat, because it's quite likely this is a scam or false promise designed to separate you from your money. Instead, take responsibility for your career, learn how to conduct an effective job search (a resume writer can certainly help), and equip yourself to manage your career for the rest of your working life.

- **Make you eligible for jobs for which you are not qualified.** Maybe you think that a professional resume writer can make you look like the perfect candidate for your dream job. Quite possibly that's true—as long as you actually are qualified for that job. No matter how snazzy the writing or how effective the makeover of your resume is, you must have the basic qualifications to be considered for a position. Don't expect your resume writer to be able to fulfill a dream that's not (yet) possible. However, consider working with a career coach to identify what you need to do to be qualified for that job, or what other related jobs you might pursue that you are qualified for. It's good to dream!
- **Lie about your credentials.** It seems that every month or so we read in the news a high-profile case of someone lying on their resume—and getting caught and losing their job. Simply, don't lie on your resume, and don't expect your resume writer to knowingly falsify your information. Not only is it unethical, it's not worth the risk.

  The reason many people exaggerate, stretch the truth, or flat-out invent material for their resume is usually because they're insecure about how competitive they will be for their desired jobs. Or they have what they feel is an insurmountable deficit that will prevent them from getting any job. Often, they don't know how to conduct an effective job search—one where they won't immediately be disqualified if they don't have a specific degree, credential, or knowledge listed on their resume. But lying is not the answer—and it's not necessary! A well-written resume should position you strongly for your target jobs. Combined with a well-thought-out search strategy, your truthful, powerful resume will open doors for you.

Little White Resume Lies

A survey conducted in October 2006 by CareerBuilder.com reported that 57 percent of hiring managers say they have caught a lie on a candidate's resume. The most common lies are "stretched" dates to cover an employment gap, falsification of past employers, and falsification of academic credentials.

The outcome? According to the CareerBuilder survey, 93 percent of those managers refused to hire the candidate.

- **Exaggerate your capabilities.** You might be tempted to stretch some information to better position yourself, but an exaggeration is a close cousin to a lie. Professional resume writers do a great job of stressing the right information and downplaying less-positive information without crossing the line by embellishing or embroidering the truth.

- **Invent successes or experiences.** When you work with a professional writer, you'll be asked to describe what you've done in your career and how well you've done it. If your success stories aren't that impressive, don't expect your writer to make things up to make you sound better. However, in some instances writers will make assumptions based on their vast experience of various professions and job functions. You might see some of those assumptions in the draft version of your resume, and your resume writer will probably point them out to you. If they are not truthful, it's up to you to correct your writer and ensure 100 percent accuracy of the document that bears *your* name.
- **Do their job without your cooperation and input.** When you hire a writer, you enter into a partner relationship. Guided by your writer, you must supply the fundamental information to include in your resume. This will take some time and effort on your part; you won't be able to simply hand over your credit-card information and walk away from the process. But you'll find that the end result is well worth the effort. Not only will you have a great resume, you'll have a clear understanding of your value in the market and a great foundation for a successful interview.
- **Tell you what you should do with your career or your life.** One of the biggest challenges resume writers face is the client who can't or won't specify a job target. If you're uncertain about where you're going, no resume—no matter how good—will be effective. It's essential for you to do the work necessary to define, at least in general terms, the kind of work you want to do. Then your writer can help you examine and frame your experiences to position you as a qualified candidate for those roles.

Is It Really Okay to Have Someone Else Write My Resume for Me?

The growth of the career services industry means that more and more people are taking advantage of career experts to help them choose a career and land a job. It's now mainstream, not unusual, for people who are serious about their careers to hire an interview coach, a career counselor, or a resume writer.

Employers and recruiters may or may not be able to tell that you've had professional help. And even if you have, they don't necessarily view it as a negative. If a career advisor helps you write a resume that better represents your skills and capabilities, it makes the hiring manager's job easier. If an interview coach helps you communicate effectively during the stress of a job interview, so much the better!

Thus, you can dispel any lingering doubts you might have about whether it's okay to have someone else write your resume. It's perfectly okay and extremely beneficial. Just be sure that you participate in the process and that the final document is an accurate reflection of you and your talents.

How Do You Answer the Question, "Did You Write This Yourself?"

First off, don't get defensive. Don't assume the interviewer is trying to trick you into revealing information that will harm you. Maybe he or she simply wants to know who wrote such a great resume! (I've had plenty of calls from recruiters and HR professionals who want me to write their resumes or who want to refer their job-seeking clients, friends, and colleagues.)

A good way to answer this question might be, "I did work with a professional to make sure that I was including the right information on my resume. I found it to be really valuable in helping me to focus on the most relevant details of my career. Do you have questions about a particular section?"

Or you might say, "I place a lot of importance on my career, and working with a career coach has been very beneficial in identifying my greatest passions and skills. I'm excited about using those passions and skills in this position, and I'm glad that my resume made it clear to you that I have what you're looking for."

Or, "Like a lot of people, I found it hard to be objective about myself and my career. Working with a professional resume writer helped me to see the big picture as well as the details and has been extremely helpful in guiding my career direction. I'm glad you like the resume!"

How Important Is Your Career?

Investing in the services of a professional resume writer signals that you are serious about your career. You understand the far-reaching consequences of each career transition, and you want to do everything possible to ensure that you land a job that is a close fit for your talents and interests. Not only that, you want to be sure you are getting paid what you're worth and not sabotaging yourself by undervaluing your experience and expertise.

In brief, working with a career professional is an investment in yourself.

CHAPTER 2

How to Choose the Writer Who's Right for You

Do you remember the last time you shopped for an important purchase—a car, maybe, or a flat-screen TV or a new computer? You started out gathering lots of information about many different models that *might* suit your needs and narrowed down your choices by evaluating the data, comparing different options, and matching each "possible" to your needs and preferences. Then, when you made your choice, you felt certain that you had selected the product that fit your needs to a "T."

The same approach will work to select the professional resume writer who best matches your needs, circumstances, personality, and preferences. This chapter gives tips on the process of selecting just the right writer.

Weigh Your Options

In this chapter, I review 11 different factors to consider when choosing a writer, along with details and data that will help you evaluate each factor and weigh how important it is to you. Armed with this data, you can narrow down the "possibles" to a few "probables" and compare those directly to make your selection.

But first, consider where you might start looking to make up your list of potential writers:

- **Referrals from friends and colleagues:** Your personal network is a great place to start looking. You'll get unbiased opinions from people you trust.
- **Articles in print and online:** Many published articles are written by professional resume writers as a way to share their expertise and raise their visibility among potential customers. Other articles, written by journalists, quote career experts as credible sources. When you read career advice that makes sense, check the source and follow up to learn more about that person and whether he or she offers services that meet your needs.
- **Local advertising (newspaper and Yellow Pages):** Although the Internet has become the preferred method of marketing most career services, some professionals still prefer to work with local clients and thus will advertise in local media. Because these writers might have inside expertise on the job market in your area, they might be the ideal choice for you.

- **Resume books:** Many resume sample books include contributions from dozens of different writers. These books are an excellent resource for comparing styles and selecting writers whose work you have already seen and admired. And if the sample you choose represents your professional field, you can be sure that writer has specific expertise working with people who have a background similar to yours.
- **Internet search:** If you enter the term "resume writer" into Google, you will get more than 350,000 results! You can certainly start clicking and surfing, but you might want to first narrow down your search by using more specific search terms—"executive resume writer" or "hospitality industry resume" or "healthcare resume," for example—to boost your chances of finding a writer with the expertise you need.

Of course, turning up a list of possible resume writers is only the first step. Whatever your initial source, be sure you carefully evaluate each potential writer according to the nine factors detailed in the following section. And don't miss the two important sections that conclude this chapter:

- How Much Should It Cost?
- Warning Signs of a Bad Fit

Above all, be an educated buyer to make sure you are entrusting your career to someone who has the right match of skills, experience, and style for you.

Factors for Evaluating Resume Writers

Although not every one of these factors will be equally important to you, I suggest that you review each one to build your awareness of features and qualifications you should consider in your quest for the ideal writer.

What Are the Right Answers?

You will note that I don't provide answers to the suggested questions that appear throughout this chapter. That's because there is never one "right" answer. Different writers take different approaches and have different models. Just as importantly, you have your own preferences for how you want to work with a resume writer.

Use the questions to gather the information and winnow down multiple choices. You'll find that some answers will be deal-breakers for you: The writer can't do an evening consultation, perhaps, or hasn't updated his skills through training or conferences in the last five years. For each person, the deal-breakers will be different. The questions are important, and the answers will help you. Just don't expect your selection process to fit into a formula.

1. Experience

It's true that some people have a natural knack for writing resumes. (When I was looking for my first job out of college, the recruiter asked me—somewhat suspiciously—if I had written my resume myself!) But in a field where training is inconsistent and there are no licensing requirements, length of experience is a good indicator of skill level and expertise. If nothing else, writing hundreds or thousands of resumes means your writer has been exposed to different professions and job levels, different client personalities, and a vast array of career-related information.

As you make your queries, you will find writers whose experience ranges from a few months to a few decades. One guideline is to look for someone whose level of experience matches your own or slightly outpaces you.

Be sure also to weigh relevant experience; someone who's been writing resumes full-time for just a few months but has years of experience as a recruiter, coach, counselor, or human resources professional brings loads of expertise to the challenge.

Keep in mind that you shouldn't make your final call based on any single factor. You might find a naturally talented writer who perfectly meets your needs and has only six months of experience; or you might find a 30-year industry veteran who simply doesn't "get" your circumstances. Experience is just one aspect of the writer's qualifications.

Questions to ask about experience include the following:

- *How many years of resume-writing experience do you have?*
- *Is that full-time or part-time?*
- *Have you dealt with situations like mine?* (This is especially relevant if you have an unusual or challenging employment situation, such as returning to work after a long absence, changing careers, reaching for your first C-level position, downsizing your career, or explaining multiple gaps in employment.)
- *What other experience do you have in the careers field?*

2. Areas of Specialization

Part 2 of this book is a directory of resume writers broken down by area of specialization. Some of these are functional specialties, such as sales or accounting; others are industry niches, such as hospitality or healthcare; and still others relate to special circumstances, such as returning to work after an absence.

Of course, there's no guarantee that a writer who specializes will produce a better resume than a generalist. (In fact, many of the writers in this directory selected numerous specialty areas; so in a way, they can be considered generalists.) But the advantage to working with a writer who knows your niche is that he will be familiar with the terminology, typical challenges, and work environments of your field and experienced using a variety of resume techniques appropriate to your circumstances.

Questions to ask about areas of specialization include the following:

- *What is your area of specialization?*
- *What are the challenges you typically encounter in this niche?*
- *How do you address them?*
- *How did you come to specialize in this area?*
- *What other areas do you specialize in?*

3. Credentials

I've mentioned that there is no licensing or accreditation required for professional resume writers. But there are numerous training and certification programs that help build skills in key areas: resume writing, job search, interviewing, career planning, and so forth.

All of the professional associations whose members are included in this book offer at least one resume-writing certification. Some are more rigorous than others; some require continuing education, whereas others do not; and some certify different levels of expertise, from basic up to advanced or "master" level. Here's a rundown of these associations and their resume-writing certifications:

Association of Online Resume and Career Professionals

- Certified Master Resume Specialist (CMRS)

Career Directors International

- Certified Advanced Resume Writer (CARW)
- Certified Expert Resume Writer (CERW)
- Certified Federal Resume Writer (CFRW)
- Certified Military Resume Writer (CMRW)

Career Management Alliance (formerly Career Masters Institute)

- Master Resume Writer (MRW)

Career Professionals of Canada

- Certified Resume Strategist (CRS)

National Resume Writers' Association

- Nationally Certified Resume Writer (NCRW)

Professional Association of Resume Writers and Career Coaches

- Certified Professional Resume Writer (CPRW)

Don't worry about evaluating each of these credentials, but *do* look for a writer who has a writing credential. If you are interested, ask her or him about the credential and what was required to earn it.

One thing to watch out for is writers who pooh-pooh the idea of a credential and tell you that "they can be bought by anyone." That's simply not true. Earning the credential usually requires passing a test on resume standards, writing techniques, and job search strategies; actually writing one or more resumes; and perhaps submitting a portfolio of resumes written for clients. Some certifications call for a minimum number of years of experience in the careers industry or as a resume writer.

I myself am partial to the Master Resume Writer (MRW) credential because I was the first person to earn it! It demands a comprehensive portfolio of resume work, supported by an explanation of the strategies chosen, and it must be renewed (with another full portfolio) every two years.

All of the credential applications are reviewed by a panel of experienced resume writers, usually a rotating team of volunteers selected from the organization's leading members. Speaking from experience, judges can be extremely nitpicky and demanding; we want credentialed writers to uphold the standard of the industry and the prestige of the credential.

Questions to ask about credentials include the following:

- *Are you a professionally certified resume writer?*
- *What is your certification, and what did you do to earn it?*
- *Is your certification renewable or permanent?*
- *How long have you had the certification?*
- *What other certifications do you have? Why did you earn them, and how do they help you write good resumes?*

4. Professional Associations

Like most fields, the careers industry is constantly changing. In just the last few years, career professionals have had to bone up on emerging trends such as online social networking, video resumes, blogging as a career management tool, increasing globalization, and totally new professions such as robot programmer or stem-cell researcher.

One of the best ways to stay informed of the latest trends is to join professional associations that keep their members up-to-date via training programs, conferences, newsletters, and member exchanges. If your resume writer does not belong to a professional association, he could be relying on knowledge that hasn't kept up with the fast pace of today's job market, possibly using resume styles, language, and strategies that are outdated and stale. Joining an association means he considers himself a professional and is willing to invest in his own career development.

In addition to the six resume-writing associations mentioned in this book, there are dozens of other professional organizations catering to coaches, counselors, outplacement experts, and other areas of the careers and employment industry. Belonging to these associations means your writer is striving to stay abreast of changes across the entire industry.

Questions to ask about professional associations include the following:

- *What professional associations do you belong to?*
- *Do you volunteer with the organization? In what capacity?*
- *Have you attended a conference in the last year?*
- *What other training programs have you taken?*
- *What else do you do to keep your skills and knowledge up-to-date?*

5. Guarantee

Because resume writing is a service and not a product that can be put back on the shelf and resold, few resume-writing firms offer unconditional money-back guarantees. After all, by the time you receive your proof copy, your writer will have spent hours consulting, writing, and formatting to create a unique resume for you.

However, resume writers understand that guarantees create consumer confidence, so they might offer a guarantee that will help to reassure customers nervous about spending a good deal of money on a product that can't be viewed or evaluated until it is nearly complete.

One guarantee offered by numerous resume firms states that if you don't get interviews "we'll rewrite for free." Of course, to protect themselves, the businesses that offer this guarantee hedge it with very specific criteria about what you must do before they'll rewrite your resume. These requirements usually entail responding to *x* number of job postings or ads, using your resume (unaltered from the way it was prepared for you) and perhaps a companion cover letter also prepared by the resume writer. You have to document your efforts before earning a rewrite.

Writers who don't offer the guarantee say they'd prefer to "write it right the first time" and not tweak an already good resume simply because you haven't had responses in a competitive job market. After all, responding to ads is just one method of searching for a job, and one of the least effective. (See chapter 3 for guidance on how to launch your job search with your new resume.)

Another guarantee, the one that I use, is that you will be "100 percent satisfied" with the work that is done for you. No rewrites are offered after the fact, but you will have the opportunity to review and revise the initial draft until you are fully happy with it. Again, this guarantee is designed primarily to build customer trust and confidence in a somewhat unknown process.

If a guarantee is important to you, you can certainly find a writer who offers one. However, I think it's more important to have a clear understanding of the process, fees, and deliverables so that you have a very explicit expectation for what will happen and what you'll receive. If everything is not clear to you, keep asking questions and ensure everything is fully explained, preferably in writing, before you sign an agreement.

Finally, be sure to check out the section in chapter 3, "Resolving Problems," for some guidance on how to handle the situation if you are seriously unhappy with your resume product.

Questions to ask about guarantees include the following:

- *Do you offer a guarantee?*
- *What happens if I'm not happy with my resume?*
- *How many resumes have you had to rewrite in the last six months?*
- *What does "satisfied" mean?*

6. Examples of Work

What better way to evaluate a writer's skill than to look at examples of his or her work? Many resume writers post samples on their Web sites or have a portfolio available in their offices. If you don't see samples, be sure to ask. Some writers will point you in the direction of a book of resumes where their work has been published; others might send you a few samples as a PDF file.

Some writers don't like to provide samples because they fear it sets up an expectation that your resume will look exactly like the sample. Or, just the opposite, that you will be dissatisfied if your resume reads or looks like the sample rather than being unique to you. It's up to you whether refusal to provide a sample is a deal-breaker.

Don't expect to find a sample for someone exactly like you. It's really not necessary—in fact, it might raise expectations about your resume that will not be fulfilled because your situation is unique to you. Plus, it's a lot of work to create custom samples; the resume writer must "fictionalize" the document to protect the original client's confidentiality.

When looking at samples, ask yourself these questions:

- *What is the overall impression?*
- *Is the document readable and well designed?*
- *Are the focus and expertise crystal-clear?*
- *Is there a logical flow to the resume?*
- *Do I pick up essential information in a quick skim?*
- *When reading more closely, do I get a sense of the candidate's "story"—where he's been, what he's good at?*
- *Am I impressed by the accomplishments? Are the accomplishments quantified with numbers and other hard results?*
- *Is it well written?*

- *Is it grammatically correct?*
- *Is the resume distinctive? Does the candidate seem to be one of a kind, or would she blend in with a host of other candidates?*
- *In looking at multiple samples from the same writer, do they all look and sound the same—are similar phrases and formats used in every resume?*

7. Reputation and References

Recommendations from reliable sources are one of the best ways to judge just about any product or service you are considering—a restaurant, a refrigerator, a plumber, the latest iPod, and even a resume writer. When asking your friends, family, and colleagues for recommendations, be as specific as you can about what you're looking for. Consider the different referrals you might get in response to each of these requests:

- "I'm looking for a low-cost resume firm that can tweak and polish my existing resume for my interview next week."
- "I need to find a resume writer who understands the IT field and will make my resume more than a collection of technical terms."
- "I'm worried that having spent 15 years to raise my family will really harm my chances of finding a job now. I need a resume writer who understands how to deal with this situation."
- "I'm looking for another CEO job and I'd like to find a resume writer who understands how to create a succinct yet powerful synopsis of my 30-year career."

You can also request one or two client references from a resume-writing firm that you are considering. Note that I do not suggest that you make this request of *every* firm; save it for the final tie-breaker between two firms or to confirm your first choice. Because of the need for strict client confidentiality, it is not always quick or easy for the writer to provide a reference to you. He has to track down the former client, get her permission, and pass along to you the client's preferred contact information. But a former client can be an exceedingly valuable resource.

Finally, be alert to other clues about the resume writer's reputation. If you hear from multiple sources that she is "the best," that's a good sign! If you keep stumbling across her name as you browse online career information in your field, that's a plus. If you mention her name to other career professionals (coaches, counselors, other resume writers) and they tell you you've made a good choice, that's reassuring.

Use these questions to dig more deeply into the recommendations you receive:

- *What did you like about working with him?*
- *What didn't you like? What could have gone better?*
- *Tell me how the process worked.*

- *What were your specific challenges, and how did the resume writer address them?*
- *Are you satisfied with the value you received for the amount you paid?*
- *How much did he charge? What did that include?*
- *Were there any surprises—good or bad?*
- *Does he specialize in your field?*
- *How did you find out about him?*
- *Were you happy with the first draft? If not, how many rewrites did it take to get it right?*
- *How did having a professionally written resume help your job search?*
- *If you had to do it again, would you choose the same writer? Why or why not?*

8. Process, Services, Deliverables, Quality, and Customer Satisfaction

How does a resume writer work, anyway? What will you actually end up with, and what's the process you'll be following to transform the raw material of your career into a brilliantly polished resume? This is important because you'll be going through that process with the writer—and it's your career!

First consider who you'll really be working with. If you've chosen a private practice with a single resume writer, then obviously you'll be working with one person start to finish on every aspect of developing your resume. Some firms have administrative help—people who might set appointments, arrange follow-up meetings, manage payment processes, and work with you on final edits and formatting details. At larger firms, it's likely you'll first connect with a salesperson who is responsible for converting prospects to paying customers and then turns them over to the writing team. Within that writing team, you might have direct contact with one person while another person, perhaps a subcontract writer, actually develops your resume.

All of the preceding models are perfectly valid and can produce excellent resumes. But it's a good idea for you to know precisely who will be responsible for each stage of the process and what each process entails. Use the following questions to ensure that you are fully informed about and comfortable with the process of producing your resume. Clear expectations reduce surprises.

Information Gathering

- *Do you use a questionnaire, a consultation, or both?*
- *How can I be sure your questionnaire is going to get all the right information? I know I overlooked things when I tried to write the resume myself.*
- *Will my consultation be in person (or by phone) with my writer, or will someone else handle this part of the process?*

- *Do you welcome additional materials beyond your questionnaire—items such as performance reviews, letters of recommendation, job descriptions, and my own draft versions of the resume?*
- *What happens if I think of more things to add after the consultation is complete?*
- *Can I schedule the consultation in the evening or on a weekend, so as not to conflict with my current job?*

Writing

- *Who will actually be writing my resume?*
- *What are that person's credentials, and how much experience does he or she have?*
- *Will I have direct access to my writer, or do I need to go through an intermediary?*
- *How long will it take to get my draft resume?*

Review and Revision

- *How many opportunities will I have to revise the draft?*
- *Does the editing process include phone consultation, or will I be expected to provide all of my input via e-mail? What if I have follow-up questions?*
- *Will my writer be handling my revisions, or will someone else?*
- *What limitations or restrictions do you have on the revision process?*
- *Can I see the resume in more than one format before making my final choice?*

Deliverables

- *What will I actually receive (hard copy, files, etc.)?*
- *Will I have a fully editable MS Word file?*
- *What if I have problems with the files or if there are formatting glitches?*
- *Will I receive text files for online use? Is there an extra charge for that?*
- *Will I receive printed copies? Is there an extra charge?*
- *What else is included with my resume service?*
- *What else do you offer as an add-on to the resume?*
- *What additional services does your firm offer?*
- *If I purchase other services at a later time, will I be working with the same writer?*
- *If I purchase other services at a later time, will the price be higher?*

Quality and Customer Satisfaction

- *Can I view samples of your work (or the work of my writer)?*
- *How long will the process take, start to finish?*
- *What if you miss your deadline?*
- *Is there any way to speed up the process?*
- *What is your quality-control process—how do you make sure your resumes are accurate, error free, grammatically correct, and professionally formatted?*
- *If I don't agree with my writer's approach or advice, who can I talk to about that?*
- *What if I find mistakes in the resume after it's been finalized?*

9. Resume Review and Recommendations

Many resume writers begin their evaluation of your situation by reviewing your existing resume. This is a great strategy for your selection purposes, too, because it allows you to quickly compare different approaches and get a feel for the style and expertise of each potential writer.

If the review is provided orally, either on the phone or in person, you will want to take notes about the recommendations and observations the resume writer shares. If the review is in writing, typically via e-mail, you will be able to review the details at your leisure and compare it to the other proposals you've received.

I suggest that you request two to four evaluations. Asking for more than that is a waste of time (yours and the resume writers'); fewer than that, and you won't have enough data for comparison. When you review the recommendations, look for trends and similarities. These are probably key areas where your resume needs to be improved. Next, look at how each report is different. What does one person say that another doesn't? Which approach rings true to you?

From the perspective of a professional resume writer, most self-written resumes share similar failings. They tend to be short on quantifiable achievements and overly detailed about job duties and descriptions. Quite often they lack a strong introduction and fail to clearly communicate who the job seeker is and his or her unique value in the market. Because they see the same trends over and over, most resume writers have designed a standardized response that includes their most frequent recommendations. So don't be surprised if you receive what seems a bit like a form letter; however, do look for personalization and customization of that response to address the specific circumstances of your job search and your resume.

10. Fit and Feel

This is one of the most subjective areas for consideration. Because the resume-writing process is intense and personal, it's important that you feel comfortable with your writer and fully confident in his or her ability to represent you on paper.

Your personalities don't need to mesh fully—after all, you'll be working together for just a few days or weeks. But if there is a real personality clash or you feel he or she doesn't respect you or value your input, move on to the next writer.

The process of creating your resume should increase your knowledge of yourself and help you appreciate your value in the job market. Not only that, talking to your resume writer and reading your new resume should give you jolt of self-confidence. It should be a positive experience with long-term career benefits.

To evaluate fit and feel, quiz yourself about the experience of interacting with each specific resume writer during your evaluation process:

- *Was she a good listener?*
- *Did she understand my circumstances?*
- *Did her initial recommendations make sense and sound like the right approach?*
- *Did she answer all my questions?*
- *Was it easy to reach her?*
- *Did she respond promptly to e-mail and voice-mail messages?*
- *Did I feel a good rapport?*
- *Would I enjoy working with her?*

11. Cost

It's no coincidence that I've left cost for last. Although the price you'll pay is, of course, an important consideration, it should never be the only or the most significant factor in your decision.

Fees for professional resume writing vary widely. (See the next section for a more detailed discussion of this topic.) You will need to evaluate the cost based on the value received and your own budget. Just be sure that you understand fully what's being charged, what's included and what costs more, and what you'll receive for your money.

Questions to ask about cost include the following:

- *What does the fee include?*
- *What might I need that would cost extra?*
- *If I make multiple changes, will you charge more?*
- *Are there any circumstances in which I would be charged more than this amount?*
- *Is there anything I can do beforehand that would reduce the fee?*
- *How do you establish your fees?*
- *If I return for an update, how will you determine the fee?*

How Much Should It Cost?

Just like any other product or service that you purchase, the price for having a resume professionally written can vary greatly from one provider to another. In general, higher fees signify more specialized expertise and often a more intensive level of service. But you can find good writers at all price points and must weigh your own circumstances when making your choice.

Average Prices

All of the writers listed in this directory were asked to supply information about pricing along with other details such as specialty areas, credentials, and services offered. Although this data represents only the 229 writers in this book, it will help you start to understand what the "going rate" is for the service you are seeking (see table 2.1).

Table 2.1: Average Price for a Resume

Price Range	% of Respondents
Under $100	4%
$100–$199	18%
$200–$349	26%
$350–$499	26%
$500–$699	13%
$700–$999	7%
$1,000–$1,399	3%
$1,400–$1,799	2%
$1,800 or higher	1%

As shown more graphically in the following chart, more than half the writers—54 percent—are positioned in the middle-to-lower price range of $200 to $499, with 22 percent charging under $200 and 26 percent charging above $500.

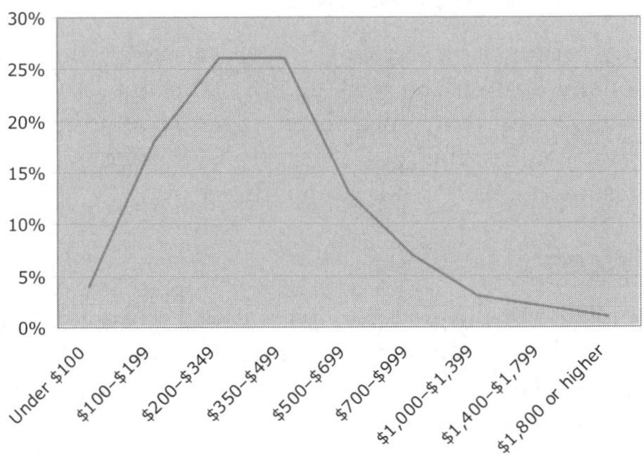

You might think that the writer's experience and the candidate's expertise correlate with price, and to some degree that's true. For example:

- More than half (56 percent) who specialize in writing resumes for new graduates charge less than $350 per resume.
    - Explanation: In general, new-grad resumes tend to be less complex and lengthy than resumes for experienced professionals and thus tend to be priced in a lower range.
- Those who are at the very bottom of the price range (less than $200) are relatively inexperienced—59 percent have been writing resumes for 10 years or less.
    - Explanation: Just as in most careers, new resume writers usually start out toward the bottom of the ladder and work their way up as they gather experience, gain confidence in their writing skills, and build a steady stream of business through repeat and referral customers.
- Of those whose practice is limited to senior executives, 79 percent have 11-plus years of experience, 71 percent write only one to three resumes per week, and 57 percent charge $700 or more for a resume.
    - Explanation: Although most resume writers serve the professional/executive market, a select few write only for the topmost executives. It's rare for a writer to limit her practice to this relatively narrow niche until he or she has built the expertise and the reputation needed to command the highest prices and appeal to this demanding group.
- In the lowest price groups (less than $200), 51 percent write four to eight resumes a week, 10 percent produce nine to 14 resumes a week, and a full 12 percent write more than 15.

- At low price points, volume is key! Otherwise the resume writer will not be able to stay in business. Thus, resumes are produced more quickly to allow the higher volume.

The Effect of a Personal Consultation on Price

Resume writers gather information from clients in a variety of ways, supplementing any existing materials with worksheets, consultations, or both. Gathering and analyzing additional materials takes time, and therefore you might expect writers who include a personal consultation to charge a higher fee.

However, the survey data did not bear this out. Ninety-five percent of respondents supplement a written worksheet with a consultation or follow-up questions, and their fees vary from below $100 to above $1,800. Thus, regardless of price, you can expect to have the opportunity to spend some time discussing your career with your writer.

Price Differences Between Service Models

Next you might wonder whether meeting in person makes a difference in price. Here's what the survey showed for three different service models. Note that numbers exceed 100 percent because some writers use more than one model.

- **Remote (via phone or e-mail):** 93 percent of writers work with clients in this manner, and pricing encompasses all ranges.
- **In person:** 51 percent of writers will meet with you in person; however, almost none (only 1 percent) of the highest-priced services (above $1,000) will do so.
- **While-you-wait:** This specialized segment was represented by only 12 percent of respondents, and pricing varied from below $100 to $999.

Price Advice

You can find experienced writers in all price ranges, and you will most likely have the opportunity for a personal consultation regardless of the price or service model. That's the good news! The challenge, then, is deciding when and why to pay more for your resume.

In general, the more complex your situation, and the higher your salary, the more you should consider opting for a higher-priced service. As in any field, resume writers who specialize can command a higher fee. That specialty might represent your level (senior executive), your specific circumstance (many gaps in your career history), your function (legal), or your industry (federal government). Use the criteria presented earlier in this chapter to screen several writers who have the expertise you need, and consider price as one (but not the only) factor when making your choice.

Samples, references, and the elusive "fit and feel" factor are much better ways to judge a resume writer than price. Don't be penny-wise, by choosing the cheapest service, and career-foolish, by putting your future in the hands of a writer who won't represent you in the most powerful way.

Resume Writer Red Flags

Steer clear of any resume-writing services that display the following danger signs:

- **Lack of direct contact:** Your career is too important to trust to an anonymous Web site. Never sign up for a service or provide payment if you have not had direct contact with a real person. If that contact is by e-mail, be sure you have a phone number and a name, someone with whom you can follow up should questions or problems arise.
- **Not knowing who you're working with:** Don't put your career in the hands of "our writers." Ask specifically who will be writing your resume, what his/her credentials are, and who your contact is for review and revision. You don't want to be a cog in the impersonal machinery of a resume-writing "mill."
- **No information-gathering process:** If your current resume contained everything it should, you probably wouldn't need professional help. Your writer must have a way to get additional information from you—a worksheet, a consultation, or both. Otherwise, your new resume will probably suffer from "garbage-in, garbage-out" syndrome.
- **Unrealistic promises:** When your gut instinct tells you a promise is too good to be true, listen. Remember, it's your career and your job search. No resume-writing, coaching, outplacement, or other career-services firm can find a job for you or give you access to the so-called "hidden job market." Don't be seduced by a great sales pitch.

Be alert to these warning signs, and when you see them, move on to a reputable service.

Stumbling Blocks

Sometimes, in spite of your best efforts, there might be a mismatch between you and your resume writer. Although these situations don't fall into the "danger" categories described above, you should pay serious attention to any of the following issues and be proactive in resolving them before they become problems.

- **Confusion or lack of clarity regarding fees, processes, timeline, and expectations:** Despite your best "due diligence" efforts before signing on with a writer, sometimes communication styles don't mesh and the process doesn't go as you expected. Never hesitate to ask for clarification, and don't continue the process until you have all your questions answered and feel comfortable about what has happened and will happen.

- **Inability to connect with your writer:** You can't expect your resume writer to be on call 24/7 just for you, but it is reasonable to expect a return phone call or e-mail when you contact your writer with a question at any point during the process. Same-day or next-day response is normal and appropriate—at least to acknowledge your questions, even if she can't answer them immediately.
- **Unwillingness or inability to allay your concerns:** If you feel like your resume writer is giving you the brush-off, be firm about expressing your feelings and concerns—and don't move on until all your questions have been answered. You should feel like an important client both before and after the sale has been made.
- **Disagreement regarding the strategy for your resume:** You need to respect your writer as a professional and an expert in his field, but you must also feel comfortable about the way he is positioning and portraying you in your resume. Your writer might want to eliminate some of your jobs, for example, or group several under one heading. Although these are perfectly legitimate strategies, and might be the perfect solution for your circumstances, you should feel free to probe a bit to discover why he plans to take this approach, and how he recommends you address it during interviews. Ultimately, it is your resume and your job search, and your writer needs to respect your concerns.
- **Lack of empathy or otherwise a poor fit with your personal style:** Perhaps you were swayed by the great samples or stellar reputation of your writer, but now that you are into the process you find that she doesn't seem to care much about you or doesn't communicate well. A perfect style fit is not necessary, but you should feel comfortable, valued, and respected throughout the process.
- **Dissatisfying or confusing consultation:** Most people come away from their career consultation feeling uplifted and excited. The consultation is an essential building block for the resume-development process, so during that time you should be discussing significant career experiences and challenges. If you don't understand your writer's questions, or if you find you spent most of your time on insignificant career experiences, you might wonder how the end result is going to reflect your career and your potential.

The best strategy for all of these stumbling blocks is clear and open communication. Whether via phone or e-mail, you should ask your questions and persist until you get the answers you need. Don't let the situation fester, and certainly don't sit and fret without bringing up the issue. You have made a large investment, and you should feel good about your choice and satisfied with the process.

Most of these issues are simply miscommunication and can be resolved easily. Your writer will appreciate knowing about your concerns and being able to deal with them quickly.

In the next chapter, you'll find an in-depth discussion of what to expect from the resume-writing process, including some guidelines on what you should do if you are seriously dissatisfied with the result.

On a more positive note, you can expect to emerge from the process with a clear perception of yourself and your value in the job market. You'll be armed with powerful and appropriate documents to market yourself to employers—giving you a decided advantage over the competition.

CHAPTER 3

What to Expect from the Resume Development Process

You are one of a kind, and your career circumstances are unique. So your individual experience of working with a resume writer will not be exactly like anyone else's. Yet there are certain steps you can expect as you move through the process, from making an inquiry to finalizing your new resume. This chapter spells out those steps and helps you understand what will happen and why, when, and how the resume writer will do what he does to create a powerful career marketing document for you.

Getting Started

As discussed in chapter 2, you will probably be making inquiries of several different writers. That first step for you is also the first opportunity for the resume writer to evaluate your needs, develop an initial strategy, and present a proposal for your consideration.

Your inquiry will begin with a phone call, an e-mail, a Web site form, or even an in-person visit. If you have an existing resume, it's a good idea to share that with the resume writer as the first step. She will review your resume—and tell you what's wrong with it! If you're looking for help, you probably know that the resume is not perfect, so you're probably expecting to hear some criticism. Don't take it personally. Listen to or read your critique carefully, looking for the following:

- Insightful comments about your specific situation and your resume, in addition to more generalized comments about what works and what doesn't in today's job market.
- A sensible plan for improving your resume—what needs to be different, why, and how the resume writer will fix it.
- A general sense that the resume writer knows what he's talking about and understands the job market.
- Responses to any specific concerns you addressed in your initial inquiry.

- Evidence of good writing, language, and grammar skills. If your writer can't speak or write properly when communicating with you, how can she write a great resume?
- A clear proposal for working together, describing the process, timeline, deliverables, and cost.

If you don't have an existing resume, engage the writer in a brief discussion about your specific circumstances and then look for a plan and proposal to meet your needs. Use the questions in chapter 2 to evaluate several potential writers and make your selection. It's thoughtful to let any other writers who are in the running know that you've finalized your decision. You don't have to go into detail as to why you didn't choose them. Just let them know that you've chosen another writer.

Payment and Paperwork

To initiate your project, most resume writers will prepare a contract or agreement that spells out policies for payment, proofreading, revisions, timely completion of the work, and any other factors that they consider an essential part of doing business together. Read it carefully and make sure you understand everything before signing and returning the agreement.

If there's something in the contract that you don't agree with or contradicts your understanding, bring this up to the resume writer before signing. It might be something that he can alter, or his explanation might make you comfortable with the issue. Or it could be a deal-breaker—and you certainly want to learn about it prior to committing yourself and your resources.

I noted earlier that 93 percent of resume writers featured in this book work with at least some of their clients remotely—never meeting in person, even if they live in the same area. For this reason, most writers have established policies that make it easy for them to transmit documents to you, manage the editing process by phone and/or e-mail, and collect their fees in advance. Even if you're working in person, similar policies will apply. So pay attention to the policies and respect them. They are designed to make it easy for the writer to focus on doing what she does best (writing your resume) instead of managing administrative processes.

Contracts Protect Both Parties

The contract you sign is a legal agreement that commits you to paying for the work you have requested. Even with this protection, most resume writers collect payment in advance via credit card, check, or even cash if you meet face-to-face.

With a written agreement, you'll know what to expect, what you'll receive, and possibly when you'll receive it. You'll have a written record of fees and payments. Just as the resume writer can hold you accountable for your part of the project, you too can use the agreement to ensure that you receive the entire service that you've paid for.

A good contract avoids misunderstandings and creates clear expectations for both you and your writer. It's a good thing!

Remember, resume writing is a customized, one-on-one, time-intensive service that requires about 95 percent of the work to be completed before you see your draft. The resume writer wants to be sure he'll be paid for this work, and the industry has trended toward the payment-up-front policy after too many writers experienced situations like these:

- Clients walk away with their draft resume without paying the fee.
- Midstream, clients change their mind, cancel the project, and assume they won't be charged a fee because they haven't received any "goods" yet.
- Clients take weeks and even months making small tweaks to their resume drafts and withhold payment until the project is 100 percent complete.
- A situation occurs that causes clients to put a job search on hold and therefore they don't get around to finalizing the draft.

By collecting in advance, resume writers are protected from these situations and also can avoid spending time pursuing "stalled" clients or collecting overdue amounts—nobody's favorite activity!

The bottom line is that you can expect to pay in advance for the custom service you are requesting, and most agreements include a no-refund policy. If your situation changes before your project is done, contact your resume writer immediately to discuss it. Most writers understand that unusual circumstances sometimes arise and are willing to bend their policies if it's truly warranted.

Of utmost importance in any agreement is that you comprehend what you're signing and understand the policies and processes that will be followed, as well as deliverables you'll receive. If you're in doubt, ask your writer before moving forward.

Information Gathering

Now it's time for your resume writer to perform one of his most amazing feats: gathering the information he needs to write a stellar resume for you. This encompasses so much more than your career history, education, and other credentials. There is an art and a science to asking the right questions—in the right way—to uncover rough gems that the writer will shape and polish to make your resume sparkle.

Most writers use more than one method for gathering this essential information. Here are some of the most popular and effective ones:

- **Your existing resume:** Before submitting it to your writer, be certain that all dates, spellings, names, numbers, and other details are correct. Your writer will probably not quiz you too much on what's in the resume—we're more interested in what you *didn't* put in. But we will use this as a key source of basic information, such as your employment chronology, education, affiliations, community activities, and other fundamentals of your professional persona.

- **Supplemental materials:** You might have performance reviews or letters of recommendation that talk about what you did and how well you did it. These are fantastic resources for the fertile imagination of a resume writer. As well, if you have additional materials that you think help to explain who you are and what you have done in your career, by all means pass these along to your writer.
- **Job postings:** It's a good idea to gather a few postings of jobs that match your interests. Your writer will use these to cross-check your new resume to be sure that essential keywords are included and to identify any areas where experience seems to be missing, thus requiring follow-up questions.
- **Worksheets:** Many resume writers request that you fill out the questionnaires they have developed as a primary source of information-gathering. Every question is included for a reason that is important to that writer, so don't skimp on your responses, and don't assume your writer can get this information from your existing resume. Take the time and make the effort to give your writer what she needs.
- **Consultation:** Whether it's a short 15-minute follow-up to an extensive questionnaire, or an in-depth, hour-long investigation into the story of your career, the consultation is an intensely valuable part of the resume-development process. It helps the writer understand who you are, helps you feel comfortable with the writer, lets you share any issues that are of concern to you, and allows your writer to approach important subjects in a number of different ways to get you to reveal the essential information. Be sure you allot enough time in a quiet spot where you can speak freely and won't be interrupted.
- **Homework:** Sometimes you might be required to provide more information after the consultation. What's requested could be essential facts and figures or more detailed descriptions of some of your major career activities. Be sure to complete this assignment thoroughly and on schedule so that you don't slow down the completion of your resume.

Writing

Ahh... sit back and relax while your resume writer takes care of this step. Your writer will be reviewing and synthesizing all the information gathered from every source and selecting just the right mix of material to best showcase you and your career. He'll be writing, rewriting, editing, and polishing the phrases, sentences, and paragraphs. He'll select a font, format, and design to highlight key information and promote readability. And he'll be proofreading, tightening, and fine-tuning your resume until it is ready to be presented to you for approval.

Review, Revision, and Finalization

Now it's your turn again. You'll want to carefully review your draft resume several times. First, give it the once-over. How does it look? How does it sound? What impression does it give from a quick read? Hopefully you'll be among the majority who react with awe and amazement when they see their new resumes. But whatever your initial response, make note of it before you delve too deeply into the content of the resume.

Next, read every word and highlight any areas that you think are inaccurate or confusing. Call attention to any sections whose meaning is not clear to you—after all, you'll be the one sitting across from the interviewer, and you'll need to feel entirely comfortable with what's in your resume. Never hesitate to ask your writer, "What did you mean by that?" If it's not clear to you, chances are it won't be clear to someone else.

Next, proofread carefully, double- and triple-checking dates, degrees, names, and other facts that can be easily checked and where it would be embarrassing—if not disastrous—to include an inaccuracy. Read every phrase and sentence to be sure it makes sense and that the grammatical structure and punctuation are absolutely accurate. Speak up if you have a question about a comma, semicolon, or sentence structure. If it's wrong, you're the one whose career could be affected. In fact, most agreements include a clause that specifically assigns responsibility to you for proofreading. Your resume writer will do his very best, but it's ultimately on your shoulders to be sure there are no errors in your document.

Some writers give very specific instructions for how they want you to provide feedback; many request you to use the "Track Changes" feature in Microsoft Word to insert your comments and corrections. Others are more flexible and will welcome your input via a marked-up hard copy, an e-mail message, a phone conversation, or a sit-down meeting.

After you've shared your feedback and discussed your questions, your writer will produce an updated draft for your review and additional edits. Read this version just as carefully, and communicate questions or changes in the same manner as before.

In rare instances, a first draft is deemed to be perfect. But most people go through two or three drafts en route to the final version. After you've given your final approval, your resume writer will prepare and deliver whatever's been promised in your agreement. Typically you'll receive a Microsoft Word version (fully editable by you). You might also receive printed copies, a plain-text version for Internet use, a PDF file, and additional "goodies" shared by your writer to help you in your career transition.

As you're winding up your resume project, now is the time to discuss additional services for which you might want to engage your writer—services such as cover letter writing, biography writing, job search coaching, or interview coaching. Be sure to ask your writer to recommend services based on your circumstances.

Even if you don't want to purchase them now, you'll know what's available if you need them down the road.

A Draft Is a Draft

Resume writers prefer to provide a draft or proof copy in as near to final form as possible. The strategy, structure, writing, and design should be impeccable, and any edits or changes should be minor rewording, not major reconstruction. Most likely that's the experience you'll have.

But if the draft doesn't meet your expectations, keep in mind that it is a work in progress. Changes can be made and issues addressed with your writer. Never despair that a rough draft can't be polished.

Share all of your questions and concerns with your writer in a respectful manner, and he will work with you to resolve them. Chances are, you'll be entirely satisfied with the finished product. If you do have major issues that can't be resolved, see the box at the end of this chapter, "What to Do If You're Seriously Unhappy with Your Resume."

Your Contribution to the Process

Yes, you've hired a professional to write your resume. But that doesn't absolve you from all responsibility. The resume can't be written without your participation, and the more energetically and positively you approach the task, the better the results will be.

Your resume writer will appreciate you for doing the following:

- **Know what you're looking for.** Your resume writer can't tell you what career to pursue and can't write one resume that will position you for every job under the sun. Know where you're going, and your writer will help you get there.
- **Provide all information as requested and in a timely fashion.** If worksheets are required, spend the time and effort to complete them thoroughly. If completing a questionnaire is an onerous burden on you, select a writer who relies on consultation rather than worksheets. For all other parts of the process, pay attention to deadlines and stay on top of the tasks you've been assigned. This will keep your resume project on track and your career moving forward.
- **Be introspective, thoughtful, and comprehensive in answering questions during the consultation or on worksheets.** Resume writers can only write about what you tell us. Think carefully about why you love your work, what you're really good at, and what work-related activities you have most enjoyed. Share all of that with your resume writer, with emphasis on your greatest successes. Don't be modest!

- **Review drafts promptly.** Keep the process moving by reviewing proof copies expeditiously and getting back quickly to your writer. Be aware that your contract may include a time limit for reviewing and revising your document. Resume writers include this clause because if we have to revisit your circumstances after several weeks or months have passed, your situation is not as fresh in our minds and we have to expend a good deal of time and effort to get back up to speed. It's much better for everyone to review and finalize the material while it's fresh.
- **Clearly articulate your feedback.** Hearing "I love it! It's perfect!" is the resume writer's dream. Our highest aspiration is to hear that you're thrilled with our work. But we know that every resume won't be a perfect 10 on the very first try. When reviewing your resume with your writer, be as specific as you can about what you don't like. Is it tone, language, format, layout, facts? Any or all of those things can be adjusted. Saying "I'm just not happy with it" is not effective because your writer won't know how to make it right.
- **Be open to your writer's viewpoint and respect your writer's expertise.** Ask your questions and share your comments, and then let your writer explain the rationale behind the decision. Does it make sense? Even if it's a bit outside your comfort zone, be willing to stretch yourself a bit, and keep in mind that your writer is a pro with a ton of experience regarding resumes and job search. However, don't bend so far that you're uncomfortable with your resume. You know yourself, your industry, and your career, and you (not your writer) will be discussing all of the above at the interviews. Never settle for a resume that you think is ineffective, misleading, or out of touch with reality.

What to Do If You're Seriously Unhappy with Your Resume

In the vast majority of cases, the process from first review to final document is swift and cordial. But perhaps you are one of those rare instances of deep dissatisfaction. What should you do? Follow these steps in their escalating order, stopping at the point where you are satisfied with your resume.

- **Articulate your dissatisfaction in a professional manner.** Try to steer away from emotional words like "hate," "lousy," "stinks," and "unprofessional." Instead, be as specific as possible about what you dislike. Use examples of other resumes to support your case.
- **Give the resume writer a chance to respond and address your concerns.** Be open-minded when reviewing subsequent drafts, and be realistic about how well your background stacks up to your example resumes.
- **Get third-party opinions from people you respect who are in a position to know.** Perhaps these are work colleagues, a former boss, a mentor, or a

(continued)

(continued)

recruiter—not just your family and close friends. Share their feedback with your resume writer, again in a professional manner.

- **Consider asking another resume writer for an opinion.** If repeated revisions bring you no closer to your ideal resume, contact another resume writer, perhaps one of your initial "possibles," and be frank about the situation. Ask for a professional opinion without revealing the name of your writer.
- **Give your resume a few test flights to see what response you get.** Unless your resume is error-filled or clearly unprofessional, why not give your writer the benefit of the doubt and test-drive your new resume in a variety of circumstances? Share it with network contacts, send it directly to targeted companies, and respond to postings. See what happens. You might be pleasantly surprised! Be sure to document all of this activity and any reaction you get so that you'll have evidence of your case.
- **Go back to your resume writer with all of the evidence and invoke the money-back, rewrite, or satisfaction guarantee.**

If you've gone through all of these steps and remain deeply dissatisfied, there's little chance that your writer can do more for you. Resume writers get tremendous satisfaction from helping people with their careers. They will feel terrible that they've disappointed you, and they'll want to make it right. However, in these cases there is often disagreement about the quality of the work and the degree to which expectations were met. Be clear about what you expect now, and be willing to hear your writer's side of the story. Resolve the issue as best you can, and then put it behind you and reapply your energies to your job search.

In the vast majority of cases, the resume development process is intense but enjoyable and extremely rewarding in helping you appreciate your value in the job market. At the end of the process, you'll feel energized, excited, and eager to put your new resume to work.

Move On to Your Job Search

Every professional resume writer will tell you that the cycle of review and revision can be never-ending. We can always find just one more sentence to tweak or format to try. But after you've reviewed your document, approved its strategy and contents, corrected any errors, and given it a final eagle-eyed examination, it's time to finish the review process and put your resume to work.

Although you want to be thorough and careful, don't get obsessive about your resume. Changing one word here or there is not going to make the difference in your career. The most critical factor is what you do with the resume—how you execute your search strategy. The next section gives you a blueprint for doing just that.

If you find yourself going over and over the resume, aiming for perfection while doing nothing about actually looking for a job, dig deep to find out what's stopping you. Are you afraid you won't be successful? Nervous about networking? Apprehensive about interviewing, concerned about your job history, or worried about a reference from your latest boss? It's natural to feel some apprehension at the start of a major transition, but if you find yourself stuck and unable to move forward, it's time to call in a coach or counselor to help you uncover and resolve the issues so that you can advance toward your goals.

Putting Your New Resume to Work

Attack your job search by crafting a plan that incorporates as many as possible of the different avenues you might pursue to learn about jobs and land interviews.

The following nine strategies are presented in order from *least* to *most* effective. Most people get busy with items #1 through #4, zapping out their resume to any and all places they can think of. That's a good way to *feel* like you're working hard on your job search. You'll be busy... but you won't be very productive.

For best results, spend most of your time on activities #5 through #9. These might not be as easy or as direct, but they usually yield the best leads, and they usually position you ahead of the competition.

Less Effective Strategies

1. **Post your resume online.**
   Success tips: Focus on specialty rather than general sites. If a professional association or industry-specific Web site has a posting page, employers often go there first because they can find a highly concentrated source of resumes in a particular field. You can use an automated service to mass-post your resume on the sites you select. Post it, refresh or update it periodically, but don't obsess about plastering your resume everywhere online. Finally, be aware of identity-theft issues with any material that you post online.
2. **Respond to print ads and online postings.**
   Success tips: Take just a few minutes to fine-tune your resume so that it responds as closely as possible to the specifics called out in the ad. Send it and forget it—don't waste a lot of time following up, especially if there's no name included in the posting. If you do have a name, a quick phone call two or three days after sending your resume is appropriate. Be aware that employers are flooded with hundreds if not thousands of responses to every ad, and don't get discouraged if your "hit" rate is low.
3. **Mass-mail or e-mail your resume to companies.**
   Success tips: You can purchase a mailing list of companies that fit your criteria for industry, size, and location, and then send them a resume in hopes that they'll have an interest if not an opening. Hard-copy mailing is much more costly but much more classy and probably more effective, especially if

you are contacting senior executives and hiring managers rather than the human resources department.

4. **Mass e-mail your resume to recruiters.**
   Success tips: Put your material into hundreds of recruiter databases in hopes that you'll be a match for a current or future search. Multiple services exist to automate and handle this task for you. Hit rates tend to be low, but it's a low-risk, low-effort, relatively low-cost activity—typically a few hundred dollars or less.

More Effective Strategies

5. **Connect with recruiters.**
   Success tips: If you have past relationships with recruiters, now is the time to get back in touch. You can also identify a handful of recruiters who specialize in your profession or your industry and reach out to them one at a time to see if they have an interest. Be aware that recruiters *do* specialize, and don't be surprised if they ignore you unless you are a great fit for one of their current searches.
6. **Apply directly at your companies of choice.**
   Success tips: Spend some time on the career sites of the companies you're most interested in. Browse their openings, learn more about career paths and company culture, and gather information about what it's really like to work there. Then, go ahead and apply for jobs that are a good fit. Follow all instructions carefully, and do tailor your resume to fit the job specs, as appropriate.
7. **Use online networking sites.**
   Success tips: Just as in offline networking (see #9 below), focus on building relationships and giving before getting. Be clear about what you're looking for and how—precisely—your contacts can help you. In everything you do, be sure you are creating an online identity that presents a positive professional image, so that when network contacts and future employers look you up they'll receive positive reinforcement about who you are.
8. **Get referrals to your target companies.**
   Success tips: What better way to get an "in" at a target company than to get a personal referral? This approach requires that you first develop your target list, and continue to expand and refine it as your search continues. Then, when meeting with your contacts, ask for specific referrals to your top companies.
9. **Tap into your network for ideas, advice, recommendations, and referrals.**
   Success tips: Who you know counts… but even more important are the people your contacts know. Ask your friends, relatives, colleagues, former co-workers, members of professional groups, and anyone and everyone you can think of for ideas, leads, referrals to influential people, and referrals to your target companies. Have a prepared message that clearly communicates who you are, what your greatest value is, and how they can help you.

You may be astonished at how helpful people are. It's sometimes difficult to get started with networking, but it is truly the most valuable tool in your job search toolbox.

If the challenge of looking for a job seems overwhelming, ask for help. Many professional resume writers also provide coaching services. They can help you create an action plan and execute every step of the way until you land your next job.

PART 2

The Directory of Professional Resume Writers

How This Section Is Organized

This directory is a rich lode of information about some of the best resume writers in the English-speaking world. Knowing that you will want to search for a writer with the specific expertise to fit your circumstances, I have arranged this section into several lists that will help you quickly locate several "possibles" as the starting point for your search.

Chapter 4: Resume Writers by Specialty Areas

In this chapter, you'll find a listing of writers sorted by functional area, industries, and special circumstances. After browsing this chapter, turn to chapter 6 (the alphabetic listing) to find out more details and full contact information for the writers you've selected.

Chapter 5: Geographic Directory of Professional Resume Writers

Where your resume writer is located might not be an important factor for you. The vast majority (95 percent) of the resume writers featured in this book work remotely, communicating with clients by phone and e-mail and sending documents electronically. In fact, you might find it advantageous to work with a writer in a different time zone, so that you can more easily schedule phone consultations without conflicting with your work schedule.

But perhaps you prefer to work with a writer who is located where you live now or where you want to live. For that reason, I have provided a geographic breakdown of all the writers featured in the book.

Note that if you prefer to work in person or even get your resume prepared while-you-wait, be sure to cross-check your local writers with the "Business Model" section in chapter 4.

Chapter 6: Alphabetic Directory of Resume Writers

Finally, in chapter 6, I present a complete alphabetic listing of all the resume writers featured in this book. You will find each resume writer's credentials, contact information (phone and e-mail), Web site, and a brief self-written description of what sets them apart from others.

Use this chapter to narrow down your choices and connect with a few writers. Read what they say about themselves and review the content on their Web sites. Then contact your top choices and begin asking questions (as detailed in chapter 2) to select the right writer for your specific circumstances.

A Note About Professional Associations

I'm a big believer in the value of belonging to professional associations. In the careers field, like any other, it's essential to stay abreast of trends and changes in our profession, keep our skills sharp, pursue professional development, and connect with a group of peers and acknowledged experts.

The five associations profiled here exist to serve professional resume writers, and membership in one of these organizations was the only criteria for a resume writer to be included in this book. All members of all the associations were invited, and I listed every writer who took the time to complete my survey.

You can visit the association Web sites if you are interested in learning more about any of the organizations, or to check the current roster to be sure your selected writers haven't let their memberships lapse.

Following is a brief profile of all five of these organizations.

Association of Online Resume and Career Professionals (AORCP)
Year Founded: 2001
Members: 100
Certifications Awarded: Certified Master Resume Specialist (CMRS)
Description: The Association of Online Résumé and Career Professionals (AORCP) was formed specifically targeting Internet-based career coaches and resume writers who perform their business utilizing online technologies. The organization provides resume writers with an opportunity to network on both a professional and personal level to foster professional development and business growth.

Web site: www.aorcp.com
Additional Contact Information: Karen M. Silins, (816) 942-3019, karen@aorcp.com

Career Directors International (CDI)
Year Founded: 2000
Members: 300
Certifications Awarded: Certified Advanced Resume Writer (CARW)
Certified Expert Resume Writer (CERW)
Master Career Director (MCD)
Certified Employment Interview Consultant (CEIC)
Certified Career Research Expert (CCRE)
Corrections Career Transition Certified (CCTC)
Certified Military Resume Writer (CMRW)
Certified Federal Resume Writer (CFRW)
Certified Web Portfolio Practitioner (CWPP)
Certified Electronic Career Coach (CECC)
Description: CDI is the premier educational, research, and credentialing organization for career professionals. A professional association committed to delivering industry innovation and unlimited potential for career professionals, CDI places top priority on introducing new member opportunities in education, connection, and empowerment. Its global membership spans all career disciplines and includes resume writers, career coaches and counselors, job developers, recruiters, outplacement specialists, HR practitioners, and other specialists from private practice, civil service, academia, and military.
Web site: www.careerdirectors.com

Additional Contact Information: Laura DeCarlo, (321) 752-0442, (888) 867-7972, laura@careerdirectors.com

Career Management Alliance (formerly Career Masters Institute)
Year Founded: 1999
Members: 550
Certifications Awarded: Master Resume Writer (MRW)
Credentialed Career Master (CCM)
Description: The world's leading and most trusted association of career professionals, Career Management Alliance is your gateway to fulfillment and profits. Our community members come from every sector of the careers industry—career coaches, counselors, outplacement consultants, resume writers, recruiters, HR professionals, college and university career development professionals, government and military career transition specialists, and more. Together, we've formed the most vibrant careers community in the world!
Web site: www.careermanagementalliance.com
Additional Contact Information: Wendy Enelow, (434) 299-5600, wendy@careermanagementalliance.com

Career Professionals of Canada
Year Founded: 2004
Members: 150
Certifications Awarded: Certified Resume Strategist (CRS)
Certified Interview Strategist (CIS)
Certified Career Strategist (CCS)
Description: Career Professionals of Canada (CPC) is setting the Canadian standard for excellence in resume, interview, and career strategy. We are the leading Canadian member-driven career services organization. Our members come from all sectors and regions across Canada including universities and colleges, government organizations, non-profit services, outplacement firms, and independent practitioners. Our mandate is to enable Canadians to achieve their career, business, and organizational development goals by promoting quality, ethics, and expertise within the industry. Working together, we provide quality services, comply with a strict ethical standard, and offer career expertise to assist Canadians. We connect individuals and organizations to a nationwide network of advisors. We help people achieve success as they take their career and business to new horizons.
Web site: www.CareerProCanada.ca
Additional Contact Information: Sharon Graham, (905) 878-8768, (866) 622-1464, info@CareerProCanada.ca

The National Resume Writers' Association (NRWA)
Year Founded: 1997
Members: 400
Certifications Awarded: Nationally Certified Resume Writer (NCRW)
Description: The National Resume Writers' Association (NRWA) is the industry's leading not-for-profit, member-driven organization dedicated to promoting the highest standards of excellence in resume writing through certification, education, and mentoring programs. Our membership is made up of a diverse and global group of resume writers, career coaches, government and military career transition specialists, college and university career development professionals, and outplacement consultants.
Many of our members have been recipients of one or more industry writing or coaching certifications; published in national career-relevant books and industry publications; quoted as a career-industry expert in national, regional, and local newspapers; requested to speak on career topics for television and radio broadcasts; and guest speakers at professional association events, conferences, and career fairs.
NRWA members' commitment to continual learning in the career services field equates to the utmost professionalism and the highest ethical standards.
Web site: www.nrwaweb.com
Additional Contact Information: (877) 843-6792, adminmanager@nrwaweb.com

Professional Association of Resume Writers & Career Coaches (PARW/CC)
Year Founded: 1990
Members: 650
Certifications Awarded: Certified Professional Resume Writer (CPRW)
Certified Employment Interview Professional (CEIP)
Certified Professional Career Coach (CPCC)
Description: The oldest and largest association for professional resume writers and career coaches.
Web site: www.parw.com
Additional Contact Information: Frank Fox, (800) 822-7279, parwhq@aol.com

CHAPTER 4

Resume Writers by Specialty Areas

This chapter breaks down writers by Functional Specialties, Special Circumstances, Industry Specialities, and Business Model (remote, in person, or while-you-wait).

Starting your search with resume writers who specialize in your particular function, industry, or circumstance is a smart approach. After you review the lists below, you can find full contact information for each writer in chapter 6. Most writers have a Web site that you can check out to get further information—and often view some sample resumes, in addition to the resumes showcased in chapter 7.

Functional Specialties

Blue Collar/Trades

Margaret Anderson
Elizabeth J. Axnix
Ann Baehr
Janet L. Beckstrom
Mark D. Berkowitz
Marian Bernard
Julie Bernardin
Arnold G. Boldt
Nancy Boyer
Shannon D. Branson
Anne Brunelle
LeRachel H. Buffkins
Margaret Burkholder
Nita Busby
Ron Cail
Clay Cerny
Freddie Cheek
Stephanie Clark
Sally Cofer-Lindberg
Pat Cort
Pat Criscito
Norine Dagliano
Robert Dagnall
Dian R. Davis
Laura DeCarlo
Jessica Dillard
Patricia Duckers
Deloris J. (Dee) Duff

(continued)

Blue Collar/Trades (continued)

Nina Ebert

Lynn Eischen

Wilson W. Elliott

Donna Farrise

Dayna Feist

Audrey Field

Art Frank

Gail Frank

Fred Frazier Jr.

Stephen R. Gallison

Susan Geary

Wendy Gelberg

Betty Geller

Don Goodman

Will W. Grant

Jill Grindle

Meg Guiseppi

Beate Hait

Makini Theresa Harvey

Terri W. Henderson

Susan Hoopes

Phyllis Houston

Kim Isaacs

Caroline M. Jagot

Deborah James

La-Dana Renee Jenkins

Jerry D. Johnson

Suzette Jolly

Angela Jones

Denette Jones

Billie P. Jordan

Wally C. Keenan

Gillian Kelly

Pat Kendall

Kathy Keshemberg

Frost Krist

Malloy Lacktman

Lynda Lucas

Tamelynda Lux

Irene Marshall

Sharon McCormick

Debbie McMahan

Carol Nason

Patricia Navin

Beverley Neil

Katie Newton

Samantha Nolan

Debra O'Reilly

Tracy M. Parish

Kris Plantrich

Robert Prock

Julie Rains

Michelle Mastruserio Reitz

Jane Roqueplot

Teena Rose

Nancy Rozum

Jennifer Rushton

Robin Schlinger

Debbie Shalom

Harriet Shea

Janice M. Shepherd
William (Bill) Smith
Chris Starkey
Ann Stewart
Denise Stewart
Marilyn Stollon
Billie R. Sucher
Lonnie L. Swanson
Kathy Sweeney
Tanya Taylor
Kevin Tucker
Edward Turilli
Christine Tutor
Ilona Vanderwoude
Chris Van Petten
Roleta Fowler Vasquez
Judith Vince
Kathy Voska
Julie Walraven
Jill Walser
Kendra Walters
Judy Ware
Kathleen Weston
Pearl White
Amy Whitmer
Beth Woodworth
Jeremy Worthington
Angela P. Zimmer

Creative Professions

Christopher Aune
Ann Baehr
Lorraine Beaman
Mark D. Berkowitz
Marian Bernard
Julie Bernardin
Anne Brunelle
LeRachel H. Buffkins
Margaret Burkholder
Nita Busby
Tammy W. Chisholm
Stephanie Clark
Pat Criscito
Annemarie Cross
Robert Dagnall
Laura DeCarlo
Jessica Dillard
Patricia Duckers
Michelle Dumas
Nina Ebert
Clifford W. Eischen
Wilson W. Elliott
Donna Farrise
Marilyn A. Feldstein
Cliff Flamer
Louise Fletcher
Art Frank
Gail Frank
Stephen R. Gallison
Louise Garver

(continued)

Creative Professions (continued)

Susan Geary
Betty Geller
Don Goodman
Will W. Grant
Susan Guarneri
Meg Guiseppi
Terri W. Henderson
Karen Hughes
Kim Isaacs
La-Dana Renee Jenkins
Jerry D. Johnson
Denette Jones
Wally C. Keenan
Gillian Kelly
Pat Kendall
Erin Kennedy
Jeanne Knight
Frost Krist
Malloy Lacktman
Lorie Lebert
Lynda Lucas
Tamelynda Lux
Murray A. Mann
Jan Melnik
Sharon McCormick
Debbie McMahan
Joan Murrin
Katie Newton
Samantha Nolan
John M. O'Connor
Tracy M. Parish
Stephanie Peacocke
Judit Price
Robert Prock
Edie Rische
Camille Carboneau Roberts
Martha Rockwell
Jane Roqueplot
Teena Rose
Nancy Rozum
Lori Russel
Evelyn U. Salvador
Robin Schlinger
Kimberly Schneiderman
Debbie Shalom
Harriet Shea
Janice M. Shepherd
Karen M. Silins
Ann Stewart
Denise Stewart
Marilyn Stollon
Billie R. Sucher
Lonnie L. Swanson
Wendy J. Terwelp
Kevin Tucker
Edward Turilli
Christine Tutor
Claudine Vainrub
Ilona Vanderwoude
Vivian VanLier

Chris Van Petten
Roleta Fowler Vasquez
Judith Vince
Kathy Voska
Julie Walraven
Jill Walser
Kendra Walters
Martin Weitzman
Pearl White
Amy Whitmer
Beth Woodworth
Janice Worthington
Jeremy Worthington
Angela P. Zimmer

Administration and Customer Service

Georgia Adamson
Tom Albano
Margaret Anderson
Don Arthur
Christopher Aune
Elizabeth J. Axnix
Ann Baehr
Lorraine Beaman
Janet L. Beckstrom
Mark D. Berkowitz
Marian Bernard
Julie Bernardin
Nancy Boyer
Shannon D. Branson
Anne Brunelle
LeRachel H. Buffkins
Margaret Burkholder
Diane Hudson Burns
Nita Busby
Ron Cail
Franchesca Carrington
Clay Cerny
Lisa Chapman
Freddie Cheek
Tammy W. Chisholm
Stephanie Clark
Sally Cofer-Lindberg
Beth Colley
Pat Cort
Pat Criscito
Annemarie Cross
Norine Dagliano
Robert Dagnall
Dian R. Davis
Michael S. Davis
Laura DeCarlo
Jessica Dillard
John Donovan
Patricia Duckers
Deloris J. (Dee) Duff
Michelle Dumas
Nina Ebert
Cory Edwards
Clifford W. Eischen

(continued)

Administration and Customer Service (continued)

Lynn Eischen
Wilson W. Elliott
Donna Farrise
Dayna Feist
Robyn L. Feldberg
Marilyn A. Feldstein
Cliff Flamer
Art Frank
Gail Frank
Fred Frazier Jr.
Stephen R. Gallison
Louise Garver
Susan Geary
Wendy Gelberg
Betty Geller
Don Goodman
Will W. Grant
Jill Grindle
Susan Guarneri
Meg Guiseppi
Beate Hait
Makini Theresa Harvey
Terri W. Henderson
Susan Hoopes
Phyllis Houston
Karen Hughes
Diane Irwin
Kim Isaacs
Caroline M. Jagot
Deborah James
La-Dana Renee Jenkins
Jerry D. Johnson
Suzette Jolly
Angela Jones
Denette Jones
Billie P. Jordan
Karen P. Katz
Wally C. Keenan
Fran Kelley
Gillian Kelly
Pat Kendall
Erin Kennedy
Kathy Keshemberg
Myriam-Rose Kohn
Frost Krist
Laura Labovich
Malloy Lacktman
Lorie Lebert
Lynda Lucas
Tamelynda Lux
Murray A. Mann
Irene Marshall
Sharon McCormick
Debbie McMahan
Cheryl Minnick
Carol Nason
Patricia Navin
Beverley Neil
Sari Neudorf
Katie Newton

JoAnn Nix
Samantha Nolan
Debra O'Reilly
Ethan Pang
Tracy M. Parish
Stephanie Peacocke
Kris Plantrich
Judit Price
Robert Prock
Julie Rains
Michelle Mastruserio Reitz
Edie Rische
Camille Carboneau Roberts
Martha Rockwell
Jane Roqueplot
Teena Rose
Nancy Rozum
Jennifer Rushton
Lori Russel
Robin Schlinger
Joellyn Wittenstein Schwerdlin
Nancy H. Segal
Debbie Shalom
Harriet Shea
Janice M. Shepherd
Igor Shpudejko
Karen M. Silins
Kelley Smith
William (Bill) Smith
Chris Starkey
Ann Stewart
Denise Stewart
Marilyn Stollon
Billie R. Sucher
Lonnie L. Swanson
Kathy Sweeney
Tanya Taylor
Kevin Tucker
Edward Turilli
Christine Tutor
Claudine Vainrub
Ilona Vanderwoude
Vivian VanLier
Chris Van Petten
Ellie Vargo
Roleta Fowler Vasquez
Judith Vince
Debra M. Vinikour
Kathy Voska
Julie Walraven
Jill Walser
Kendra Walters
Judy Ware
Kathleen Weston
Pearl White
Amy Whitmer
Beth Woodworth
Jeremy Worthington
Daisy Wright
Angela P. Zimmer

Finance and Accounting

Georgia Adamson
Margaret Anderson
Michele Angello
Deanne Arnath
Elizabeth J. Axnix
Ann Baehr
Mark D. Berkowitz
Marian Bernard
Julie Bernardin
Anne Brunelle
LeRachel H. Buffkins
Margaret Burkholder
Nita Busby
Franchesca Carrington
Clay Cerny
Lisa Chapman
Freddie Cheek
Tammy W. Chisholm
Stephanie Clark
Pat Criscito
Annemarie Cross
Robert Dagnall
Michael S. Davis
Laura DeCarlo
Jessica Dillard
John Donovan
Patricia Duckers
Deloris J. (Dee) Duff
Michelle Dumas
Nina Ebert
Clifford W. Eischen
Wilson W. Elliott
Debbie Ellis
Donna Farrise
Dayna Feist
Robyn L. Feldberg
Marilyn A. Feldstein
Cliff Flamer
Louise Fletcher
Art Frank
Gail Frank
Fred Frazier Jr.
Stephen R. Gallison
Louise Garver
Wendy Gelberg
Betty Geller
Don Goodman
Will W. Grant
Susan Guarneri
Meg Guiseppi
Beate Hait
Tina Harlan
Makini Theresa Harvey
Maria E. Hebda
Terri W. Henderson
Phyllis Houston
Gayle Howard
Karen Hughes

Diane Irwin
Kim Isaacs
Deborah James
Jerry D. Johnson
Angela Jones
Billie P. Jordan
Wally C. Keenan
Gillian Kelly
Pat Kendall
Erin Kennedy
Kathy Keshemberg
Jeanne Knight
Myriam-Rose Kohn
Frost Krist
Malloy Lacktman
Lorie Lebert
Sandra Lim
Lynda Lucas
Tamelynda Lux
Murray A. Mann
Irene Marshall
Sharon McCormick
Debbie McMahan
Jan Melnik
Doug Morrison
Joan Murrin
Carol Nason
Katie Newton
JoAnn Nix
Samantha Nolan
John M. O'Connor
Tracy M. Parish
Sharon Pierce-Williams
Kris Plantrich
Judit Price
Robert Prock
Julie Rains
Michelle Mastruserio Reitz
Edie Rische
Camille Carboneau Roberts
Martha Rockwell
Jane Roqueplot
Teena Rose
Nancy Rozum
Jennifer Rushton
Lori Russel
Barbara Safani
Robin Schlinger
Kimberly Schneiderman
Joellyn Wittenstein Schwerdlin
Nancy H. Segal
Debbie Shalom
Harriet Shea
Janice M. Shepherd
Igor Shpudejko
Karen M. Silins
Kelley Smith
Chris Starkey
Ann Stewart
Denise Stewart

(continued)

Finance and Accounting (continued)

Marilyn Stollon
Billie R. Sucher
Lonnie L. Swanson
Kathy Sweeney
Tanya Taylor
Kevin Tucker
Edward Turilli
Claudine Vainrub
Ilona Vanderwoude
Vivian VanLier
Chris Van Petten
Ellie Vargo
Roleta Fowler Vasquez
Judith Vince
Debra M. Vinikour
Kathy Voska
Julie Walraven
Jill Walser
Kendra Walters
Judy Ware
Martin Weitzman
Pearl White
Betty H. Williams
Beth Woodworth
Janice Worthington
Jeremy Worthington
Daisy Wright
Angela P. Zimmer

Human Resources

Georgia Adamson
Tom Albano
Margaret Anderson
Michele Angello
Deanne Arnath
Don Arthur
Elizabeth J. Axnix
Ann Baehr
Lorraine Beaman
Janet L. Beckstrom
Mark D. Berkowitz
Marian Bernard
Julie Bernardin
Arnold G. Boldt
Nancy Boyer
Shannon D. Branson
Anne Brunelle
LeRachel H. Buffkins
Margaret Burkholder
Diane Hudson Burns
Nita Busby
Franchesca Carrington
Clay Cerny
Lisa Chapman
Freddie Cheek
Tammy W. Chisholm
Stephanie Clark
Sally Cofer-Lindberg
Beth Colley
Pat Criscito

Annemarie Cross
Norine Dagliano
Robert Dagnall
Michael S. Davis
Laura DeCarlo
Jessica Dillard
John Donovan
Patricia Duckers
Deloris J. (Dee) Duff
Michelle Dumas
Nina Ebert
Cory Edwards
Clifford W. Eischen
Wilson W. Elliott
Debbie Ellis
Donna Farrise
Dayna Feist
Robyn L. Feldberg
Marilyn A. Feldstein
Cliff Flamer
Louise Fletcher
Art Frank
Gail Frank
Julianne Franke
Fred Frazier Jr.
Stephen R. Gallison
Louise Garver
Susan Geary
Wendy Gelberg
Betty Geller
Don Goodman
Will W. Grant
Jill Grindle
Susan Guarneri
Meg Guiseppi
Beate Hait
Makini Theresa Harvey
Maria E. Hebda
Terri W. Henderson
Susan Hoopes
Phyllis Houston
Karen Hughes
Diane Irwin
Kim Isaacs
Deborah James
La-Dana Renee Jenkins
Jerry D. Johnson
Suzette Jolly
Angela Jones
Denette Jones
Billie P. Jordan
Karen P. Katz
Fran Kelley
Gillian Kelly
Wally C. Keenan
Pat Kendall
Erin Kennedy
Kathy Keshemberg
Jeanne Knight
Myriam-Rose Kohn

(continued)

Human Resources (continued)

Frost Krist

Laura Labovich

Malloy Lacktman

Lorie Lebert

Sandra Lim

Lynda Lucas

Tamelynda Lux

Murray A. Mann

Irene Marshall

Sharon McCormick

Debbie McMahan

Jan Melnik

Meg Montford

Joan Murrin

Carol Nason

Patricia Navin

Beverley Neil

Katie Newton

JoAnn Nix

Samantha Nolan

John M. O'Connor

Debra O'Reilly

Tracy M. Parish

Stephanie Peacocke

Sharon Pierce-Williams

Kris Plantrich

Judit Price

Robert Prock

Michelle Mastruserio Reitz

Edie Rische

Camille Carboneau Roberts

Martha Rockwell

Jane Roqueplot

Teena Rose

Nancy Rozum

Jennifer Rushton

Lori Russel

Barbara Safani

Robin Schlinger

Kimberly Schneiderman

Joellyn Wittenstein Schwerdlin

Nancy H. Segal

Debbie Shalom

Harriet Shea

Janice M. Shepherd

Igor Shpudejko

Karen M. Silins

William (Bill) Smith

Chris Starkey

Ann Stewart

Denise Stewart

Marilyn Stollon

Billie R. Sucher

Lonnie L. Swanson

Kathy Sweeney

Tanya Taylor

Kevin Tucker

Edward Turilli

Christine Tutor

Claudine Vainrub

Ilona Vanderwoude

Vivian VanLier

Chris Van Petten

Ellie Vargo

Roleta Fowler Vasquez

Judith Vince

Debra M. Vinikour

Kathy Voska

James Walker

Julie Walraven

Jill Walser

Kendra Walters

Martin Weitzman

Pearl White

Amy Whitmer

Betty H. Williams

Janice Worthington

Jeremy Worthington

Daisy Wright

Angela P. Zimmer

Advertising, Public Relations, Sales and Marketing, and Business Development

Georgia Adamson

Tom Albano

Carol Altomare

Margaret Anderson

Michele Angello

Deanne Arnath

Don Arthur

Christopher Aune

Elizabeth J. Axnix

Ann Baehr

Jacqui D. Barrett

Janet L. Beckstrom

Mark D. Berkowitz

Marian Bernard

Julie Bernardin

Arnold G. Boldt

Nancy Boyer

Anne Brunelle

LeRachel H. Buffkins

Margaret Burkholder

Diane Hudson Burns

Nita Busby

Ron Cail

Franchesca Carrington

Clay Cerny

Lisa Chapman

Freddie Cheek

Tammy W. Chisholm

Stephanie Clark

Sally Cofer-Lindberg

Beth Colley

Pat Cort

Pat Criscito

Annemarie Cross

Norine Dagliano

Robert Dagnall

(continued)

Advertising, Public Relations, Sales and Marketing, and Business Development (continued)

Michael S. Davis
Laura DeCarlo
Jessica Dillard
John Donovan
Patricia Duckers
Deloris J. (Dee) Duff
Michelle Dumas
George Dutch
Nina Ebert
Clifford W. Eischen
Lynn Eischen
Wilson W. Elliott
Debbie Ellis
Donna Farrise
Dayna Feist
Robyn L. Feldberg
Marilyn A. Feldstein
Audrey Field
Cliff Flamer
Louise Fletcher
Art Frank
Gail Frank
Julianne Franke
Fred Frazier Jr.
Stephen R. Gallison
Roberta Gamza
William Garner
Louise Garver
Susan Geary
Wendy Gelberg
Betty Geller
Don Goodman
Will W. Grant
Jill Grindle
Susan Guarneri
Meg Guiseppi
Beate Hait
Tina Harlan
Makini Theresa Harvey
Maria E. Hebda
Terri W. Henderson
Gayle Howard
Karen Hughes
Diane Irwin
Kim Isaacs
Caroline M. Jagot
Deborah James
La-Dana Renee Jenkins
Jerry D. Johnson
Suzette Jolly
Angela Jones
Denette Jones
Billie P. Jordan
Karen P. Katz
Wally C. Keenan
Fran Kelley
Gillian Kelly
Pat Kendall
Erin Kennedy
Kathy Keshemberg

Jeanne Knight
Myriam-Rose Kohn
Frost Krist
Laura Labovich
Malloy Lacktman
Lorie Lebert
Sandra Lim
Lynda Lucas
Tamelynda Lux
Murray A. Mann
Irene Marshall
Sharon McCormick
Debbie McMahan
Jan Melnik
Meg Montford
Doug Morrison
Joan Murrin
Carol Nason
Patricia Navin
Beverley Neil
Sari Neudorf
Katie Newton
JoAnn Nix
Samantha Nolan
John M. O'Connor
Debra O'Reilly
Ethan Pang
Tracy M. Parish
Stephanie Peacocke
Sharon Pierce-Williams
Kris Plantrich
Judit Price
Robert Prock
Julie Rains
Michelle Mastruserio Reitz
Edie Rische
Camille Carboneau Roberts
Martha Rockwell
Barbara Romano
Jane Roqueplot
Teena Rose
Nancy Rozum
Jennifer Rushton
Lori Russel
Evelyn U. Salvador
Robin Schlinger
Kimberly Schneiderman
Joellyn Wittenstein Schwerdlin
Debbie Shalom
Harriet Shea
Janice M. Shepherd
Igor Shpudejko
Karen M. Silins
Kelley Smith
William (Bill) Smith
Chris Starkey
Ann Stewart
Denise Stewart
Marilyn Stollon
Billie R. Sucher

(continued)

Advertising, Public Relations, Sales and Marketing, and Business Development (continued)

Lonnie L. Swanson
Kathy Sweeney
Tanya Taylor
Wendy J. Terwelp
Kevin Tucker
Edward Turilli
Christine Tutor
Claudine Vainrub
Ilona Vanderwoude
Vivian VanLier
Chris Van Petten
Ellie Vargo
Roleta Fowler Vasquez
Judith Vince
Debra M. Vinikour
Kathy Voska
Julie Walraven
Jill Walser
Kendra Walters
Judy Ware
Martin Weitzman
Kathleen Weston
Pearl White
Amy Whitmer
Betty H. Williams
Beth Woodworth
Janice Worthington
Jeremy Worthington
Daisy Wright
Angela P. Zimmer

Technology, Science, and Engineering

Georgia Adamson
Carol Altomare
Margaret Anderson
Deanne Arnath
Don Arthur
Elizabeth J. Axnix
Ann Baehr
Jacqui D. Barrett
Mark D. Berkowitz
Julie Bernardin
LeRachel H. Buffkins
Margaret Burkholder
Diane Hudson Burns
Nita Busby
Lisa Chapman
Freddie Cheek
Tammy W. Chisholm
Stephanie Clark
Pat Criscito
Annemarie Cross
Robert Dagnall
Michael S. Davis
Laura DeCarlo
Jessica Dillard
Anne-Marie Ditta
John Donovan

Patricia Duckers
Michelle Dumas
George Dutch
Nina Ebert
Cory Edwards
Wilson W. Elliott
Debbie Ellis
Donna Farrise
Marilyn A. Feldstein
Audrey Field
Cliff Flamer
Art Frank
Stephen R. Gallison
Roberta Gamza
William Garner
Louise Garver
Don Goodman
Will W. Grant
Susan Guarneri
Tina Harlan
Maria E. Hebda
Terri W. Henderson
Gayle Howard
Karen Hughes
Kim Isaacs
Angela Jones
Denette Jones
Billie P. Jordan
Karen P. Katz
Wally C. Keenan
Gillian Kelly
Pat Kendall
Erin Kennedy
Kathy Keshemberg
Jeanne Knight
Frost Krist
Bonnie Kurka
Malloy Lacktman
Lorie Lebert
Sandra Lim
Lynda Lucas
Tamelynda Lux
Murray A. Mann
Irene Marshall
Sharon McCormick
Debbie McMahan
Jan Melnik
Doug Morrison
Joan Murrin
Carol Nason
Patricia Navin
Katie Newton
JoAnn Nix
Samantha Nolan
John M. O'Connor
Debra O'Reilly
Ethan Pang
Tracy M. Parish
Stephanie Peacocke
Kris Plantrich

(continued)

Technology, Science and Engineering (continued)

Judit Price

Robert Prock

Edie Rische

Camille Carboneau Roberts

Martha Rockwell

Teena Rose

Jennifer Rushton

Lori Russel

Barbara Safani

Robin Schlinger

Kimberly Schneiderman

Harriet Shea

Igor Shpudejko

Karen M. Silins

Chris Starkey

Denise Stewart

Marilyn Stollon

Billie R. Sucher

Lonnie L. Swanson

Kathy Sweeney

Kevin Tucker

Edward Turilli

Christine Tutor

Claudine Vainrub

Ilona Vanderwoude

Chris Van Petten

Ellie Vargo

Roleta Fowler Vasquez

Judith Vince

Debra M. Vinikour

Kathy Voska

Julie Walraven

Jill Walser

Martin Weitzman

Michael B. Wetherington

Pearl White

Betty H. Williams

Janice Worthington

Jeremy Worthington

Angela P. Zimmer

Professionals

Georgia Adamson

Tom Albano

Carol Altomare

Margaret Anderson

Michele Angello

Deanne Arnath

Don Arthur

Elizabeth J. Axnix

Ann Baehr

Jacqui D. Barrett

Lorraine Beaman

Mark D. Berkowitz

Marian Bernard

Julie Bernardin

Arnold G. Boldt

Shannon D. Branson

Anne Brunelle

Shauna C. Bryce

Margaret Burkholder
Diane Hudson Burns
Nita Busby
Ron Cail
Franchesca Carrington
Clay Cerny
Lisa Chapman
Tammy W. Chisholm
Stephanie Clark
Sally Cofer-Lindberg
Beth Colley
Darlene Cook
Fred Coon
Pat Cort
Pat Criscito
Annemarie Cross
Norine Dagliano
Robert Dagnall
Michael S. Davis
Laura DeCarlo
Jessica Dillard
Anne-Marie Ditta
John Donovan
Patricia Duckers
Deloris J. (Dee) Duff
Michelle Dumas
George Dutch
Nina Ebert
Cory Edwards
Clifford W. Eischen
Lynn Eischen
Wilson W. Elliott
Donna Farrise
Dayna Feist
Robyn L. Feldberg
Marilyn A. Feldstein
Audrey Field
Cliff Flamer
Louise Fletcher
Art Frank
Gail Frank
Julianne Franke
Stephen R. Gallison
Louise Garver
Susan Geary
Wendy Gelberg
Betty Geller
Don Goodman
Will W. Grant
Jill Grindle
Susan Guarneri
Meg Guiseppi
Beate Hait
Tina Harlan
Makini Theresa Harvey
Maria E. Hebda
Terri W. Henderson
Gayle Howard
Karen Hughes
Diane Irwin

(continued)

Professionals (continued)

Kim Isaacs
Caroline M. Jagot
Deborah James
La-Dana Renee Jenkins
Jerry D. Johnson
Suzette Jolly
Angela Jones
Denette Jones
Billie P. Jordan
Karen P. Katz
Wally C. Keenan
Fran Kelley
Gillian Kelly
Pat Kendall
Erin Kennedy
Kathy Keshemberg
Jeanne Knight
Myriam-Rose Kohn
Bonnie Kurka
Laura Labovich
Malloy Lacktman
Lorie Lebert
Sandra Lim
Lynda Lucas
Tamelynda Lux
Murray A. Mann
Irene Marshall
Maureen McCann
Sharon McCormick
Debbie McMahan
Jan Melnik
Cheryl Minnick
Doug Morrison
Joan Murrin
Carol Nason
Patricia Navin
Beverley Neil
Sari Neudorf
Katie Newton
JoAnn Nix
Samantha Nolan
John M. O'Connor
Debra O'Reilly
Ethan Pang
Tracy M. Parish
Stephanie Peacocke
Sharon Pierce-Williams
Kris Plantrich
Judit Price
Robert Prock
Julie Rains
Michelle Mastruserio Reitz
Edie Rische
Camille Carboneau Roberts
Martha Rockwell
Jane Roqueplot
Teena Rose
Nancy Rozum
Jennifer Rushton
Lori Russel

Barbara Safani
Evelyn U. Salvador
Robin Schlinger
Kimberly Schneiderman
Joellyn Wittenstein Schwerdlin
Nancy H. Segal
Debbie Shalom
Harriet Shea
Janice M. Shepherd
Igor Shpudejko
Karen M. Silins
William (Bill) Smith
Chris Starkey
Ann Stewart
Denise Stewart
Marilyn Stollon
Billie R. Sucher
Lonnie L. Swanson
Kathy Sweeney
Tanya Taylor
Kevin Tucker
Edward Turilli
Christine Tutor
Claudine Vainrub
Ilona Vanderwoude
Vivian VanLier
Chris Van Petten
Ellie Vargo
Roleta Fowler Vasquez
Judith Vince
Debra M. Vinikour
Kathy Voska
Julie Walraven
Jill Walser
Kendra Walters
Martin Weitzman
Kathleen Weston
Michael B. Wetherington
Pearl White
Betty H. Williams
Beth Woodworth
Janice Worthington
Jeremy Worthington
Daisy Wright
Angela P. Zimmer

Managers and Executives

Barbara A. Adams
Georgia Adamson
Tom Albano
Carol Altomare
Margaret Anderson
Michele Angello
Deanne Arnath
Don Arthur
Christopher Aune
Elizabeth J. Axnix
Ann Baehr
Jacqui D. Barrett

(continued)

Managers and Executives (continued)

Lorraine Beaman
Mark D. Berkowitz
Marian Bernard
Julie Bernardin
Arnold G. Boldt
Anne Brunelle
Margaret Burkholder
Diane Hudson Burns
Nita Busby
Ron Cail
Clay Cerny
Lisa Chapman
Tammy W. Chisholm
Stephanie Clark
Sally Cofer-Lindberg
Darlene Cook
Fred Coon
Pat Criscito
Annemarie Cross
Robert Dagnall
Michael S. Davis
Laura DeCarlo
Jessica Dillard
Anne-Marie Ditta
John Donovan
Patricia Duckers
Deloris J. (Dee) Duff
Michelle Dumas
George Dutch
Nina Ebert
Cory Edwards
Clifford W. Eischen
Lynn Eischen
Wilson W. Elliott
Debbie Ellis
Donna Farrise
Dayna Feist
Robyn L. Feldberg
Marilyn A. Feldstein
Audrey Field
Cliff Flamer
Louise Fletcher
Art Frank
Gail Frank
Julianne Franke
Stephen R. Gallison
Roberta Gamza
Louise Garver
Wendy Gelberg
Betty Geller
Don Goodman
Will W. Grant
Jill Grindle
Susan Guarneri
Meg Guiseppi
Beate Hait
Tina Harlan
Makini Theresa Harvey
Maria E. Hebda
Terri W. Henderson

Phyllis Houston
Gayle Howard
Karen Hughes
Diane Irwin
Kim Isaacs
Caroline M. Jagot
Deborah James
La-Dana Renee Jenkins
Jerry D. Johnson
Angela Jones
Denette Jones
Billie P. Jordan
Karen P. Katz
Wally C. Keenan
Fran Kelley
Gillian Kelly
Pat Kendall
Erin Kennedy
Kathy Keshemberg
Jeanne Knight
Myriam-Rose Kohn
Frost Krist
Bonnie Kurka
Laura Labovich
Malloy Lacktman
Lorie Lebert
Sandra Lim
Lynda Lucas
Tamelynda Lux
Murray A. Mann

Irene Marshall
Maureen McCann
Sharon McCormick
Debbie McMahan
Jan Melnik
Meg Montford
Doug Morrison
Joan Murrin
Carol Nason
Patricia Navin
Beverley Neil
Sari Neudorf
Katie Newton
JoAnn Nix
Samantha Nolan
John M. O'Connor
Debra O'Reilly
Tracy M. Parish
Stephanie Peacocke
Sharon Pierce-Williams
Kris Plantrich
Judit Price
Robert Prock
Julie Rains
Michelle Mastruserio Reitz
Edie Rische
Camille Carboneau Roberts
Martha Rockwell
Barbara Romano
Jane Roqueplot

(continued)

Managers and Executives (continued)

Teena Rose

Nancy Rozum

Jennifer Rushton

Lori Russel

Barbara Safani

Evelyn U. Salvador

Robin Schlinger

Linda Schnabel

Kimberly Schneiderman

Joellyn Wittenstein Schwerdlin

Nancy H. Segal

Debbie Shalom

Harriet Shea

Igor Shpudejko

Karen M. Silins

Kelley Smith

Chris Starkey

Ann Stewart

Denise Stewart

Marilyn Stollon

Billie R. Sucher

Lonnie L. Swanson

Kathy Sweeney

Tanya Taylor

Wendy J. Terwelp

Kevin Tucker

Edward Turilli

Christine Tutor

Claudine Vainrub

Ilona Vanderwoude

Vivian VanLier

Chris Van Petten

Ellie Vargo

Roleta Fowler Vasquez

Judith Vince

Debra M. Vinikour

Kathy Voska

Julie Walraven

Jill Walser

Kendra Walters

Martin Weitzman

Kathleen Weston

Michael B. Wetherington

Susan Britton Whitcomb

Pearl White

Amy Whitmer

Betty H. Williams

Beth Woodworth

Janice Worthington

Daisy Wright

Angela P. Zimmer

Practice Limited to Executives

Martin Buckland

Jean Cummings

Deb Dib

Sharon Graham

Michele Haffner

Beverly Harvey

Cindy Kraft
Louise Kursmark
Linsey Levine
Abby Locke
Don Orlando
Phyllis B. Shabad
Laurie J. Smith
Beth W. Stefani
Kathy Warwick

Special Circumstances

Military Transition

Barbara A. Adams
Tom Albano
Michele Angello
Don Arthur
Christopher Aune
Elizabeth J. Axnix
Ann Baehr
Mark D. Berkowitz
Shannon D. Branson
Margaret Burkholder
Diane Hudson Burns
Nita Busby
Ron Cail
Clay Cerny
Lisa Chapman
Tammy W. Chisholm
Beth Colley
Fred Coon
Pat Cort
Pat Criscito
Annemarie Cross
Robert Dagnall
Dian R. Davis
Jessica Dillard
John Donovan
Patricia Duckers
Deloris J. (Dee) Duff
George Dutch
Nina Ebert
Clifford W. Eischen
Wilson W. Elliott
Debbie Ellis
Donna Farrise
Marilyn A. Feldstein
Audrey Field
Cliff Flamer
Art Frank
Fred Frazier Jr.
Stephen R. Gallison
William Garner
Louise Garver
Don Goodman
Will W. Grant
Beate Hait
Tina Harlan
Makini Theresa Harvey

(continued)

Military Transition (continued)

Terri W. Henderson

Phyllis Houston

Gayle Howard

Diane Irwin

Kim Isaacs

Caroline M. Jagot

Suzette Jolly

Angela Jones

Billie P. Jordan

Wally C. Keenan

Gillian Kelly

Pat Kendall

Erin Kennedy

Bonnie Kurka

Lynda Lucas

Murray A. Mann

Maureen McCann

Sharon McCormick

JoAnn Nix

John M. O'Connor

Debra O'Reilly

Don Orlando

Tracy M. Parish

Stephanie Peacocke

Judit Price

Robert Prock

Julie Rains

Michelle Mastruserio Reitz

Edie Rische

Camille Carboneau Roberts

Jane Roqueplot

Teena Rose

Lori Russel

Robin Schlinger

Nancy H. Segal

Janice M. Shepherd

Igor Shpudejko

Karen M. Silins

Laurie J. Smith

William (Bill) Smith

Marilyn Stollon

Lonnie L. Swanson

Kathy Sweeney

Kevin Tucker

Edward Turilli

Chris Van Petten

Ellie Vargo

Roleta Fowler Vasquez

James Walker

Jill Walser

Kendra Walters

Pearl White

Amy Whitmer

Betty H. Williams

Beth Woodworth

Janice Worthington

Jeremy Worthington

Angela P. Zimmer

Government (Federal Resumes)

Barbara A. Adams
Don Arthur
Shannon D. Branson
LeRachel H. Buffkins
Margaret Burkholder
Diane Hudson Burns
Clay Cerny
Tammy W. Chisholm
Beth Colley
Pat Criscito
Norine Dagliano
Jessica Dillard
Patricia Duckers
Deloris J. (Dee) Duff
George Dutch
Cory Edwards
Wilson W. Elliott
Debbie Ellis
Donna Farrise
Cliff Flamer
Art Frank
Stephen R. Gallison
Louise Garver
Will W. Grant
Tina Harlan
Makini Theresa Harvey
Terri W. Henderson
Phyllis Houston
Kim Isaacs
Billie P. Jordan
Gillian Kelly
Pat Kendall
Bonnie Kurka
Lynda Lucas
Tamelynda Lux
Murray A. Mann
Sharon McCormick
JoAnn Nix
John M. O'Connor
Don Orlando
Stephanie Peacocke
Julie Rains
Camille Carboneau Roberts
Jane Roqueplot
Teena Rose
Robin Schlinger
Nancy H. Segal
Karen M. Silins
Lonnie L. Swanson
Kathy Sweeney
Kevin Tucker
Ellie Vargo
Roleta Fowler Vasquez
Judith Vince
Jill Walser
Kendra Walters
Amy Whitmer
Janice Worthington
Jeremy Worthington

Return-to-Work

Carol Altomare
Margaret Anderson
Michele Angello
Don Arthur
Christopher Aune
Elizabeth J. Axnix
Ann Baehr
Jacqui D. Barrett
Lorraine Beaman
Mark D. Berkowitz
Marian Bernard
Nancy Boyer
Shannon D. Branson
Anne Brunelle
Margaret Burkholder
Nita Busby
Ron Cail
Franchesca Carrington
Freddie Cheek
Tammy W. Chisholm
Stephanie Clark
Beth Colley
Fred Coon
Pat Cort
Annemarie Cross
Norine Dagliano
Robert Dagnall
Dian R. Davis
Laura DeCarlo
Jessica Dillard
John Donovan
Deloris J. (Dee) Duff
Michelle Dumas
Nina Ebert
Clifford W. Eischen
Lynn Eischen
Wilson W. Elliott
Donna Farrise
Dayna Feist
Marilyn A. Feldstein
Audrey Field
Cliff Flamer
Art Frank
Gail Frank
Julianne Franke
Fred Frazier Jr.
Stephen R. Gallison
Louise Garver
Susan Geary
Wendy Gelberg
Betty Geller
Don Goodman
Sharon Graham
Will W. Grant
Jill Grindle
Susan Guarneri
Meg Guiseppi
Beate Hait

Makini Theresa Harvey
Terri W. Henderson
Phyllis Houston
Gayle Howard
Kim Isaacs
Caroline M. Jagot
Deborah James
La-Dana Renee Jenkins
Jerry D. Johnson
Suzette Jolly
Angela Jones
Billie P. Jordan
Wally C. Keenan
Gillian Kelly
Pat Kendall
Erin Kennedy
Myriam-Rose Kohn
Frost Krist
Malloy Lacktman
Lorie Lebert
Linsey Levine
Lynda Lucas
Tamelynda Lux
Murray A. Mann
Irene Marshall
Sharon McCormick
Debbie McMahan
Jan Melnik
Cheryl Minnick
Doug Morrison
Joan Murrin
Carol Nason
Patricia Navin
Sari Neudorf
Katie Newton
JoAnn Nix
Samantha Nolan
John M. O'Connor
Debra O'Reilly
Tracy M. Parish
Stephanie Peacocke
Sharon Pierce-Williams
Kris Plantrich
Judit Price
Robert Prock
Julie Rains
Michelle Mastruserio Reitz
Camille Carboneau Roberts
Martha Rockwell
Jane Roqueplot
Teena Rose
Nancy Rozum
Jennifer Rushton
Lori Russel
Kimberly Schneiderman
Joellyn Wittenstein Schwerdlin
Debbie Shalom
Harriet Shea
Janice M. Shepherd
Igor Shpudejko

(continued)

Return-to-Work (continued)

William (Bill) Smith

Chris Starkey

Ann Stewart

Marilyn Stollon

Billie R. Sucher

Lonnie L. Swanson

Kevin Tucker

Edward Turilli

Christine Tutor

Claudine Vainrub

Ilona Vanderwoude

Vivian VanLier

Chris Van Petten

Roleta Fowler Vasquez

Judith Vince

Jill Walser

Kendra Walters

Pearl White

Amy Whitmer

Betty H. Williams

Beth Woodworth

Janice Worthington

Jeremy Worthington

Angela P. Zimmer

Changing Careers

Barbara A. Adams

Georgia Adamson

Tom Albano

Carol Altomare

Margaret Anderson

Michele Angello

Deanne Arnath

Don Arthur

Christopher Aune

Elizabeth J. Axnix

Ann Baehr

Jacqui D. Barrett

Lorraine Beaman

Mark D. Berkowitz

Marian Bernard

Julie Bernardin

Nancy Boyer

Shannon D. Branson

Anne Brunelle

Martin Buckland

LeRachel H. Buffkins

Margaret Burkholder

Diane Hudson Burns

Nita Busby

Ron Cail

Franchesca Carrington

Clay Cerny

Lisa Chapman

Freddie Cheek

Tammy W. Chisholm

Stephanie Clark

Sally Cofer-Lindberg

Beth Colley

Darlene Cook

Fred Coon
Pat Cort
Pat Criscito
Annemarie Cross
Norine Dagliano
Robert Dagnall
Dian R. Davis
Michael S. Davis
Laura DeCarlo
Jessica Dillard
Anne-Marie Ditta
John Donovan
Deloris J. (Dee) Duff
Michelle Dumas
George Dutch
Nina Ebert
Clifford W. Eischen
Lynn Eischen
Wilson W. Elliott
Debbie Ellis
Donna Farrise
Dayna Feist
Robyn L. Feldberg
Marilyn A. Feldstein
Audrey Field
Cliff Flamer
Art Frank
Gail Frank
Julianne Franke
Fred Frazier Jr.

Stephen R. Gallison
Roberta Gamza
Louise Garver
Susan Geary
Wendy Gelberg
Betty Geller
Don Goodman
Sharon Graham
Will W. Grant
Jill Grindle
Susan Guarneri
Meg Guiseppi
Beate Hait
Beverly Harvey
Makini Theresa Harvey
Terri W. Henderson
Susan Hoopes
Karen Hughes
Diane Irwin
Kim Isaacs
Caroline M. Jagot
Deborah James
La-Dana Renee Jenkins
Jerry D. Johnson
Suzette Jolly
Angela Jones
Denette Jones
Billie P. Jordan
Karen P. Katz
Wally C. Keenan

(continued)

Changing Careers (continued)

Fran Kelley

Gillian Kelly

Pat Kendall

Erin Kennedy

Kathy Keshemberg

Myriam-Rose Kohn

Frost Krist

Bonnie Kurka

Laura Labovich

Malloy Lacktman

Lorie Lebert

Linsey Levine

Sandra Lim

Abby Locke

Lynda Lucas

Tamelynda Lux

Murray A. Mann

Irene Marshall

Sharon McCormick

Debbie McMahan

Jan Melnik

Cheryl Minnick

Meg Montford

Doug Morrison

Joan Murrin

Carol Nason

Patricia Navin

Sari Neudorf

Katie Newton

JoAnn Nix

Samantha Nolan

John M. O'Connor

Debra O'Reilly

Don Orlando

Ethan Pang

Tracy M. Parish

Stephanie Peacocke

Sharon Pierce-Williams

Kris Plantrich

Judit Price

Robert Prock

Michelle Mastruserio Reitz

Edie Rische

Camille Carboneau Roberts

Martha Rockwell

Jane Roqueplot

Teena Rose

Nancy Rozum

Jennifer Rushton

Lori Russel

Robin Schlinger

Linda Schnabel

Kimberly Schneiderman

Joellyn Wittenstein Schwerdlin

Nancy H. Segal

Phyllis B. Shabad

Debbie Shalom

Harriet Shea

Janice M. Shepherd

Igor Shpudejko

Karen M. Silins
William (Bill) Smith
Chris Starkey
Ann Stewart
Denise Stewart
Marilyn Stollon
Billie R. Sucher
Lonnie L. Swanson
Wendy J. Terwelp
Kevin Tucker
Edward Turilli
Christine Tutor
Claudine Vainrub
Ilona Vanderwoude
Vivian VanLier
Chris Van Petten
Roleta Fowler Vasquez
Judith Vince
Kathy Voska
Jill Walser
Kendra Walters
Judy Ware
Michael B. Wetherington
Pearl White
Amy Whitmer
Betty H. Williams
Beth Woodworth
Janice Worthington
Jeremy Worthington
Daisy Wright
Angela P. Zimmer

New Graduates

Deanne Arnath
Christopher Aune
Elizabeth J. Axnix
Ann Baehr
Lorraine Beaman
Mark D. Berkowitz
Marian Bernard
Janet L. Beckstrom
Nancy Boyer
Shannon D. Branson
Anne Brunelle
LeRachel H. Buffkins
Margaret Burkholder
Nita Busby
Ron Cail
Franchesca Carrington
Clay Cerny
Lisa Chapman
Tammy W. Chisholm
Stephanie Clark
Sally Cofer-Lindberg
Beth Colley
Pat Cort
Pat Criscito
Annemarie Cross
Norine Dagliano

(continued)

New Graduates (continued)

Robert Dagnall
Dian R. Davis
Michael S. Davis
Laura DeCarlo
Jessica Dillard
Anne-Marie Ditta
John Donovan
Patricia Duckers
Michelle Dumas
George Dutch
Nina Ebert
Clifford W. Eischen
Lynn Eischen
Wilson W. Elliott
Donna Farrise
Dayna Feist
Robyn L. Feldberg
Marilyn A. Feldstein
Cliff Flamer
Art Frank
Gail Frank
Julianne Franke
Fred Frazier Jr.
Stephen R. Gallison
Louise Garver
Susan Geary
Wendy Gelberg
Betty Geller
Don Goodman
Will W. Grant
Jill Grindle
Susan Guarneri
Meg Guiseppi
Beate Hait
Makini Theresa Harvey
Terri W. Henderson
Susan Hoopes
Phyllis Houston
Gayle Howard
Kim Isaacs
Caroline M. Jagot
Deborah James
La-Dana Renee Jenkins
Jerry D. Johnson
Suzette Jolly
Angela Jones
Billie P. Jordan
Wally C. Keenan
Gillian Kelly
Pat Kendall
Erin Kennedy
Myriam-Rose Kohn
Frost Krist
Laura Labovich
Malloy Lacktman
Lorie Lebert
Sandra Lim
Lynda Lucas
Tamelynda Lux
Murray A. Mann

Irene Marshall
Sharon McCormick
Debbie McMahan
Jan Melnik
Marti Miller
Cheryl Minnick
Doug Morrison
Carol Nason
Patricia Navin
Sari Neudorf
Katie Newton
JoAnn Nix
Samantha Nolan
John M. O'Connor
Debra O'Reilly
Ethan Pang
Tracy M. Parish
Stephanie Peacocke
Sharon Pierce-Williams
Kris Plantrich
Judit Price
Robert Prock
Julie Rains
Michelle Mastruserio Reitz
Edie Rische
Jane Roqueplot
Teena Rose
Nancy Rozum
Jennifer Rushton
Kimberly Schneiderman
Nancy H. Segal
Debbie Shalom
Janice M. Shepherd
Igor Shpudejko
Harriet Shea
Karen M. Silins
William (Bill) Smith
Chris Starkey
Ann Stewart
Marilyn Stollon
Lonnie L. Swanson
Kathy Sweeney
Kevin Tucker
Edward Turilli
Christine Tutor
Claudine Vainrub
Vivian VanLier
Chris Van Petten
Roleta Fowler Vasquez
Judith Vince
Kathy Voska
Julie Walraven
Jill Walser
Kendra Walters
Judy Ware
Michael B. Wetherington
Pearl White
Amy Whitmer
Betty H. Williams
Beth Woodworth

(continued)

New Graduates (continued)

Janice Worthington

Jeremy Worthington

Angela P. Zimmer

Over 50

Barbara A. Adams

Margaret Anderson

Michele Angello

Deanne Arnath

Don Arthur

Christopher Aune

Elizabeth J. Axnix

Ann Baehr

Jacqui D. Barrett

Lorraine Beaman

Mark D. Berkowitz

Marian Bernard

Julie Bernardin

Nancy Boyer

Shannon D. Branson

Anne Brunelle

Martin Buckland

Margaret Burkholder

Nita Busby

Clay Cerny

Lisa Chapman

Tammy W. Chisholm

Stephanie Clark

Beth Colley

Darlene Cook

Fred Coon

Pat Cort

Pat Criscito

Annemarie Cross

Norine Dagliano

Robert Dagnall

Dian R. Davis

Michael S. Davis

Laura DeCarlo

Deb Dib

Jessica Dillard

Deloris J. (Dee) Duff

Michelle Dumas

Nina Ebert

Clifford W. Eischen

Lynn Eischen

Wilson W. Elliott

Debbie Ellis

Donna Farrise

Dayna Feist

Robyn L. Feldberg

Marilyn A. Feldstein

Audrey Field

Cliff Flamer

Art Frank

Gail Frank

Julianne Franke

Fred Frazier Jr.
Stephen R. Gallison
Roberta Gamza
William Garner
Louise Garver
Susan Geary
Wendy Gelberg
Betty Geller
Don Goodman
Sharon Graham
Will W. Grant
Jill Grindle
Susan Guarneri
Meg Guiseppi
Beverly Harvey
Makini Theresa Harvey
Karen Hughes
Diane Irwin
Kim Isaacs
Caroline M. Jagot
Deborah James
Jerry D. Johnson
Suzette Jolly
Angela Jones
Billie P. Jordan
Karen P. Katz
Wally C. Keenan
Pat Kendall
Gillian Kelly
Kathy Keshemberg
Myriam-Rose Kohn
Frost Krist
Bonnie Kurka
Louise Kursmark
Malloy Lacktman
Lorie Lebert
Linsey Levine
Abby Locke
Lynda Lucas
Tamelynda Lux
Murray A. Mann
Irene Marshall
Sharon McCormick
Debbie McMahan
Jan Melnik
Meg Montford
Doug Morrison
Joan Murrin
Carol Nason
Patricia Navin
Katie Newton
JoAnn Nix
Samantha Nolan
John M. O'Connor
Debra O'Reilly
Don Orlando
Tracy M. Parish
Stephanie Peacocke
Sharon Pierce-Williams
Kris Plantrich

(continued)

Over 50 (continued)

Judit Price

Robert Prock

Julie Rains

Michelle Mastruserio Reitz

Camille Carboneau Roberts

Martha Rockwell

Jane Roqueplot

Teena Rose

Lori Russel

Robin Schlinger

Kimberly Schneiderman

Joellyn Wittenstein Schwerdlin

Phyllis B. Shabad

Debbie Shalom

Harriet Shea

Igor Shpudejko

Karen M. Silins

Laurie J. Smith

William (Bill) Smith

Chris Starkey

Ann Stewart

Marilyn Stollon

Billie R. Sucher

Lonnie L. Swanson

Kevin Tucker

Edward Turilli

Christine Tutor

Claudine Vainrub

Vivian VanLier

Chris Van Petten

Ellie Vargo

Roleta Fowler Vasquez

Judith Vince

Kathy Voska

Jill Walser

Kendra Walters

Judy Ware

Pearl White

Amy Whitmer

Betty H. Williams

Beth Woodworth

Janice Worthington

Jeremy Worthington

Daisy Wright

Angela P. Zimmer

Underemployed

Tom Albano

Deanne Arnath

Don Arthur

Christopher Aune

Elizabeth J. Axnix

Ann Baehr

Jacqui D. Barrett

Lorraine Beaman

Mark D. Berkowitz

Marian Bernard

Nancy Boyer
Shannon D. Branson
Anne Brunelle
Nita Busby
Lisa Chapman
Freddie Cheek
Tammy W. Chisholm
Stephanie Clark
Beth Colley
Pat Cort
Annemarie Cross
Norine Dagliano
Robert Dagnall
Dian R. Davis
Michael S. Davis
Laura DeCarlo
Jessica Dillard
John Donovan
Michelle Dumas
Nina Ebert
Wilson W. Elliott
Donna Farrise
Cliff Flamer
Art Frank
Gail Frank
Julianne Franke
Fred Frazier Jr.
Stephen R. Gallison
Roberta Gamza
Susan Geary
Wendy Gelberg
Betty Geller
Don Goodman
Sharon Graham
Will W. Grant
Jill Grindle
Susan Guarneri
Meg Guiseppi
Makini Theresa Harvey
Susan Hoopes
Gayle Howard
Diane Irwin
Kim Isaacs
Caroline M. Jagot
La-Dana Renee Jenkins
Jerry D. Johnson
Suzette Jolly
Angela Jones
Billie P. Jordan
Wally C. Keenan
Gillian Kelly
Pat Kendall
Kathy Keshemberg
Frost Krist
Laura Labovich
Malloy Lacktman
Lorie Lebert
Lynda Lucas
Tamelynda Lux
Murray A. Mann

(continued)

Underemployed (continued)

Irene Marshall

Sharon McCormick

Debbie McMahan

Jan Melnik

Doug Morrison

Joan Murrin

Carol Nason

Patricia Navin

Katie Newton

Samantha Nolan

John M. O'Connor

Don Orlando

Ethan Pang

Tracy M. Parish

Stephanie Peacocke

Judit Price

Robert Prock

Jane Roqueplot

Teena Rose

Kimberly Schneiderman

Joellyn Wittenstein Schwerdlin

Harriet Shea

Kelley Smith

William (Bill) Smith

Chris Starkey

Marilyn Stollon

Lonnie L. Swanson

Kevin Tucker

Edward Turilli

Christine Tutor

Claudine Vainrub

Chris Van Petten

Roleta Fowler Vasquez

Judith Vince

Jill Walser

Kendra Walters

Pearl White

Amy Whitmer

Beth Woodworth

Janice Worthington

Jeremy Worthington

Daisy Wright

Entrepreneurial

Barbara A. Adams

Tom Albano

Margaret Anderson

Michele Angello

Deanne Arnath

Don Arthur

Christopher Aune

Elizabeth J. Axnix

Ann Baehr

Jacqui D. Barrett

Mark D. Berkowitz

Marian Bernard

Julie Bernardin

Shannon D. Branson

Martin Buckland
Margaret Burkholder
Nita Busby
Lisa Chapman
Tammy W. Chisholm
Stephanie Clark
Sally Cofer-Lindberg
Beth Colley
Fred Coon
Pat Criscito
Annemarie Cross
Jean Cummings
Robert Dagnall
Dian R. Davis
Michael S. Davis
Laura DeCarlo
Deb Dib
Jessica Dillard
John Donovan
Patricia Duckers
Deloris J. (Dee) Duff
Michelle Dumas
Nina Ebert
Clifford W. Eischen
Lynn Eischen
Donna Farrise
Dayna Feist
Marilyn A. Feldstein
Cliff Flamer
Art Frank
Gail Frank
Julianne Franke
Stephen R. Gallison
Louise Garver
Betty Geller
Don Goodman
Sharon Graham
Will W. Grant
Jill Grindle
Susan Guarneri
Meg Guiseppi
Makini Theresa Harvey
Gayle Howard
Karen Hughes
Kim Isaacs
Caroline M. Jagot
Deborah James
La-Dana Renee Jenkins
Jerry D. Johnson
Suzette Jolly
Angela Jones
Denette Jones
Billie P. Jordan
Wally C. Keenan
Gillian Kelly
Pat Kendall
Erin Kennedy
Kathy Keshemberg
Myriam-Rose Kohn
Frost Krist

(continued)

Entrepreneurial (continued)

Bonnie Kurka

Louise Kursmark

Malloy Lacktman

Lorie Lebert

Linsey Levine

Sandra Lim

Abby Locke

Lynda Lucas

Tamelynda Lux

Murray A. Mann

Sharon McCormick

Debbie McMahan

Meg Montford

Doug Morrison

Carol Nason

Katie Newton

JoAnn Nix

Samantha Nolan

John M. O'Connor

Don Orlando

Ethan Pang

Tracy M. Parish

Stephanie Peacocke

Judit Price

Robert Prock

Julie Rains

Michelle Mastruserio Reitz

Camille Carboneau Roberts

Martha Rockwell

Teena Rose

Nancy Rozum

Jennifer Rushton

Lori Russel

Robin Schlinger

Kimberly Schneiderman

Joellyn Wittenstein Schwerdlin

Phyllis B. Shabad

Debbie Shalom

Harriet Shea

Janice M. Shepherd

Igor Shpudejko

Karen M. Silins

Laurie J. Smith

Ann Stewart

Denise Stewart

Marilyn Stollon

Billie R. Sucher

Lonnie L. Swanson

Wendy J. Terwelp

Kevin Tucker

Claudine Vainrub

Ilona Vanderwoude

Vivian VanLier

Chris Van Petten

Ellie Vargo

Roleta Fowler Vasquez

Judith Vince

Julie Walraven

Jill Walser

Kendra Walters

Kathleen Weston
Michael B. Wetherington
Pearl White
Amy Whitmer
Janice Worthington
Jeremy Worthington
Daisy Wright
Angela P. Zimmer

Industry Specialties

Healthcare

Barbara A. Adams
Tom Albano
Carol Altomare
Margaret Anderson
Deanne Arnath
Don Arthur
Christopher Aune
Elizabeth J. Axnix
Ann Baehr
Jacqui D. Barrett
Lorraine Beaman
Janet L. Beckstrom
Mark D. Berkowitz
Marian Bernard
Julie Bernardin
Arnold G. Boldt
Nancy Boyer
Shannon D. Branson
Anne Brunelle
Martin Buckland
LeRachel H. Buffkins
Nita Busby
Ron Cail
Franchesca Carrington
Clay Cerny
Lisa Chapman
Freddie Cheek
Tammy W. Chisholm
Stephanie Clark
Sally Cofer-Lindberg
Beth Colley
Fred Coon
Pat Criscito
Annemarie Cross
Jean Cummings
Norine Dagliano
Robert Dagnall
Dian R. Davis
Laura DeCarlo
Deb Dib
Jessica Dillard
Anne-Marie Ditta
Patricia Duckers
Deloris J. (Dee) Duff
Nina Ebert
Clifford W. Eischen

(continued)

Healthcare (continued)

Lynn Eischen
Wilson W. Elliott
Debbie Ellis
Donna Farrise
Dayna Feist
Robyn L. Feldberg
Marilyn A. Feldstein
Cliff Flamer
Art Frank
Gail Frank
Julianne Franke
Fred Frazier Jr.
Stephen R. Gallison
Louise Garver
Susan Geary
Betty Geller
Don Goodman
Sharon Graham
Will W. Grant
Jill Grindle
Susan Guarneri
Meg Guiseppi
Michele Haffner
Beate Hait
Tina Harlan
Beverly Harvey
Makini Theresa Harvey
Maria E. Hebda
Terri W. Henderson
Phyllis Houston
Karen Hughes
Diane Irwin
Kim Isaacs
Deborah James
La-Dana Renee Jenkins
Jerry D. Johnson
Suzette Jolly
Angela Jones
Billie P. Jordan
Karen P. Katz
Wally C. Keenan
Fran Kelley
Gillian Kelly
Pat Kendall
Erin Kennedy
Kathy Keshemberg
Jeanne Knight
Myriam-Rose Kohn
Frost Krist
Louise Kursmark
Malloy Lacktman
Lorie Lebert
Linsey Levine
Abby Locke
Lynda Lucas
Tamelynda Lux
Murray A. Mann
Irene Marshall
Sharon McCormick
Debbie McMahan

Jan Melnik
Meg Montford
Doug Morrison
Joan Murrin
Carol Nason
Katie Newton
JoAnn Nix
Samantha Nolan
John M. O'Connor
Debra O'Reilly
Don Orlando
Tracy M. Parish
Stephanie Peacocke
Sharon Pierce-Williams
Kris Plantrich
Judit Price
Robert Prock
Michelle Mastruserio Reitz
Edie Rische
Camille Carboneau Roberts
Martha Rockwell
Jane Roqueplot
Teena Rose
Nancy Rozum
Jennifer Rushton
Lori Russel
Evelyn U. Salvador
Robin Schlinger
Linda Schnabel
Phyllis B. Shabad
Debbie Shalom
Harriet Shea
Janice M. Shepherd
Igor Shpudejko
Karen M. Silins
Kelley Smith
Chris Starkey
Beth W. Stefani
Marilyn Stollon
Billie R. Sucher
Lonnie L. Swanson
Kathy Sweeney
Tanya Taylor
Wendy J. Terwelp
Kevin Tucker
Edward Turilli
Christine Tutor
Claudine Vainrub
Ilona Vanderwoude
Vivian VanLier
Chris Van Petten
Roleta Fowler Vasquez
Judith Vince
Debra M. Vinikour
Kathy Voska
Julie Walraven
Jill Walser
Kendra Walters
Kathy Warwick
Martin Weitzman

(continued)

Healthcare (continued)

Michael B. Wetherington

Pearl White

Amy Whitmer

Betty H. Williams

Beth Woodworth

Janice Worthington

Jeremy Worthington

Daisy Wright

Angela P. Zimmer

Education

Barbara A. Adams

Georgia Adamson

Michele Angello

Deanne Arnath

Don Arthur

Elizabeth J. Axnix

Ann Baehr

Jacqui D. Barrett

Lorraine Beaman

Janet L. Beckstrom

Mark D. Berkowitz

Marian Bernard

Julie Bernardin

Arnold G. Boldt

Nancy Boyer

Shannon D. Branson

Anne Brunelle

LeRachel H. Buffkins

Margaret Burkholder

Diane Hudson Burns

Nita Busby

Ron Cail

Franchesca Carrington

Clay Cerny

Lisa Chapman

Freddie Cheek

Tammy W. Chisholm

Stephanie Clark

Sally Cofer-Lindberg

Beth Colley

Fred Coon

Pat Cort

Pat Criscito

Annemarie Cross

Robert Dagnall

Dian R. Davis

Laura DeCarlo

Deb Dib

Jessica Dillard

Anne-Marie Ditta

John Donovan

Patricia Duckers

Deloris J. (Dee) Duff

Michelle Dumas

Nina Ebert

Clifford W. Eischen

Lynn Eischen

Wilson W. Elliott

Debbie Ellis
Donna Farrise
Dayna Feist
Robyn L. Feldberg
Marilyn A. Feldstein
Audrey Field
Cliff Flamer
Art Frank
Gail Frank
Julianne Franke
Fred Frazier Jr.
Stephen R. Gallison
Louise Garver
Betty Geller
Don Goodman
Sharon Graham
Will W. Grant
Susan Guarneri
Meg Guiseppi
Michele Haffner
Beate Hait
Beverly Harvey
Makini Theresa Harvey
Terri W. Henderson
Susan Hoopes
Phyllis Houston
Karen Hughes
Diane Irwin
Kim Isaacs
Deborah James
La-Dana Renee Jenkins
Jerry D. Johnson
Suzette Jolly
Angela Jones
Denette Jones
Billie P. Jordan
Karen P. Katz
Wally C. Keenan
Fran Kelley
Gillian Kelly
Pat Kendall
Erin Kennedy
Kathy Keshemberg
Myriam-Rose Kohn
Frost Krist
Laura Labovich
Malloy Lacktman
Lorie Lebert
Linsey Levine
Lynda Lucas
Tamelynda Lux
Murray A. Mann
Irene Marshall
Sharon McCormick
Debbie McMahan
Jan Melnik
Cheryl Minnick
Meg Montford
Joan Murrin
Carol Nason

(continued)

Education (continued)

Sari Neudorf

Katie Newton

JoAnn Nix

Samantha Nolan

John M. O'Connor

Debra O'Reilly

Don Orlando

Ethan Pang

Tracy M. Parish

Stephanie Peacocke

Sharon Pierce-Williams

Kris Plantrich

Judit Price

Robert Prock

Julie Rains

Michelle Mastruserio Reitz

Edie Rische

Camille Carboneau Roberts

Martha Rockwell

Jane Roqueplot

Teena Rose

Jennifer Rushton

Evelyn U. Salvador

Linda Schnabel

Joellyn Wittenstein Schwerdlin

Phyllis B. Shabad

Debbie Shalom

Harriet Shea

Janice M. Shepherd

Igor Shpudejko

Karen M. Silins

Kelley Smith

Chris Starkey

Beth W. Stefani

Marilyn Stollon

Billie R. Sucher

Lonnie L. Swanson

Kathy Sweeney

Tanya Taylor

Kevin Tucker

Edward Turilli

Christine Tutor

Claudine Vainrub

Ilona Vanderwoude

Vivian VanLier

Chris Van Petten

Ellie Vargo

Roleta Fowler Vasquez

Judith Vince

Kathy Voska

Julie Walraven

Jill Walser

Kendra Walters

Michael B. Wetherington

Pearl White

Amy Whitmer

Betty H. Williams

Beth Woodworth

Janice Worthington

Jeremy Worthington

Daisy Wright

Angela P. Zimmer

High-Tech and Internet

Barbara A. Adams
Georgia Adamson
Carol Altomare
Margaret Anderson
Deanne Arnath
Don Arthur
Christopher Aune
Elizabeth J. Axnix
Ann Baehr
Jacqui D. Barrett
Mark D. Berkowitz
Martin Buckland
Nita Busby
Lisa Chapman
Tammy W. Chisholm
Stephanie Clark
Fred Coon
Pat Criscito
Annemarie Cross
Jean Cummings
Robert Dagnall
Michael S. Davis
Laura DeCarlo
Deb Dib
Jessica Dillard
Anne-Marie Ditta
John Donovan
Patricia Duckers

Michelle Dumas
George Dutch
Nina Ebert
Wilson W. Elliott
Debbie Ellis
Donna Farrise
Marilyn A. Feldstein
Audrey Field
Cliff Flamer
Louise Fletcher
Art Frank
Stephen R. Gallison
Roberta Gamza
William Garner
Louise Garver
Don Goodman
Sharon Graham
Will W. Grant
Susan Guarneri
Michele Haffner
Tina Harlan
Beverly Harvey
Terri W. Henderson
Gayle Howard
Karen Hughes
Kim Isaacs
Angela Jones
Denette Jones

(continued)

High-Tech and Internet (continued)

Billie P. Jordan
Karen P. Katz
Wally C. Keenan
Fran Kelley
Gillian Kelly
Pat Kendall
Erin Kennedy
Kathy Keshemberg
Jeanne Knight
Bonnie Kurka
Louise Kursmark
Laura Labovich
Malloy Lacktman
Lorie Lebert
Linsey Levine
Sandra Lim
Abby Locke
Lynda Lucas
Tamelynda Lux
Murray A. Mann
Irene Marshall
Sharon McCormick
Debbie McMahan
Jan Melnik
Meg Montford
Doug Morrison
Joan Murrin
Carol Nason
Katie Newton
JoAnn Nix
Samantha Nolan
John M. O'Connor
Debra O'Reilly
Ethan Pang
Tracy M. Parish
Stephanie Peacocke
Kris Plantrich
Judit Price
Robert Prock
Camille Carboneau Roberts
Teena Rose
Jennifer Rushton
Lori Russel
Barbara Safani
Robin Schlinger
Linda Schnabel
Kimberly Schneiderman
Phyllis B. Shabad
Harriet Shea
Igor Shpudejko
Karen M. Silins
Kelley Smith
Laurie J. Smith
Chris Starkey
Beth W. Stefani
Billie R. Sucher
Lonnie L. Swanson
Kathy Sweeney
Christine Tutor
Claudine Vainrub

Ilona Vanderwoude
Vivian VanLier
Chris Van Petten
Ellie Vargo
Roleta Fowler Vasquez
Judith Vince
Debra M. Vinikour
Kathy Voska
Julie Walraven
Jill Walser
Kathy Warwick
Martin Weitzman
Kathleen Weston
Michael B. Wetherington
Pearl White
Betty H. Williams
Janice Worthington
Jeremy Worthington

Manufacturing

Barbara A. Adams
Tom Albano
Carol Altomare
Margaret Anderson
Michele Angello
Deanne Arnath
Don Arthur
Christopher Aune
Elizabeth J. Axnix
Ann Baehr
Jacqui D. Barrett
Janet L. Beckstrom
Mark D. Berkowitz
Marian Bernard
Julie Bernardin
Arnold G. Boldt
Nancy Boyer
Anne Brunelle
Martin Buckland
Diane Hudson Burns
Nita Busby
Ron Cail
Lisa Chapman
Freddie Cheek
Tammy W. Chisholm
Stephanie Clark
Darlene Cook
Fred Coon
Pat Criscito
Annemarie Cross
Jean Cummings
Norine Dagliano
Robert Dagnall
Michael S. Davis
Laura DeCarlo
Deb Dib
Jessica Dillard
John Donovan
Patricia Duckers
Deloris J. (Dee) Duff

(continued)

Manufacturing (continued)

Michelle Dumas

Nina Ebert

Clifford W. Eischen

Debbie Ellis

Donna Farrise

Dayna Feist

Robyn L. Feldberg

Audrey Field

Cliff Flamer

Art Frank

Gail Frank

Julianne Franke

Fred Frazier Jr.

Stephen R. Gallison

William Garner

Louise Garver

Susan Geary

Betty Geller

Don Goodman

Sharon Graham

Will W. Grant

Jill Grindle

Susan Guarneri

Meg Guiseppi

Michele Haffner

Beate Hait

Tina Harlan

Beverly Harvey

Makini Theresa Harvey

Terri W. Henderson

Karen Hughes

Diane Irwin

Kim Isaacs

Deborah James

La-Dana Renee Jenkins

Jerry D. Johnson

Suzette Jolly

Angela Jones

Denette Jones

Billie P. Jordan

Karen P. Katz

Wally C. Keenan

Gillian Kelly

Pat Kendall

Erin Kennedy

Kathy Keshemberg

Jeanne Knight

Myriam-Rose Kohn

Frost Krist

Louise Kursmark

Malloy Lacktman

Lorie Lebert

Linsey Levine

Lynda Lucas

Tamelynda Lux

Murray A. Mann

Irene Marshall

Sharon McCormick

Debbie McMahan

Jan Melnik

Doug Morrison
Carol Nason
Katie Newton
JoAnn Nix
Samantha Nolan
John M. O'Connor
Don Orlando
Tracy M. Parish
Stephanie Peacocke
Sharon Pierce-Williams
Kris Plantrich
Judit Price
Robert Prock
Julie Rains
Michelle Mastruserio Reitz
Edie Rische
Martha Rockwell
Jane Roqueplot
Teena Rose
Jennifer Rushton
Lori Russel
Robin Schlinger
Linda Schnabel
Joellyn Wittenstein Schwerdlin
Debbie Shalom
Harriet Shea
Janice M. Shepherd
Igor Shpudejko
Karen M. Silins
Kelley Smith
Laurie J. Smith
Chris Starkey
Beth W. Stefani
Marilyn Stollon
Billie R. Sucher
Lonnie L. Swanson
Kathy Sweeney
Tanya Taylor
Wendy J. Terwelp
Kevin Tucker
Edward Turilli
Christine Tutor
Claudine Vainrub
Ilona Vanderwoude
Vivian VanLier
Chris Van Petten
Ellie Vargo
Roleta Fowler Vasquez
Judith Vince
Kathy Voska
Julie Walraven
Jill Walser
Kendra Walters
Judy Ware
Martin Weitzman
Kathleen Weston
Michael B. Wetherington
Pearl White
Amy Whitmer
Betty H. Williams

(continued)

Manufacturing (continued)

Beth Woodworth
Janice Worthington
Jeremy Worthington
Daisy Wright
Angela P. Zimmer

Hospitality and Entertainment

Barbara A. Adams
Georgia Adamson
Margaret Anderson
Michele Angello
Don Arthur
Christopher Aune
Elizabeth J. Axnix
Ann Baehr
Jacqui D. Barrett
Lorraine Beaman
Janet L. Beckstrom
Mark D. Berkowitz
Marian Bernard
Julie Bernardin
Nancy Boyer
Anne Brunelle
LeRachel H. Buffkins
Nita Busby
Ron Cail
Clay Cerny
Lisa Chapman
Stephanie Clark
Beth Colley
Fred Coon
Pat Cort
Pat Criscito
Annemarie Cross
Norine Dagliano
Robert Dagnall
Dian R. Davis
Laura DeCarlo
Deb Dib
Jessica Dillard
John Donovan
Patricia Duckers
Deloris J. (Dee) Duff
Michelle Dumas
Nina Ebert
Clifford W. Eischen
Lynn Eischen
Wilson W. Elliott
Debbie Ellis
Donna Farrise
Dayna Feist
Cliff Flamer
Louise Fletcher
Art Frank
Gail Frank
Julianne Franke
Fred Frazier Jr.
Stephen R. Gallison
Louise Garver

Susan Geary
Betty Geller
Don Goodman
Sharon Graham
Will W. Grant
Jill Grindle
Susan Guarneri
Meg Guiseppi
Beverly Harvey
Makini Theresa Harvey
Terri W. Henderson
Phyllis Houston
Karen Hughes
Diane Irwin
Kim Isaacs
Deborah James
La-Dana Renee Jenkins
Jerry D. Johnson
Suzette Jolly
Denette Jones
Karen P. Katz
Wally C. Keenan
Gillian Kelly
Pat Kendall
Erin Kennedy
Myriam-Rose Kohn
Frost Krist
Louise Kursmark
Laura Labovich
Malloy Lacktman
Lorie Lebert
Linsey Levine
Abby Locke
Lynda Lucas
Tamelynda Lux
Murray A. Mann
Irene Marshall
Debbie McMahan
Jan Melnik
Meg Montford
Doug Morrison
Carol Nason
Katie Newton
JoAnn Nix
Samantha Nolan
John M. O'Connor
Don Orlando
Tracy M. Parish
Stephanie Peacocke
Sharon Pierce-Williams
Kris Plantrich
Judit Price
Robert Prock
Julie Rains
Michelle Mastruserio Reitz
Edie Rische
Camille Carboneau Roberts
Martha Rockwell
Jane Roqueplot
Teena Rose

(continued)

Hospitality and Entertainment (continued)

Jennifer Rushton
Linda Schnabel
Kimberly Schneiderman
Joellyn Wittenstein Schwerdlin
Phyllis B. Shabad
Debbie Shalom
Harriet Shea
Janice M. Shepherd
Igor Shpudejko
Karen M. Silins
Kelley Smith
Chris Starkey
Beth W. Stefani
Marilyn Stollon
Billie R. Sucher
Lonnie L. Swanson
Kathy Sweeney
Tanya Taylor
Kevin Tucker
Edward Turilli
Christine Tutor
Claudine Vainrub
Vivian VanLier
Chris Van Petten
Roleta Fowler Vasquez
Judith Vince
Debra M. Vinikour
Kathy Voska
Julie Walraven
Jill Walser
Kendra Walters
Martin Weitzman
Pearl White
Amy Whitmer
Betty H. Williams
Beth Woodworth
Janice Worthington
Jeremy Worthington
Daisy Wright
Angela P. Zimmer

Legal

Barbara A. Adams
Elizabeth J. Axnix
Ann Baehr
Mark D. Berkowitz
Anne Brunelle
Shauna C. Bryce
Martin Buckland
Nita Busby
Ron Cail
Franchesca Carrington
Stephanie Clark
Fred Coon
Pat Criscito
Annemarie Cross
Laura DeCarlo
Jessica Dillard
Patricia Duckers
Nina Ebert

Clifford W. Eischen
Lynn Eischen
Debbie Ellis
Donna Farrise
Marilyn A. Feldstein
Cliff Flamer
Gail Frank
Stephen R. Gallison
Louise Garver
Don Goodman
Sharon Graham
Will W. Grant
Makini Theresa Harvey
Terri W. Henderson
Phyllis Houston
Karen Hughes
Diane Irwin
Kim Isaacs
Jerry D. Johnson
Suzette Jolly
Billie P. Jordan
Wally C. Keenan
Gillian Kelly
Pat Kendall
Jeanne Knight
Myriam-Rose Kohn
Malloy Lacktman
Linsey Levine
Abby Locke
Lynda Lucas
Tamelynda Lux
Murray A. Mann
Irene Marshall
Sharon McCormick
Debbie McMahan
Jan Melnik
Joan Murrin
Carol Nason
Katie Newton
JoAnn Nix
Samantha Nolan
John M. O'Connor
Tracy M. Parish
Kris Plantrich
Judit Price
Robert Prock
Camille Carboneau Roberts
Jane Roqueplot
Teena Rose
Jennifer Rushton
Lori Russel
Robin Schlinger
Linda Schnabel
Kimberly Schneiderman
Phyllis B. Shabad
Harriet Shea
Karen M. Silins
Kelley Smith
Chris Starkey
Beth W. Stefani

(continued)

Legal (continued)

Billie R. Sucher
Lonnie L. Swanson
Kathy Sweeney
Wendy J. Terwelp
Kevin Tucker
Claudine Vainrub
Vivian VanLier
Chris Van Petten
Ellie Vargo
Roleta Fowler Vasquez
Judith Vince
Debra M. Vinikour
Kathy Voska
Jill Walser
Martin Weitzman
Pearl White
Janice Worthington
Jeremy Worthington
Angela P. Zimmer

Banking/Finance

Barbara A. Adams
Tom Albano
Margaret Anderson
Michele Angello
Deanne Arnath
Elizabeth J. Axnix
Ann Baehr
Jacqui D. Barrett
Janet L. Beckstrom
Mark D. Berkowitz
Marian Bernard
Julie Bernardin
Arnold G. Boldt
Anne Brunelle
Martin Buckland
Nita Busby
Franchesca Carrington
Lisa Chapman
Freddie Cheek
Tammy W. Chisholm
Stephanie Clark
Darlene Cook
Fred Coon
Pat Criscito
Annemarie Cross
Jean Cummings
Robert Dagnall
Michael S. Davis
Laura DeCarlo
Deb Dib
Jessica Dillard
Anne-Marie Ditta
John Donovan
Patricia Duckers
Deloris J. (Dee) Duff
Michelle Dumas

Nina Ebert
Clifford W. Eischen
Debbie Ellis
Donna Farrise
Dayna Feist
Marilyn A. Feldstein
Robyn L. Feldberg
Cliff Flamer
Art Frank
Gail Frank
Fred Frazier Jr.
Stephen R. Gallison
Louise Garver
Betty Geller
Don Goodman
Sharon Graham
Will W. Grant
Susan Guarneri
Beate Hait
Tina Harlan
Beverly Harvey
Makini Theresa Harvey
Maria E. Hebda
Terri W. Henderson
Phyllis Houston
Gayle Howard
Karen Hughes
Diane Irwin
Kim Isaacs
Deborah James
Suzette Jolly
Angela Jones
Billie P. Jordan
Karen P. Katz
Wally C. Keenan
Fran Kelley
Gillian Kelly
Pat Kendall
Erin Kennedy
Kathy Keshemberg
Jeanne Knight
Myriam-Rose Kohn
Cindy Kraft
Frost Krist
Louise Kursmark
Malloy Lacktman
Lorie Lebert
Sandra Lim
Abby Locke
Lynda Lucas
Tamelynda Lux
Murray A. Mann
Irene Marshall
Sharon McCormick
Debbie McMahan
Jan Melnik
Meg Montford
Doug Morrison
Joan Murrin
Carol Nason

(continued)

Banking and Finance (continued)

Katie Newton
JoAnn Nix
Samantha Nolan
John M. O'Connor
Don Orlando
Tracy M. Parish
Sharon Pierce-Williams
Kris Plantrich
Judit Price
Robert Prock
Julie Rains
Michelle Mastruserio Reitz
Edie Rische
Jane Roqueplot
Teena Rose
Jennifer Rushton
Lori Russel
Barbara Safani
Robin Schlinger
Linda Schnabel
Kimberly Schneiderman
Joellyn Wittenstein Schwerdlin
Nancy H. Segal
Phyllis B. Shabad
Debbie Shalom
Harriet Shea
Igor Shpudejko
Karen M. Silins
Kelley Smith
Chris Starkey
Beth W. Stefani
Marilyn Stollon
Billie R. Sucher
Lonnie L. Swanson
Kathy Sweeney
Wendy J. Terwelp
Kevin Tucker
Edward Turilli
Claudine Vainrub
Ilona Vanderwoude
Vivian VanLier
Chris Van Petten
Ellie Vargo
Roleta Fowler Vasquez
Judith Vince
Debra M. Vinikour
Kathy Voska
Julie Walraven
Jill Walser
Kendra Walters
Kathy Warwick
Martin Weitzman
Pearl White
Amy Whitmer
Betty H. Williams
Janice Worthington
Jeremy Worthington
Daisy Wright
Angela P. Zimmer

Construction and Transportation

Barbara A. Adams
Margaret Anderson
Michele Angello
Don Arthur
Christopher Aune
Elizabeth J. Axnix
Ann Baehr
Mark D. Berkowitz
Marian Bernard
Julie Bernardin
Nancy Boyer
Diane Hudson Burns
Nita Busby
Freddie Cheek
Lisa Chapman
Stephanie Clark
Sally Cofer-Lindberg
Fred Coon
Pat Cort
Pat Criscito
Annemarie Cross
Norine Dagliano
Robert Dagnall
Dian R. Davis
Michael S. Davis
Laura DeCarlo
Deb Dib
Jessica Dillard
John Donovan
Patricia Duckers
Deloris J. (Dee) Duff
Michelle Dumas
Nina Ebert
Clifford W. Eischen
Lynn Eischen
Debbie Ellis
Donna Farrise
Dayna Feist
Robyn L. Feldberg
Marilyn A. Feldstein
Audrey Field
Cliff Flamer
Art Frank
Julianne Franke
Fred Frazier Jr.
Stephen R. Gallison
Louise Garver
Susan Geary
Betty Geller
Don Goodman
Sharon Graham
Will W. Grant
Jill Grindle
Susan Guarneri
Meg Guiseppi
Beate Hait
Beverly Harvey
Makini Theresa Harvey

(continued)

Construction and Transportation (continued)

Terri W. Henderson

Karen Hughes

Diane Irwin

Kim Isaacs

Deborah James

Suzette Jolly

Angela Jones

Denette Jones

Billie P. Jordan

Karen P. Katz

Wally C. Keenan

Pat Kendall

Erin Kennedy

Kathy Keshemberg

Jeanne Knight

Frost Krist

Louise Kursmark

Malloy Lacktman

Lorie Lebert

Lynda Lucas

Tamelynda Lux

Murray A. Mann

Irene Marshall

Sharon McCormick

Debbie McMahan

Jan Melnik

Meg Montford

Doug Morrison

Carol Nason

Katie Newton

JoAnn Nix

Samantha Nolan

John M. O'Connor

Debra O'Reilly

Don Orlando

Tracy M. Parish

Kris Plantrich

Judit Price

Robert Prock

Julie Rains

Michelle Mastruserio Reitz

Camille Carboneau Roberts

Martha Rockwell

Jane Roqueplot

Teena Rose

Jennifer Rushton

Evelyn U. Salvador

Robin Schlinger

Linda Schnabel

Debbie Shalom

Harriet Shea

Janice M. Shepherd

Igor Shpudejko

Kelley Smith

William (Bill) Smith

Chris Starkey

Beth W. Stefani

Marilyn Stollon

Billie R. Sucher

Lonnie L. Swanson

Kathy Sweeney
Kevin Tucker
Edward Turilli
Claudine Vainrub
Ilona Vanderwoude
Vivian VanLier
Chris Van Petten
Roleta Fowler Vasquez
Judith Vince
Kathy Voska
Julie Walraven
Jill Walser
Kendra Walters
Judy Ware
Martin Weitzman
Kathleen Weston
Pearl White
Amy Whitmer
Betty H. Williams
Janice Worthington
Jeremy Worthington
Daisy Wright
Angela P. Zimmer

Consulting

Barbara A. Adams
Tom Albano
Carol Altomare
Michele Angello
Deanne Arnath
Don Arthur
Elizabeth J. Axnix
Ann Baehr
Jacqui D. Barrett
Lorraine Beaman
Mark D. Berkowitz
Marian Bernard
Julie Bernardin
Anne Brunelle
Martin Buckland
LeRachel H. Buffkins
Nita Busby
Franchesca Carrington
Lisa Chapman
Tammy W. Chisholm
Stephanie Clark
Sally Cofer-Lindberg
Darlene Cook
Fred Coon
Pat Cort
Jean Cummings
Robert Dagnall
Michael S. Davis
Laura DeCarlo
Deb Dib
Jessica Dillard
Anne-Marie Ditta
Patricia Duckers
Michelle Dumas

(continued)

Consulting (continued)

George Dutch
Nina Ebert
Clifford W. Eischen
Wilson W. Elliott
Debbie Ellis
Donna Farrise
Dayna Feist
Marilyn A. Feldstein
Cliff Flamer
Art Frank
Gail Frank
Julianne Franke
Stephen R. Gallison
Roberta Gamza
Louise Garver
Betty Geller
Don Goodman
Sharon Graham
Will W. Grant
Jill Grindle
Meg Guiseppi
Beverly Harvey
Makini Theresa Harvey
Terri W. Henderson
Gayle Howard
Karen Hughes
Diane Irwin
Kim Isaacs
Deborah James
La-Dana Renee Jenkins
Jerry D. Johnson
Denette Jones
Karen P. Katz
Wally C. Keenan
Fran Kelley
Gillian Kelly
Pat Kendall
Erin Kennedy
Kathy Keshemberg
Jeanne Knight
Frost Krist
Louise Kursmark
Malloy Lacktman
Laura Labovich
Lorie Lebert
Linsey Levine
Sandra Lim
Abby Locke
Lynda Lucas
Tamelynda Lux
Murray A. Mann
Irene Marshall
Sharon McCormick
Debbie McMahan
Jan Melnik
Meg Montford
Doug Morrison
Carol Nason
Katie Newton
JoAnn Nix

Samantha Nolan
John M. O'Connor
Don Orlando
Tracy M. Parish
Stephanie Peacocke
Kris Plantrich
Judit Price
Camille Carboneau Roberts
Martha Rockwell
Jane Roqueplot
Teena Rose
Jennifer Rushton
Lori Russel
Robin Schlinger
Linda Schnabel
Joellyn Wittenstein Schwerdlin
Phyllis B. Shabad
Debbie Shalom
Harriet Shea
Igor Shpudejko
Karen M. Silins
Kelley Smith
Laurie J. Smith
Beth W. Stefani
Billie R. Sucher
Lonnie L. Swanson
Wendy J. Terwelp
Kevin Tucker
Christine Tutor
Claudine Vainrub
Vivian VanLier
Chris Van Petten
Roleta Fowler Vasquez
Judith Vince
Debra M. Vinikour
Kathy Voska
Jill Walser
Kendra Walters
Martin Weitzman
Michael B. Wetherington
Pearl White
Amy Whitmer
Beth Woodworth
Janice Worthington
Jeremy Worthington
Daisy Wright

Sciences, Pharmaceuticals, and Biotechnology

Barbara A. Adams
Tom Albano
Carol Altomare
Margaret Anderson
Deanne Arnath
Don Arthur
Elizabeth J. Axnix
Ann Baehr
Jacqui D. Barrett
Mark D. Berkowitz
Martin Buckland
Diane Hudson Burns

(continued)

Sciences, Pharmaceuticals, and Biotechnology (continued)

Nita Busby

Ron Cail

Clay Cerny

Lisa Chapman

Tammy W. Chisholm

Beth Colley

Fred Coon

Pat Criscito

Jean Cummings

Norine Dagliano

Robert Dagnall

Dian R. Davis

Laura DeCarlo

Jessica Dillard

John Donovan

Patricia Duckers

Deloris J. (Dee) Duff

Nina Ebert

Clifford W. Eischen

Debbie Ellis

Donna Farrise

Dayna Feist

Audrey Field

Cliff Flamer

Art Frank

Julianne Franke

Stephen R. Gallison

Roberta Gamza

Louise Garver

Susan Geary

Sharon Graham

Don Goodman

Will W. Grant

Jill Grindle

Susan Guarneri

Beverly Harvey

Makini Theresa Harvey

Terri W. Henderson

Karen Hughes

Diane Irwin

Kim Isaacs

Deborah James

Suzette Jolly

Angela Jones

Billie P. Jordan

Karen P. Katz

Wally C. Keenan

Fran Kelley

Gillian Kelly

Pat Kendall

Erin Kennedy

Kathy Keshemberg

Jeanne Knight

Frost Krist

Bonnie Kurka

Malloy Lacktman

Lorie Lebert

Linsey Levine

Lynda Lucas

Tamelynda Lux

Murray A. Mann
Sharon McCormick
Debbie McMahan
Jan Melnik
Joan Murrin
Carol Nason
Sari Neudorf
Katie Newton
Samantha Nolan
John M. O'Connor
Debra O'Reilly
Don Orlando
Tracy M. Parish
Stephanie Peacocke
Sharon Pierce-Williams
Kris Plantrich
Judit Price
Robert Prock
Edie Rische
Camille Carboneau Roberts
Jane Roqueplot
Teena Rose
Nancy Rozum
Lori Russel
Robin Schlinger
Linda Schnabel
Kimberly Schneiderman
Phyllis B. Shabad
Igor Shpudejko
Karen M. Silins
Kelley Smith
Chris Starkey
Beth W. Stefani
Billie R. Sucher
Lonnie L. Swanson
Kathy Sweeney
Kevin Tucker
Edward Turilli
Christine Tutor
Claudine Vainrub
Ilona Vanderwoude
Vivian VanLier
Chris Van Petten
Ellie Vargo
Roleta Fowler Vasquez
Judith Vince
Kathy Voska
Julie Walraven
Martin Weitzman
Michael B. Wetherington
Pearl White
Betty H. Williams
Jeremy Worthington
Angela P. Zimmer

Retail

Margaret Anderson
Deanne Arnath
Don Arthur
Christopher Aune
Elizabeth J. Axnix
Ann Baehr
Jacqui D. Barrett
Lorraine Beaman
Janet L. Beckstrom
Mark D. Berkowitz
Marian Bernard
Julie Bernardin
Nancy Boyer
Shannon D. Branson
Anne Brunelle
Martin Buckland
LeRachel H. Buffkins
Diane Hudson Burns
Nita Busby
Ron Cail
Clay Cerny
Lisa Chapman
Stephanie Clark
Sally Cofer-Lindberg
Beth Colley
Fred Coon
Pat Cort
Pat Criscito
Annemarie Cross
Norine Dagliano
Robert Dagnall
Michael S. Davis
Laura DeCarlo
Jessica Dillard
John Donovan
Patricia Duckers
Deloris J. (Dee) Duff
Michelle Dumas
Nina Ebert
Clifford W. Eischen
Lynn Eischen
Wilson W. Elliott
Debbie Ellis
Donna Farrise
Dayna Feist
Robyn L. Feldberg
Marilyn A. Feldstein
Cliff Flamer
Art Frank
Gail Frank
Julianne Franke
Fred Frazier Jr.
Stephen R. Gallison
Louise Garver
Susan Geary
Betty Geller
Don Goodman
Sharon Graham

Will W. Grant
Jill Grindle
Susan Guarneri
Meg Guiseppi
Michele Haffner
Beate Hait
Beverly Harvey
Makini Theresa Harvey
Maria E. Hebda
Terri W. Henderson
Susan Hoopes
Phyllis Houston
Karen Hughes
Diane Irwin
Kim Isaacs
Deborah James
La-Dana Renee Jenkins
Jerry D. Johnson
Suzette Jolly
Angela Jones
Denette Jones
Billie P. Jordan
Wally C. Keenan
Fran Kelley
Gillian Kelly
Pat Kendall
Kathy Keshemberg
Myriam-Rose Kohn
Frost Krist
Malloy Lacktman
Lorie Lebert
Lynda Lucas
Tamelynda Lux
Murray A. Mann
Irene Marshall
Debbie McMahan
Jan Melnik
Meg Montford
Doug Morrison
Carol Nason
Katie Newton
JoAnn Nix
Samantha Nolan
John M. O'Connor
Ethan Pang
Tracy M. Parish
Stephanie Peacocke
Kris Plantrich
Judit Price
Robert Prock
Julie Rains
Michelle Mastruserio Reitz
Edie Rische
Martha Rockwell
Jane Roqueplot
Teena Rose
Nancy Rozum
Jennifer Rushton
Lori Russel
Evelyn U. Salvador

(continued)

Retail (continued)

Robin Schlinger
Linda Schnabel
Kimberly Schneiderman
Joellyn Wittenstein Schwerdlin
Debbie Shalom
Harriet Shea
Igor Shpudejko
Karen M. Silins
Kelley Smith
William (Bill) Smith
Chris Starkey
Beth W. Stefani
Marilyn Stollon
Billie R. Sucher
Lonnie L. Swanson
Kathy Sweeney
Tanya Taylor
Kevin Tucker
Edward Turilli
Christine Tutor
Claudine Vainrub
Ilona Vanderwoude
Vivian VanLier
Chris Van Petten
Ellie Vargo
Roleta Fowler Vasquez
Judith Vince
Debra M. Vinikour
Kathy Voska
Julie Walraven
Jill Walser
Kendra Walters
Judy Ware
Martin Weitzman
Kathleen Weston
Pearl White
Amy Whitmer
Beth Woodworth
Janice Worthington
Jeremy Worthington
Angela P. Zimmer

Public Sector/Government

Barbara A. Adams
Deanne Arnath
Don Arthur
Elizabeth J. Axnix
Ann Baehr
Jacqui D. Barrett
Lorraine Beaman
Mark D. Berkowitz
Julie Bernardin
Arnold G. Boldt
Shannon D. Branson
Anne Brunelle
Martin Buckland
LeRachel H. Buffkins

Margaret Burkholder
Diane Hudson Burns
Nita Busby
Tammy W. Chisholm
Stephanie Clark
Beth Colley
Pat Criscito
Jean Cummings
Norine Dagliano
Robert Dagnall
Laura DeCarlo
Jessica Dillard
Patricia Duckers
Deloris J. (Dee) Duff
George Dutch
Nina Ebert
Cory Edwards
Clifford W. Eischen
Wilson W. Elliott
Debbie Ellis
Donna Farrise
Audrey Field
Art Frank
Gail Frank
Stephen R. Gallison
Louise Garver
Sharon Graham
Will W. Grant
Michele Haffner
Makini Theresa Harvey

Phyllis Houston
Karen Hughes
Diane Irwin
Kim Isaacs
Deborah James
La-Dana Renee Jenkins
Suzette Jolly
Billie P. Jordan
Wally C. Keenan
Gillian Kelly
Pat Kendall
Erin Kennedy
Kathy Keshemberg
Frost Krist
Bonnie Kurka
Malloy Lacktman
Lorie Lebert
Lynda Lucas
Tamelynda Lux
Murray A. Mann
Irene Marshall
Sharon McCormick
Debbie McMahan
Katie Newton
JoAnn Nix
John M. O'Connor
Don Orlando
Ethan Pang
Tracy M. Parish
Stephanie Peacocke

(continued)

Public Sector/Government (continued)

Kris Plantrich

Judit Price

Julie Rains

Camille Carboneau Roberts

Jane Roqueplot

Teena Rose

Jennifer Rushton

Lori Russel

Robin Schlinger

Linda Schnabel

Nancy H. Segal

Debbie Shalom

Janice M. Shepherd

Karen M. Silins

Kelley Smith

William (Bill) Smith

Beth W. Stefani

Marilyn Stollon

Billie R. Sucher

Lonnie L. Swanson

Kathy Sweeney

Kevin Tucker

Edward Turilli

Chris Van Petten

Ellie Vargo

Roleta Fowler Vasquez

Judith Vince

Kathy Voska

James Walker

Julie Walraven

Jill Walser

Betty H. Williams

Beth Woodworth

Janice Worthington

Jeremy Worthington

Daisy Wright

Not-for-Profit and Association Management

Barbara A. Adams

Margaret Anderson

Deanne Arnath

Christopher Aune

Elizabeth J. Axnix

Ann Baehr

Jacqui D. Barrett

Lorraine Beaman

Janet L. Beckstrom

Mark D. Berkowitz

Marian Bernard

Julie Bernardin

Arnold G. Boldt

Shannon D. Branson

Anne Brunelle

Martin Buckland

LeRachel H. Buffkins

Nita Busby

Ron Cail

Franchesca Carrington

Lisa Chapman

Freddie Cheek

Stephanie Clark
Sally Cofer-Lindberg
Beth Colley
Fred Coon
Pat Cort
Pat Criscito
Annemarie Cross
Norine Dagliano
Robert Dagnall
Michael S. Davis
Laura DeCarlo
Jessica Dillard
Anne-Marie Ditta
John Donovan
Patricia Duckers
Deloris J. (Dee) Duff
Michelle Dumas
George Dutch
Nina Ebert
Clifford W. Eischen
Wilson W. Elliott
Debbie Ellis
Donna Farrise
Dayna Feist
Marilyn A. Feldstein
Cliff Flamer
Art Frank
Gail Frank
Julianne Franke
Stephen R. Gallison
Louise Garver
Betty Geller
Don Goodman
Sharon Graham
Will W. Grant
Susan Guarneri
Meg Guiseppi
Michele Haffner
Beate Hait
Beverly Harvey
Makini Theresa Harvey
Karen Hughes
Diane Irwin
Kim Isaacs
Deborah James
La-Dana Renee Jenkins
Jerry D. Johnson
Suzette Jolly
Denette Jones
Billie P. Jordan
Karen P. Katz
Wally C. Keenan
Fran Kelley
Gillian Kelly
Pat Kendall
Erin Kennedy
Kathy Keshemberg
Jeanne Knight
Frost Krist
Malloy Lacktman

(continued)

Not-for-Profit and Association Management (continued)

Lorie Lebert
Linsey Levine
Sandra Lim
Abby Locke
Lynda Lucas
Tamelynda Lux
Murray A. Mann
Irene Marshall
Sharon McCormick
Debbie McMahan
Jan Melnik
Meg Montford
Carol Nason
Katie Newton
JoAnn Nix
Samantha Nolan
John M. O'Connor
Don Orlando
Ethan Pang
Tracy M. Parish
Stephanie Peacocke
Kris Plantrich
Judit Price
Robert Prock
Julie Rains
Edie Rische
Martha Rockwell
Teena Rose
Jane Roqueplot
Nancy Rozum
Jennifer Rushton
Linda Schnabel
Kimberly Schneiderman
Joellyn Wittenstein Schwerdlin
Phyllis B. Shabad
Debbie Shalom
Harriet Shea
Janice M. Shepherd
Igor Shpudejko
Karen M. Silins
William (Bill) Smith
Chris Starkey
Beth W. Stefani
Marilyn Stollon
Billie R. Sucher
Lonnie L. Swanson
Kathy Sweeney
Tanya Taylor
Kevin Tucker
Edward Turilli
Christine Tutor
Claudine Vainrub
Ilona Vanderwoude
Vivian VanLier
Chris Van Petten
Roleta Fowler Vasquez
Judith Vince
Debra M. Vinikour
Kathy Voska
Jill Walser

Julie Walraven

Kendra Walters

Judy Ware

Martin Weitzman

Pearl White

Amy Whitmer

Betty H. Williams

Beth Woodworth

Janice Worthington

Jeremy Worthington

Private Equity/Venture Capital

Tom Albano

Michele Angello

Deanne Arnath

Christopher Aune

Ann Baehr

Jacqui D. Barrett

Mark D. Berkowitz

Marian Bernard

Martin Buckland

Nita Busby

Lisa Chapman

Tammy W. Chisholm

Fred Coon

Laura DeCarlo

Deb Dib

Jessica Dillard

Patricia Duckers

Nina Ebert

Clifford W. Eischen

Debbie Ellis

Donna Farrise

Cliff Flamer

Gail Frank

Stephen R. Gallison

Don Goodman

Sharon Graham

Will W. Grant

Jill Grindle

Beverly Harvey

Makini Theresa Harvey

Karen Hughes

Diane Irwin

Kim Isaacs

Deborah James

Wally C. Keenan

Pat Kendall

Jeanne Knight

Louise Kursmark

Malloy Lacktman

Lynda Lucas

Tamelynda Lux

Murray A. Mann

Debbie McMahan

Jan Melnik

Katie Newton

JoAnn Nix

Samantha Nolan

John M. O'Connor

(continued)

Private Equity/Venture Capital (continued)

Tracy M. Parish
Kris Plantrich
Judit Price
Robert Prock
Camille Carboneau Roberts
Teena Rose
Jennifer Rushton
Lori Russel
Robin Schlinger
Linda Schnabel
Kimberly Schneiderman
Phyllis B. Shabad
Debbie Shalom
Harriet Shea
Karen M. Silins
Kelley Smith
Beth W. Stefani
Billie R. Sucher
Lonnie L. Swanson
Tanya Taylor
Kevin Tucker
Claudine Vainrub
Vivian VanLier
Roleta Fowler Vasquez
Judith Vince
Debra M. Vinikour
Kathy Voska
Martin Weitzman
Kathleen Weston
Michael B. Wetherington
Pearl White
Janice Worthington
Jeremy Worthington

Business Model

Remote (via Phone and/or E-mail)

Barbara A. Adams
Georgia Adamson
Tom Albano
Carol Altomare
Margaret Anderson
Michele Angello
Deanne Arnath
Don Arthur
Christopher Aune
Elizabeth J. Axnix
Ann Baehr
Jacqui D. Barrett
Lorraine Beaman
Mark D. Berkowitz
Marian Bernard
Julie Bernardin
Arnold G. Boldt
Nancy Boyer
Shannon D. Branson
Anne Brunelle

Shauna C. Bryce
Martin Buckland
LeRachel H. Buffkins
Margaret Burkholder
Diane Hudson Burns
Nita Busby
Ron Cail
Franchesca Carrington
Lisa Chapman
Freddie Cheek
Tammy W. Chisholm
Stephanie Clark
Sally Cofer-Lindberg
Beth Colley
Darlene Cook
Fred Coon
Pat Cort
Pat Criscito
Annemarie Cross
Jean Cummings
Norine Dagliano
Robert Dagnall
Dian R. Davis
Michael S. Davis
Laura DeCarlo
Deb Dib
Jessica Dillard
Anne-Marie Ditta
John Donovan
Patricia Duckers
Deloris J. (Dee) Duff
Michelle Dumas
George Dutch
Nina Ebert
Clifford W. Eischen
Lynn Eischen
Cory Edwards
Wilson W. Elliott
Debbie Ellis
Donna Farrise
Dayna Feist
Robyn L. Feldberg
Marilyn A. Feldstein
Audrey Field
Cliff Flamer
Louise Fletcher
Art Frank
Gail Frank
Julianne Franke
Fred Frazier Jr.
Roberta Gamza
William Garner
Louise Garver
Susan Geary
Wendy Gelberg
Betty Geller
Don Goodman
Sharon Graham
Will W. Grant
Jill Grindle

(continued)

Remote (via Phone and/or E-mail) (continued)

Susan Guarneri

Meg Guiseppi

Michele Haffner

Beate Hait

Tina Harlan

Beverly Harvey

Makini Theresa Harvey

Maria E. Hebda

Terri W. Henderson

Susan Hoopes

Phyllis Houston

Gayle Howard

Karen Hughes

Diane Irwin

Kim Isaacs

Caroline M. Jagot

Deborah James

La-Dana Renee Jenkins

Jerry D. Johnson

Angela Jones

Denette Jones

Billie P. Jordan

Karen P. Katz

Wally C. Keenan

Fran Kelley

Gillian Kelly

Pat Kendall

Erin Kennedy

Kathy Keshemberg

Jeanne Knight

Myriam-Rose Kohn

Cindy Kraft

Frost Krist

Bonnie Kurka

Louise Kursmark

Laura Labovich

Malloy Lacktman

Alia Lawlor

Lorie Lebert

Linsey Levine

Sandra Lim

Abby Locke

Lynda Lucas

Tamelynda Lux

Murray A. Mann

Irene Marshall

Maureen McCann

Sharon McCormick

Debbie McMahan

Jan Melnik

Marti Miller

Meg Montford

Doug Morrison

Joan Murrin

Carol Nason

Patricia Navin

Beverley Neil

Sari Neudorf

Katie Newton

JoAnn Nix

Samantha Nolan
John M. O'Connor
Debra O'Reilly
Don Orlando
Ethan Pang
Tracy M. Parish
Stephanie Peacocke
Sharon Pierce-Williams
Kris Plantrich
Judit Price
Robert Prock
Julie Rains
Michelle Mastruserio Reitz
Edie Rische
Camille Carboneau Roberts
Martha Rockwell
Jane Roqueplot
Teena Rose
Nancy Rozum
Jennifer Rushton
Lori Russel
Robin Schlinger
Linda Schnabel
Joellyn Wittenstein Schwerdlin
Nancy H. Segal
Phyllis B. Shabad
Debbie Shalom
Harriet Shea
Janice M. Shepherd
Igor Shpudejko
Karen M. Silins
Kelley Smith
Laurie J. Smith
William (Bill) Smith
Chris Starkey
Beth W. Stefani
Ann Stewart
Denise Stewart
Marilyn Stollon
Billie R. Sucher
Lonnie L. Swanson
Kathy Sweeney
Tanya Taylor
Wendy J. Terwelp
Edward Turilli
Christine Tutor
Ilona Vanderwoude
Vivian VanLier
Chris Van Petten
Ellie Vargo
Roleta Fowler Vasquez
Judith Vince
Debra M. Vinikour
Kathy Voska
James Walker
Julie Walraven
Jill Walser
Kendra Walters
Judy Ware
Kathy Warwick

(continued)

Remote (via Phone and/or E-mail) (continued)

Martin Weitzman

Kathleen Weston

Michael B. Wetherington

Susan Britton Whitcomb

Pearl White

Amy Whitmer

Betty H. Williams

Beth Woodworth

Janice Worthington

Jeremy Worthington

Daisy Wright

Angela P. Zimmer

In Person

Barbara A. Adams

Georgia Adamson

Tom Albano

Carol Altomare

Margaret Anderson

Don Arthur

Christopher Aune

Janet L. Beckstrom

Mark D. Berkowitz

Marian Bernard

Julie Bernardin

Arnold G. Boldt

Martin Buckland

Margaret Burkholder

Nita Busby

Clay Cerny

Stephanie Clark

Beth Colley

Darlene Cook

Pat Cort

Pat Criscito

Norine Dagliano

Robert Dagnall

Dian R. Davis

Jessica Dillard

Anne-Marie Ditta

George Dutch

Deloris J. (Dee) Duff

Nina Ebert

Clifford W. Eischen

Lynn Eischen

Wilson W. Elliott

Donna Farrise

Dayna Feist

Marilyn A. Feldstein

Audrey Field

Art Frank

Fred Frazier Jr.

Stephen R. Gallison

Roberta Gamza

William Garner

Betty Geller

Will W. Grant

Michele Haffner

Beate Hait

Makini Theresa Harvey

Terri W. Henderson
Phyllis Houston
Karen Hughes
Caroline M. Jagot
Deborah James
La-Dana Renee Jenkins
Suzette Jolly
Angela Jones
Billie P. Jordan
Karen P. Katz
Wally C. Keenan
Gillian Kelly
Myriam-Rose Kohn
Frost Krist
Alia Lawlor
Linsey Levine
Abby Locke
Lynda Lucas
Tamelynda Lux
Murray A. Mann
Irene Marshall
Maureen McCann
Sharon McCormick
Marti Miller
Cheryl Minnick
Doug Morrison
Joan Murrin
Patricia Navin
Sari Neudorf
Katie Newton
John M. O'Connor
Don Orlando
Ethan Pang
Judit Price
Robert Prock
Julie Rains
Michelle Mastruserio Reitz
Edie Rische
Camille Carboneau Roberts
Martha Rockwell
Jane Roqueplot
Barbara Safani
Kimberly Schneiderman
Phyllis B. Shabad
Debbie Shalom
Harriet Shea
Janice M. Shepherd
Igor Shpudejko
Karen M. Silins
Beth W. Stefani
Marilyn Stollon
Billie R. Sucher
Lonnie L. Swanson
Wendy J. Terwelp
Kevin Tucker
Edward Turilli
Claudine Vainrub
Chris Van Petten
Ellie Vargo
Roleta Fowler Vasquez

(continued)

In Person (continued)

Debra M. Vinikour

Kathy Voska

James Walker

Julie Walraven

Jill Walser

Judy Ware

Kathleen Weston

Pearl White

Beth Woodworth

Janice Worthington

Jeremy Worthington

Daisy Wright

Angela P. Zimmer

While-You-Wait

Christopher Aune

Marian Bernard

Margaret Burkholder

Will W. Grant

Lynda Lucas

Irene Marshall

John M. O'Connor

Harriet Shea

Edward Turilli

Julie Walraven

Beth Woodworth

Jeremy Worthington

Angela P. Zimmer

CHAPTER 5

Geographic Directory of Professional Resume Writers

If the location of your resume writer is important to you, start here! You'll find all the featured resume writers sorted by country; and by cities and states, territories, or provinces within the country. In chapter 6 you will find full contact information and additional details for each of the writers listed in this chapter.

But keep in mind, the majority of resume writers do not meet with you in person. Instead, you can work with your writer from the comfort and convenience of your home or office, communicating by phone and e-mail. Thus, physical location is an unimportant matter. You might just find your perfect writer halfway around the globe!

Australia

Name	City	Territory
Jennifer Rushton	Sydney	New South Wales
Beverley Neil		Queensland
Gillian Kelly	Brisbane	Queensland
Gayle Howard	Chirnside Park	Victoria
Annemarie Cross	Hallam	Victoria

Canada

Name	City	Province
Anne Brunelle		
Audrey Field		
Sharon Graham		
Chris Starkey	Mount Pearl	Newfoundland
Marian Bernard	Aurora	Ontario

(continued)

Canada (continued)

Name	City	Province
Daisy Wright	Brampton	Ontario
Tanya Taylor	Brampton	Ontario
Linda Schnabel	Burlington	Ontario
Kathleen Weston	Holland Landing	Ontario
Stephanie Clark	Kitchener	Ontario
Tamelynda Lux	London	Ontario
Martin Buckland	Oakville	Ontario
Maureen McCann	Ottawa	Ontario
George Dutch	Ottawa	Ontario
Sandra Lim	Toronto	Ontario

Hong Kong

Name	City
Ethan Pang	Hong Kong

United States

Alabama

Name	City
Don Orlando	Montgomery

Arkansas

Name	City
JoAnn Nix	Van Buren

Arizona

Name	City
Kevin Tucker	Gilbert
Fred Coon	Phoenix

Arizona

Name	City
Kathy Sweeney	Phoenix
Martha Rockwell	Scottsdale
Chris Van Petten	Scottsdale
Margaret Burkholder	Tucson

California

Name	City
Beth Woodworth	
Jessica Dillard	Anaheim
Malloy Lacktman	Beverly Hills
Lorraine Beaman	Davis
Roleta Fowler Vasquez	Fillmore
Irene Marshall	Fremont
Lynn Eischen	Fresno
Clifford W. Eischen	Fresno
Susan Britton Whitcomb	Fresno
Pearl White	Irvine
Ron Cail	Long Beach
Vivian VanLier	Los Angeles
Makini Theresa Harvey	Menlo Park
Sally Cofer Lindberg	Modesto
William Garner	Northridge
Cliff Flamer	Oakland
William Smith (Bill)	Oakland
Marilyn Stollon	Oakland
Nita Busby	Orange
Robert Dagnall	San Diego
Georgia Adamson	San Jose
Margaret Anderson	Sylmar
Myriam-Rose Kohn	Valencia

Colorado

Name	City
Michele Angello	Aurora
Debra M. Vinikour	Boulder
Pat Criscito	Colorado Springs
Roberta Gamza	Louisville

Connecticut

Name	City
Louise Garver	Broad Brook
Jan Melnik	Durham
Frost Krist	Hebron
Suzette Jolly	Willimantic

District of Columbia

Name	City
Abby Locke	Washington, DC

Florida

Name	City
Michael B. Wetherington	
Claudine Vainrub	Aventura
Edward Turilli	Bonita Springs
Debra O'Reilly	Brandon
Marilyn A. Feldstein	Jacksonville
Laura DeCarlo	Melbourne
Beverly Harvey	Pierson
Caroline M. Jagot	Tallahassee
Gail Frank	Tampa
Cindy Kraft	Valrico

Georgia

Name	City
Robin Schlinger	Atlanta
Julianne Franke	Lawrenceville
Barbara A. Adams	Macon

Hawaii

Name	City
Denette Jones	Pahoa

Idaho

Name	City
Diane Hudson Burns	Boise
Camille Carboneau Roberts	Idaho Falls

Illinois

Name	City
Clay Cerny	Chicago
Murray A. Mann	Chicago
Nancy H. Segal	Evanston
Tracy M. Parish	Kewanee

Indiana

Name	City
Christopher Aune	Batesville
Deloris J. (Dee) Duff	Indianapolis

Iowa

Name	City
Joan Murrin	Iowa City
Elizabeth J. Axnix	Riverside
Billie R. Sucher	Urbandale

Kansas

Name	City
James Walker	Fort Riley
Marti Miller	Olathe
Kathy Voska	Overland Park

Maryland

Name	City
Darlene Cook	Baltimore
Debbie Shalom	Baltimore
Stephen R. Gallison	Columbia
Beth Colley	Crownsville
Norine Dagliano	Hagerstown
LeRachel H. Buffkins	Laurel
Phyllis Houston	Upper Marlboro

Massachusetts

Name	City
Jill Grindle	Agawam
Judit Price	Chelmsford
Jean Cummings	Concord
Carol Nason	Groton
Beate Hait	Holliston
Jeanne Knight	Melrose
Wendy Gelberg	Needham
Louise Kursmark	Reading
Julie Bernardin, M.Ed.	Wakefield
Franchesca Carrington	Waltham
Joellyn Wittenstein Schwerdlin	Worcester

Michigan

Name	City
Lorie Lebert	Brighton
Nancy Rozum	Commerce Twp.
Janet L. Beckstrom	Flint
Katie Newton	Grand Rapids
Erin Kennedy	Lapeer
Lisa Chapman	Niles
Kris Plantrich	Ortonville
Maria E. Hebda	Trenton

Mississippi

Name	City
John Donovan	Hattiesburg
Terri W. Henderson	Ridgeland

Missouri

Name	City
Jacqui D. Barrett	Kansas City
Meg Montford	Kansas City
Karen M. Silins	Kansas City
Sari Neudorf	St. Louis
Ellie Vargo	St. Louis

Montana

Name	City
Cheryl Minnick	Missoula

Nebraska

Name	City
Angela Jones	Lincoln

New Hampshire

Name	City
Lori Russel	Manchester

New Jersey

Name	City
Nancy Boyer	
Meg Guiseppi	
Shauna C. Bryce	Bloomfield
Diane Irwin	Cherry Hill
Kathy Warwick	Collingswood
Patricia Duckers	Edison
Martin Weitzman	Englishtown
Carol Altomare	Flemington
Angela P. Zimmer	Jackson
Tom Albano	Lake Hiawatha
Igor Shpudejko	Mahwah
Don Goodman	N. Caldwell
Judith Vince	Oakland
Nina Ebert	Ocean, Monmouth, & Burlington Counties
Fran Kelley	Waldwick
Barbara Romano	Wayne

New York

Name	City
Freddie Cheek	Amherst
Louise Fletcher	Bronxville
Ann Baehr	East Islip

New York

Name	City
Betty Geller	Elmira
Beth W. Stefani	Hamburg
Donna Farrise	Hauppauge
Deb Dib	Medford
Barbara Safani	New York
Kimberly Schneiderman	New York
Linsey Levine	Ossining
Phyllis B. Shabad	Ossining
Ilona Vanderwoude	Riverdale
Arnold G. Boldt	Rochester
La-Dana Renee Jenkins	Staten Island
Anne-Marie Ditta	Tuckahoe
Mark D. Berkowitz	Yorktown Heights

North Carolina

Name	City
Dayna Feist	Asheville
Christine Tutor	Cary
Tina Harlan	Charlotte
Doug Morrison	Charlotte
Julie Rains	Clemmons
Sharon McCormick	Durham
Art Frank	Flat Rock
Laurie J. Smith	Gastonia
Billie P. Jordan	Maysville
John M. O'Connor	Raleigh
Will W. Grant	Smithfield

Ohio

Name	City
Michael S. Davis	Centerville
Michelle Mastruserio Reitz	Cincinnati
Susan Hoopes	Cleveland
Alia Lawlor	Cleveland
Karen Hughes	Columbus
Samantha Nolan	Columbus
Harriet Shea	Columbus
Janice Worthington	Columbus
Jeremy Worthington	Columbus
Sharon Pierce-Williams	Findlay
Deborah James	Rossford
Teena Rose	Springfield

Oklahoma

Name	City
Debbie McMahan	Collinsville
Bonnie Kurka	Tulsa

Oregon

Name	City
Pat Kendall	Tigard

Pennsylvania

Name	City
Kim Isaacs	Doylestown
Wilson W. Elliott	Langhorne
Patricia Navin	Langhorne
Karen P. Katz	Newtown
Jane Roqueplot	Sharon

Rhode Island

Name	City
Wally C. Keenan	Cranston

South Carolina

Name	City
Debbie Ellis	Greenville
Robert Prock	Greenville

Tennessee

Name	City
Don Arthur	Collierville
Fred Frazier Jr.	Nashville

Texas

Name	City
Deanne Arnath	Arlington
Shannon D. Branson	El Paso
Lynda Lucas	El Paso
Robyn L. Feldberg	Frisco
Jerry D. Johnson	Groesbeck
Edie Rische	Lubbock
Denise Stewart	Milford
Ann Stewart	Roanoke
Kelley Smith	Sugar Land

Virginia

Name	City
Amy Whitmer	
Tammy W. Chisholm	Mechanicsville
Laura Labovich	Potomac Falls

(continued)

Virginia (continued)

Name	City
Betty H. Williams	Richmond
Susan Geary	Roanoke
Cory Edwards	Sterling

Washington

Name	City
Jill Walser	Bellevue
Janice M. Shepherd	Bellingham
Judy Ware	Camas
Stephanie Peacocke	Gig Harbor
Pat Cort	Kittitas
Lonnie L. Swanson	Poulsbo

Wisconsin

Name	City
Kathy Keshemberg	Appleton
Michele Haffner	Glendale
Wendy J. Terwelp	Mequon
Susan Guarneri	Three Lakes
Julie Walraven	Wausau
Kendra Walters	Wauwatosa

Wyoming

Name	City
Dian R. Davis	Cheyenne

CHAPTER 6

Alphabetic Directory of Professional Resume Writers

Barbara A. Adams, CPRW, CEIP, CFRWC
CareerPro Global, Inc.
173 Pierce Ave.
Macon, GA 31204
Phone: (478) 742-2442
Toll-free: (800) 471-9201
E-mail: badams@careerprocenter.net
www.careerproplus.com
www.militaryresumewriters.com
www.21stcenturyresumes.com

Career practitioner offering 20 years of direct expertise writing military resumes and federal resumes for veterans and government personnel.

Georgia Adamson, CCM, CCMC, CPRW, CEIP, JCTC
A Successful Career, div. of Adept Business Services
1096 N. Central Ave.
San Jose, CA 95128
Phone: (408) 244-6401
E-mail: success@ablueribbonresume.com
www.ablueribbonresume.com
www.asuccessfulcareer.com

My clients tell me I'm a great listener and able to bring out their "best" when they have trouble expressing it themselves, so that employers pay more attention to their resume.

Tom Albano, CARW
All Star Career Services
57 New England Dr.
Lake Hiawatha, NJ 07034
Phone: (973) 387-0134
E-mail: Tom@allstarcareer.com
www.allstarcareer.com

Tom has been developing results-driven resumes for more than a decade. He has worked with professionals, senior managers, and executives across a broad range of professions.

Carol Altomare, CPRW
World Class Resumes
Flemington, NJ 08822
Phone: (908) 237-1883
E-mail: wcr@worldclassresumes.com
www.worldclassresumes.com

Trust your resume to a true professional! Carol Altomare not only has the tools and know-how to write an effective resume, she has first-hand, in-depth knowledge of what employers are looking for.

Margaret Anderson
The Resume Connection
12861 Telfair Ave.
Sylmar, CA 91342
Phone: (818) 362-7933
Toll-free: (800) 345-9796
E-mail: margaret.anderson4@verizon.net
www.AResumeConnection.com

A preliminary draft is prepared after the interview, and then tailored precisely to each individual, as well as to the job title the client seeks, insofar as his/her qualifications/experience allow.

Michele Angello, CPRW
Corbel Communications, A+ Resumes
Aurora, CO 80013
Phone: (303) 537-3592
Toll-free: 866-5-corbel
E-mail: corbelcomm1@aol.com
http://corbelonline.com

If your job search is taking too long, you aren't confident that your resume is the best it can be, or you aren't getting interviews, make sure you get a professional resume from Corbel Communications.

Deanne Arnath, CPRW
A Resume Wizard and Services
316 McMurtry, First Floor
Arlington, TX 76002
Phone: (817) 466-0015
Toll-free: (866) 422-0800
E-mail: customerservice@aresumewizard.com
www.aresumewizard.com

"Reinventing people" through expert career document prepartion and career counseling services since 1998. If your phone is not ringing, call us for a free resume critique and price quote.

Don Arthur, CPRW
1318 Milestone Dr.
Collierville, TN 38017
Phone: (901) 861-5804 or (901) 848-0261
E-mail: arthur.don@comcast.net

With 20 years' experience as a hiring manager, I know what managers look for on a resume. Strong manufacturing background with knowledge covering a broad spectrum of disciplines.

Christopher Aune, MS, CFCC
Personal SHAPE Consulting
602 N. Main St.
Batesville, IN 47006
E-mail: lifepro@etczone.com

Special gift for career-path clarification, plus 10 years' experience in writing successful resumes, training to master the interview, and coaching to win what you're really worth.

Elizabeth J. Axnix, CPRW, IJCTC, CEIP
The Axnix Advantage
110 N. Knisel St.
Riverside, IA 52327
Phone: (319) 354-7822
Toll-free: (800) 359-7822
E-mail: axnix@earthlink.net

20+ years' experience writing resumes, targeted cover letters, executive biographies, proposals, reference pages, thank-you letters, and other career-marketing documents for job seekers in virtually all fields.

Ann Baehr, CPRW
Best Resumes of New York
49 Fern Ave.
East Islip, NY 11730
Phone: (631) 224-9300
E-mail: resumesbest@earthlink.net
www.e-bestresumes.com

Specialize in writing only resumes and cover letters.

Jacqui D. Barrett, MRW, CPRW, CEIP
Career Trend
3826 NW Barry Rd., Ste. A
Kansas City, MO 64154
Phone: (816) 468-5577
E-mail: jacqui@careertrend.net
www.careertrend.net

Jacqui—a certified Master Resume Writer from Career Masters Institute—leverages her B.A. in Writing and 15+ years' corporate experience to put "Your Value Into Words."

Lorraine Beaman, B.A., M.A.
JLB Career Consulting
426 Del Oro
Davis, CA 95616
Phone: (530) 219-9651 or (530) 219-9652
E-mail: jlbcareers@sbcglobal.net

Committed to showcasing your experience, education, talents, and skills with a strong, accurate, and attractive resume that says, "Hire Me!"

Janet L. Beckstrom, CPRW
Word Crafter
1717 Montclair Ave.
Flint, MI 48503
Phone: (810) 232-9257
Toll-free: (800) 351-9818
E-mail: wordcrafter@voyager.net

CPRW with more than 16 years of experience helping clients from diverse industries such as human services, education, health care, law enforcement, sales, and manufacturing.

Mark D. Berkowitz, CPRW, NCC, NCCC, CEIP, IJCTC
Career Development Resources
1312 Walter Rd.
Yorktown Heights, NY 10598
Phone: (914) 962-1548
Toll-free: (877) 302-2733
E-mail: cardevres@aol.com
www.careerdevresources.com

Full-service career management firm with a demonstrated track record in helping job-seeking candidates maximize their career potential, providing state-of-the-art, professional assistance from start to finish.

Marian Bernard, CPS, CPRW, JCTC, CEIP
The Regency Group
6 Morning Crescent
Aurora, Ontario L4G 2E3
Canada
Phone: (905) 841-7120
Toll-free: (866) 448-4672
E-mail: marian@neptune.on.ca
www.resumeexpert.ca

I produce exceptionally high-quality work with lightning-fast turnaround time because I operate Canada's only while-you-wait service—either in person or over the phone.

Julie Bernardin, M.Ed.
JB Consulting
8 Indian Ln.
Wakefield, MA 01880
Phone: (781) 587-1599
E-mail: julieber@aol.com
http://jbcareersuccess.com

Established in 1989. Resume writer and career coach.

Arnold G. Boldt, CPRW, JCTC
Arnold-Smith Associates
625 Panorama Trail, Bldg. 1, Ste. 120
Rochester, NY 14625
Phone: (585) 383-0350
E-mail: Arnie@ResumeSOS.com
www.ResumeSOS.com

Author of Resumes for the Rest of Us*; co-author of* No-Nonsense Resumes *and* No-Nonsense Cover Letters*; four-time TORI nominee; contributor to more than 35 resume and career books.*

Nancy Boyer, CPRW
Your Extra Hand
35 Hemlock Rd.
Columbia, NJ 07832
Phone: (908) 496-8766
Toll-free: (800) 256-5713
E-mail: nancy@nancyboyer.com
www.nancyboyer.com

Specializing in workers over 50, women returning to the workforce, career changers, new grads, and blue-collar workers. Sometimes two hands just aren't enough.

Shannon D. Branson, MS, CEIP
Shannon Branson
El Paso, TX
Phone: (678) 643-2627
E-mail: sgriffin24@hotmail.com

Specializing in the ability to analyze skill sets, creating unique, highly marketable career development documents.

Anne Brunelle
MakingChanges
Canada
Phone: (647) 224-8287
E-mail: info@makingchanges.ca
www.makingchanges.ca

MakingChanges is a holistic practice that will assist you in your search for the career, image, and life you desire. MakingChanges offers a safe environment in which you can enjoy the process, as well as the outcome.

Shauna C. Bryce, JD, CPRW
Resume Galleria LLC
P.O. Box 1003
Bloomfield, NJ 07003
E-mail: scbryce@resumegalleria.com
www.ResumeGalleria.com

Resume Galleria specializes in The Art and Craft of the Legal Resume™ and serves all types of legal professionals. At Resume Galleria, all of our resume writers are attorneys.

Martin Buckland, CPRW, CPBS, CEIP, JCTC, CJST
Elite Resumes
2020 Winston Park Dr., Ste. 100
Oakville, Ontario L6H 6X7
Canada
Phone: (905) 825-0490 or (705) 835-0951
E-mail: martin@aneliteresume.com
www.aneliteresume.com

Experience counts when selecting a professional to make you stand out from the competition. We personally conduct an interview with all clients to extract and write a dynamic document.

LeRachel H. Buffkins, MSW, CPRW, FJST
Writing For You, Inc.
14518 Cambridge Circle
Laurel, MD 20707
Phone: (301) 604-2048
E-mail: LBuffkins@writingforyouinc.com
www.writingforyouinc.com

Career advancement documents that will catch to eye of any employer and put you ahead of the pack. We specialize in complete resume packages for federal, non-profit/public/private organizations.

Margaret Burkholder
Advantage Writing Services
Tucson AZ 85747
Phone: (520) 909-5066
E-mail: advantagewriting@cox.net
www.advantagewriting.com

Get the advantage of a professionally written resume and leapfrog ahead of the competition. Job interview guaranteed! Professional resume, personal service.

Diane Hudson Burns, CPRW, CEIP, CPCC, CCM, CCMC, FJSTC, IJCTC, CLTMC
Career Marketing Techniques
3079 N. Columbine Ave.
Boise, ID 83713
Phone: (208) 323-9636
E-mail: diane@polishedresumes.com
www.polishedresumes.com

Career-change coach, specializing in executives, military transitions, federal government applications and procedures, and seminars.

Nita Busby, CPRW, CAC, JCTC, B.A., M.S.
Resumes, Etc.
438 E. Katella, Ste. G
Orange, CA 92867
Phone: (714) 633-2783
E-mail: resumes100@aol.com
http://resumesetc.net
http://heresmyresume.com
http://brightcommunications.net

Coaching clients to their career success and satisfaction is our mission. We work with clients in various parts of the world to increase their career searching success, too.

Ron Cail, CPRW, MHA
Resume Ready
375 Redondo Ave. #153
Long Beach, CA 90814
Toll-free: (888) 919-4299
E-mail: rresumerready@aol.com
http://resumereadyonline.com

Professional resume documents tailored specifically for each individual and prepared by a Certified Resume Expert. Entry level to seasoned professonals, we provide world-class resumes and world-class service.

Franchesca Carrington, M.Ed.
Waltham, MA
Phone: (781) 354-5206
E-mail: frcarrington@verizon.net

Services include writing and reworking resumes, writing cover letters, and career coaching. Thirty-minute counseling session on how to sell your resume included with purchase of resume.

Clay Cerny
AAA Targeted Writing and Coaching Services
5415 N. Clark St.
Chicago, IL 60640
Phone: (773) 907-8660
E-mail: info@aaatargeted.com
www.aaatargeted.com

Clay Cerny is dedicated to learning what makes each client unique and helping that person achieve professional success.

Lisa Chapman, CPRW
Chapman Services Group, LLC
115 Beeson Rd., Ste. 122
Niles, MI 49120
Phone: (269) 687-9700
Toll-free: (866) 687-9700
E-mail: lisa@chapmanservices.com
www.chapmanservices.com

Resumes written with your future in mind.

Freddie Cheek, CCM, CARW, CPRW, CWDP
Cheek and Associates
406 Maynard Dr.
Amherst, NY 14226
Phone: (716) 835-6945 or (716) 553-6945
E-mail: fscheek@adelphia.net
www.cheekandassociates.com

Your career solution for securing the job you deserve by providing the competitive edge through expert document preparation and interview coaching.

Tammy W. Chisholm, CPRW, CWPP
Advanced Career Marketing - MBA Resumes
P.O. Box 2403
Mechanicsville, VA 23116
Phone: (804) 878-9296
E-mail: twchisholm@advancedcareermarketing.com
www.advancedcareermarketing.com
www.mba-resumes.com

We have a targeted package that will work for you and your campaign. Whether you are a professional, executive, student, new MBA grad, or are returning to work, there is a marketing strategy for you.

Stephanie Clark, B.A., CRS
New Leaf Resumes
Kitchener, Ontario
Canada
Phone: (519) 505-5627
E-mail: stephaniec@newleafresumes
www.newleafresumes.ca

With my writing background and several years' experience in human resources, I provide sound advice and sound resume strategies.

Sally Cofer-Lindberg, CPRW, CCDT
Career Directions
PMB 201, 2401 E. Orangeburg Ave., #675
Modesto, CA 95355
Phone: (209) 575-4924
E-mail: sallys_c@earthlink.net
www.thecareerlighthouse.com

With more than 20 years of experience, Sally Cofer-Lindberg offers personal, professional, and powerful career-search techniques including hard-hitting resumes, interview coaching, and goals development.

Beth Colley, CPRW, CFJST
Chesapeake Resume Writing Service
P.O. Box 117
Crownsville, MD 21032
Phone: (410) 533-2457
E-mail: resume@chesres.com
www.chesres.com

Chart a new course to success with Chesapeake. Through continuous professional development, we guarantee that our work is on the cutting edge of today's hiring trends.

Darlene Cook, CRRC
Resumes & Beyond
P.O. Box 9952
Baltimore, MD 21224
Phone: (410) 342-6336
E-mail: dcookcoach@msn.com
www.ResumesandBeyond.com
www.QuantumQuizics.com

Trained life and certified retirement coach offering full career and job change services. Creator of landmark Quantum Quizics™ career-change method.

Fred Coon, LEA, CRW, JCTC
Stewart, Cooper & Coon, Inc.
2111 E. Highland, Ste. B-190
Phoenix, AZ 85016
Phone: (602) 385-3000
E-mail: fcoon@stewartcoopercoon.com
www.stewartcoopercoon.com
www.thegladiator.info
www.executivecareersearchadvice.com
www.readyaimhired.com

Stewart, Cooper & Coon has provided executive career transition, executive employment services, and executive counseling to 75,000 executives seeking career assistance and placement.

Pat Cort
Pat Cort's Word Processing
100 N. Main St.
P.O. Box 1262
Kittitas, WA 98934
Phone: (509) 968-9622
E-mail: pcwp@elltel.net
www.patcortswordprocessing.com

11 years experience in the employment and training field, providing resumes and job search skills.

Pat Criscito, CPRW
ProType, Ltd.
20070 Roaming Dr.
Colorado Springs, CO 80908
Phone: (719) 592-1999
Toll-free: (800) 446-2408
E-mail: pat@protypeltd.com
www.protypeltd.com

Pat Criscito is the author of Barron's Designing the Perfect Resume, e-Resumes, How to Write Better Resumes and Cover Letters, *and* Interview Answers in a Flash.

Annemarie Cross, CECC, CCM, CWPP, CERW, CPRW, CEIP
Advanced Employment Concepts
P.O. Box 91
Hallam, Victoria 3803
Australia
Phone: +613 9708 6930
E-mail: success@aresumewriter.net
www.aresumewriter.net

Multiple award-winning resume writer, career and master NLP coach, and author of 10 Key Steps to Ace that Interview. *Fast track the job offer and your career. Your catalyst to success!*

Jean Cummings, M.A.T., CPBS, SPRW, CEIP
A Resume For Today and Gig Resumes
123 Minot Rd.
Concord, MA 01742
Phone: (978) 371-9266
Toll-free: (800) 324-1699
E-mail: jc@YesResumes.com
www.aResumeForToday.com
www.GigResumes.com

Building executive and consulting careers in technology since 1992.

Norine Dagliano, NCRW, CPRW, CFRW/CC
ekm Inspirations
14 N. Potomac St., Ste. 200A
Hagerstown, MD 21740
Phone: (301) 766-2032 or (240) 217-5075
E-mail: norine@ekminspirations.com
www.ekminspirations.com

Over 20 years of personalized experience providing information, tools, and inspiration to help job seekers overcome the anxiety of looking for work.

Robert Dagnall, BA
ResumeGuru
4640 Campus Ave.
San Diego, CA 92116
Phone: (619) 297-0950
E-mail: robert@resumeguru.com
www.resumeguru.com

Resumes expertly written, not merely typed. Published expert with 6,000+ clients since 1992. Management, executives, military transition, students. Free information.

Dian R. Davis, MS, LPC, NCC, MCC
LCCC Career Center
1400 E. College Dr.
Cheyenne, WY 82007
Phone: (307) 778-1132
E-mail: ddavis@lccc.wy.edu
www.lccc.wy.edu

Specializing in resumes for new graduates, health-care professionals, job seekers with little or no education and/or experience, and mid-life job seekers in transition.

Michael S. Davis, GCDF, CPRW
Davis Consulting
940 Ashcreek Dr.
Centerville, OH 45458-3333
Phone: (937) 438-5037
E-mail: msdavis49@hotmail.com

Laura DeCarlo, MCD, CERW, CARW, CCMC, CECC, CWPP, CCRE, CCM, Reach 360, IJCTC, CEIC

A Competitive Edge Career Service, LLC
1665 Clover Circle
Melbourne, FL 32935
Phone: (321) 752-0880
Toll-free: (800) 715-3442
E-mail: success@acompetitiveedge.com
www.acompetitiveedge.com
www.careerpocketrx.com

Get an edge on your career with an award-winning and published Certified Expert Resume Writer. We are resume experts for 54 professional associations.

Deb Dib, CCM, CPBS, CCMC, NCRW, CPRW, CEIP, JCTC

Executive Power Coach, Advantage Resumes of New York
77 Buffalo Ave.
Medford, NY 11763
Phone: (631) 475-8513
E-mail: deborah.dib@advantageresumes.com
www.advantageresumes.com
www.executivepowercoach.com
www.executivepowerbrand.com
www.executivepowermarketing.com
www.executivepowergroup.com

My passion is helping visionary, gutsy, fun CEOs with a conscience build great careers, mold great companies, and even change the world a bit! I work in-depth with a few very special clients at a time.

Jessica Dillard

Dillard & Associates
3855 E. La Palma Ave. Ste. 250
Anaheim, CA 92807
Phone: (714) 632-3646 or (951) 271-2985
E-mail: resumes@dillardandassociates.com
www.dillardandassociates.com

Writing resumes that get you the interview!

Anne-Marie Ditta, CEIP, CPRW, CEIP

First Impression Career Services, LLC
58 Lincoln Ave.
Tuckahoe, NY 10707
Phone: (914) 961-0579 or (917) 576-2821
E-mail: amditta@mycareercoach.net
www.firstimpressioncareerservices.com
www.mycareercoach.net

Results-driven, insightful resume writer, career coach, and MBTI administrator serving project managers, CEOs, international executives, and young professionals.

John Donovan, CARW, CERW
CRS Resume Services
205 Beverly Lane
Hattiesburg, MS 39402
Phone: (601) 264-6663
Toll-free: (888) 264-9588
E-mail: johndonovan@crsresume.com
www.crsresume.com
www.hotelresume.com
www.teachingjobresumes.com
www.armedforcesresumes.com

I enjoy helping my clients succeed. I know people come to me because they're confident in my ability to help them achieve their career goals.

Patricia Duckers, CPRW, CERW, CEIP, CFRW, CFRWC, CPPP
P.O. Box 6434
Edison, NJ 08818-6434
Phone: (732) 239-2240
E-mail: pduckers@msn.com

Specializing in federal, military conversion, and civilian sectors. Member of the CDI Certification and Mentoring committees. Proud member of the CareerPro Global team.

Deloris J. (Dee) Duff, CPRW, CEIP, JCTC, CFRWC
Document Developers
5030 Guion Rd.
Indianapolis, IN 46254
Phone: (317) 290-0099
Toll-free: (877) 463-2034
E-mail: deesdocs@earthlink.net
www.documentdevelopers.net

An inferior resume and job search is hazardous to your wealth! Dee is a careers' professional with the knowledge, credentials, and experience to capture the essential elements of your work history.

Michelle Dumas, NCRW, CPRW, CCM, JCTC, CEIP
Distinctive Career Services, LLC
USA
Toll-free: (800) 644-9694
E-mail: mdumas@distinctiveweb.com
www.distinctivedocuments.com
www.100kcareermarketing.com

Services designed specifically for professionals, executives, and emerging executives (including VIP services exclusively for top-tier executives).

George Dutch, BA, CMF, CCM, JCTC
JobJoy
Ste. 1300, 340 Albert St.
Ottawa, Ontario K1P 6A9
Canada
Phone: (613) 563-0584
Toll-free: (800) 798-2696
E-mail: george@jobjoy.com
www.jobjoy.com

Moving you from career pain to job joy! Specializing in career transition resumes—that is, military to civilian, private to public, profit to nonprofit, and self-employment to salaried jobs.

Nina Ebert, CPRW
A Word's Worth
On the cusp of Ocean, Monmouth, and Burlington Counties
NJ 08533
USA
Phone: (609) 758-7799
Toll-free: (866) 400-7799
E-mail: nina@keytosuccessresumes.com
www.keytosuccessresumes.com

Serving clients since 1989, A Word's Worth provides resumes, cover letters, and career-coaching services that open doors to interviews. Nina is a 22-time nationally published author.

Cory Edwards, CERW, CFRW, CCMC
Partnering For Success
46890 Wesleyan Ct.
Sterling, VA 20164
Phone: (703) 444-7835
Toll-free: (800) 611-3234
E-mail: Cory@myfederalresume.com
www.myfederalresume.com
www.resumes4results.com
http://partnering4success.com

Creating federal resumes that get clients interviews. We help clients navigate through the maze of federal application rules and land federal positions. All our writers have the premier designation of CFRW.

Clifford W. Eischen, MBA, NCRW
Eischen's Professional Resume Service
Marks and Herndon Aves.
Fresno, CA 93711
Phone: (559) 435-3538
E-mail: 4resume@cvip.net
http://cvip.fresno.com/~ce082/index.html

30+ years' experience preparing career strategies and resume materials for a wide spectrum of professionals. Published author of Resumes, Cover Letters, Networking, and Interviewing, *Second Ediiton, 2007, a college textbook.*

Lynn Eischen, CPRW
Eischen's Professional Resume Service
3258 W. Spruce
Fresno, CA 93711
Phone: (559) 435-3538
E-mail: 4resume@cvip.net
http://cvip.fresno.com/~ce082/index.html

I have written professional resumes for 16 years and have been certified for 11 years. You can be assured that I possess vast knowledge in preparing resumes for various industries.

Wilson W. Elliott, JCTC, CACPD
INTRATEC, The Resume Professor
5311 Fonthill Court
Langhorne, PA 19047-3439
Phone: (215) 752-3342 or (215) 310-8060
E-mail: theresumeprofessor@comcast.net

No cookie-cutter resumes! Our mission is to help you find a job you can love. Job search packages, coaching, and interview prep. Career development and management workshops.

Debbie Ellis, MRW, CPRW
Phoenix Career Group
Greenville, SC
Toll-free: (800) 876-5506
E-mail: info@phoenixcareergroup.com
www.phoenixcareergroup.com

Serving career-minded professionals to the most senior executive managers, the Phoenix Career Group is a one-of-a-kind consortium of industry-leading professionals providing a seamless, end-to-end solution for our clients.

Donna Farrise
Dynamic Resumes of Long Island, Inc.
300 Motor Parkway, Ste. 200
Hauppauge, NY 11788
Phone: (631) 951-4120
Toll-free: (800) 528-6796
E-mail: donna@dynamicresumes.com
http://dynamicresumes.com

20+ years' experience writing 10,000+ resumes for executives, senior managers, mid-level managers, professionals, and career changers within many different fields in more than 100 industries.

Dayna Feist, CPRW, CEIP, JCTC
Gatehouse Business Services
265 Charlotte St.
Asheville, NC 28801
Phone: (828) 254-7893
E-mail: Gatehous@aol.com
www.BestJobEver.com

Dayna Feist has been writing aggressive resumes under the banner of Gatehouse Business Services since 1976. She helps clients gain a competitive advantage when interviewing for jobs and negotiating the salaries they deserve.

Robyn L. Feldberg, CCMC
Abundant Success Career Services
Frisco, TX 75035
Phone: (972) 464-1144
Toll-free: (866) WIN-AJOB
E-mail: Robyn@AbundantSuccessCareerServices.com
www.AbundantSuccessCareerServices.com

With more than 16 years' experience, I am passionate about writing resumes that consistently help my clients win interviews and position them to find rewarding work.

Marilyn A. Feldstein, M.P.A., JCTC, MBTI, PHR
Career Choices Unlimited
4465 Baymeadows Rd., #7
Jacksonville, FL 32217
Phone: (904) 443-0059 or (904) 262-9470
E-mail: mfeldstein@bellsouth.net
www.careerchoicesunlimited.com

Your resume will be written from the perspective of a hiring manager who has more than 20 years' experience in recruiting, interviewing, and staffing for three major corporations.

Audrey Field, CARW, CEIC, B.A., B.Ed.
Resume Resources
Canada
Toll-free: (877) 204-9737
E-mail: info@resumeresources.ca
www.resumeresources.ca

Canadian/US/international resumes, CVs and bios, expert engineering, IT and military-to-civilian writer interview training and outplacement. Published and award-winning global leader.

Cliff Flamer, NCRW, CPRW, MS, NCC
BrightSide Resumes
2718 Harrison St.
Oakland, CA 94612
Phone: (510) 444-1724
E-mail: writers@brightsideresumes.com
www.brightsideresumes.com

Resume-writing involves reviewing your life's work line by line to build an accurate yet favorable representation of who you are personally and professionally.

Louise Fletcher, CPRW
Blue Sky Resumes
Bronxville, NY 10708
Phone: (914) 337-5742
E-mail: lfletcher@blueskyresumes.com
www.blueskyresumes.com
www.blueskyresumesblog.com

Take charge of your career with our proprietary system for finding and communicating your unique value. We offer a 100 percent satisfaction guarantee.

Art Frank, MBA
Resumes R Us
17 Green Meadow Ct.
Flat Rock, NC 28731
Phone: (828) 696-2975
Toll-free: (866) 600-4300
E-mail: af@mchsi.com
http://PowerResumesandCoaching.com

25 years as former director of recruiting for an executive search firm enables us to construct resumes with the same mindset as the examiner. We know what they want to see and what they don't.

Gail Frank, NCRW, CPRW, JCTC, MA, CEIP
Employment U
10409 Greendale Dr.
Tampa, FL 33626
Phone: (813) 926-1353
E-mail: gailfrank@post.harvard.edu
www.EmploymentU.com
www.ResumeWritingBootCamp.com

Employment U is "the place to learn everything about job search and careers you should know...but don't!" Learn resume and job search skills from a 10-year veteran outplacement trainer.

Julianne Franke, MS, CPRW, CCMC
Breakthrough Connections
258 Shire Way
Lawrenceville, GA 30044
Phone: (770) 381-0876 or (404) 317-3316
E-mail: jfranke1@bellsouth.net
http://breakthroughconnections.typepad.com/blog/

Extensive experience writing thousands of resumes representing all industries, functions, and levels (entry-level to executive). Executive coaching to help you break through to the next level. I guarantee my clients' satisfaction.

Fred Frazier Jr., GCDF
Nashville Career Advancement Center
2200 Metro Center Blvd.
Nashville, TN 37228
Phone: (615) 253-8920, ext. 105, or (615) 862-8890
E-mail: fred.frazier@nashville.gov
www.NCACWorkforce.org

Encouraging individuals to follow the dream and purpose that God has given them. Remember, "Your dream won't work until you do!"

Stephen R. Gallison, CPRW, GCDF, CIIS, CFJTC
Professional Outplacement Assistance Center (POAC)
7161 Columbia Gateway Dr.
Columbia, MD 21046
Phone: (410) 290-2630
E-mail: sgallison@dllr.state.md.us
www.dllr.state.md.us/poac

Serves 90,000+ professional, technical, executive, and managerial workers. "Your success is our only business." We'll help guide you to your "occupassion." Free to Maryland residents.

Roberta Gamza, CEIP, CJCT, JST
Career Ink
Louisville, CO 80027
Phone: (303) 955-3065
Toll-free: (877) 581-6063
E-mail: roberta@careerink.com
www.careerink.com

Receive customized career marketing materials that support your goals. Reap the benefits of Roberta's 15-years of marketing experience with HP.

William Garner, BS, MS
Aacu Resumes
10820 Amigo Ave.
Northridge, CA 91326
Phone: (818) 368-5971
Toll-free: (866) 848-9868
E-mail: bgco@juno.com

20+ years as a technical sales and marketing rofessional. Five-plus years writing resumes for technical and all levels of technical sales and marketing personnel.

Louise Garver, CPBS, JCTC, CMP, CEIP, CPRW, CLBF, MCDP
Career Directions LLC
P.O. Box 583
Broad Brook, CT 06016
Phone: (860) 623-9476
E-mail: LouiseGarver@cox.net
www.CareerDirectionsLLC.com

Specializing in brand-driven resumes, related marketing tools, and career coaching that deliver results for executives, managers, and consultants.

Susan Geary, CERW, CEIC, CPRW, CARW
1st Rate Resumes
Roanoke, VA
Toll-free: (866) 690-4622
E-mail: info@1stRateResumes.com
www.1stRateResumes.com

Our resumes and cover letters are easy to navigate and understand, which means recruiters can quickly determine what you have to offer. Contact us for a free resume critique and quote.

Wendy Gelberg, M.Ed., IJCTC, CPRW, CEIP
Advantage Resumes/Gentle Job Search
Needham, MA 02492
Phone: (781) 444-0778
E-mail: wendy@gentlejobsearch.com
www.gentlejobsearch.com

With extensive experience creating customized resumes for people from entry level to corporate executives, I include interview preparation and job search coaching with resume writing services.

Betty Geller, NCRW, CPRW, WBE
Apple Resume and Career Services
303 W. Church St., Ste. 3
Elmira, NY 14901
Phone: (607) 734-2090
E-mail: appleresumesvc@stny.rr.com

A seasoned professional with 30 years of experience in the careers field, providing job seekers with state-of-the-art marketing tools and services. Work featured in several career-development and job search publications.

Don Goodman, CPRW, CCMC
About Jobs
18 Eton Dr., Ste. #201
North Caldwell, NJ 07006
Toll-free: (800) 909-0109
E-mail: DGoodman@GotTheJob.com
www.GotTheJob.com

Don is a nationally recognized career coach and resume writer and a graduate of the Wharton School of Business and Stanford University's Executive Program.

Sharon Graham, CRS, CIS, CCS, CPRW, CEIP
Graham Management Group
Canada
Phone: (905) 878-8768
Toll-free: (866) 622-1464
E-mail: info@GrahamManagement.com
www.GrahamManagement.com

Leading Canadian firm specializing in solutions for executives and senior-level professionals. GMG is known for excellence and innovation in resume and career strategy.

Will W. Grant
ResumesETC
102 Castle Dr.
Smithfield, NC 27577-3503
Phone: (919) 464-8794
Toll-free: (866) 386-6732
E-mail: info@resumesetc.org
www.resumesetc.org

My job is "Seeing You Succeed." You will be amazed how good you can look on paper! I answer questions and teach skills on researching companies, interviewing, job hunting, networking, and more.

Jill Grindle, CPRW
A Step Ahead Resume
Agawam, MA 1001
Phone: (413) 789-6046
E-mail: jill@astepaheadresume.com
www.astepaheadresume.com

Dedicated to helping people achieve career goals through custom, strategic marketing tools

Susan Guarneri, CERW, CPRW, MRW, CPBS, NCCC, CCMC, CEIP, DCC
6670 Crystal Lake Rd.
Three Lakes, WI 54562
Phone: (715) 546-4449
Toll-free: (866) 881-4055
E-mail: Susan@Resume-Magic.com
www.Resume-Magic.com
www.AssessmentGoddess.com

Empowering professionals and executives with personal branding and career-assessment insights, as well as resumes and job search tactics that work like magic!

Meg Guiseppi, CPRW
Resumes Plus, LLC
Andover, NJ
Phone: (973) 726-0757
E-mail: meg@resumesplusllc.com
www.resumesplusllc.com

Partnering with you to craft powerful marketing documents that distinguish you and your value. Writing career success stories since 1993 for job seekers at all levels, across diverse industries.

Michele Haffner, CPRW, JCTC
Advanced Resume Services
1314 W. Paradise Ct.
Glendale, WI 53209
Phone: (414) 247-1677
Toll-free: (888) 586-2258
E-mail: michele@resumeservices.com
www.resumeservices.com

Helping executives and professionals make successful and lucrative career moves through expertly crafted resumes, cover letters, bios, targeted campaigns, and coaching.

Beate Hait, CPRW, NCRW
Resumes Plus
80 Wingate Rd.
Holliston, MA 01746
Phone: (508) 429-1813
E-mail: bea@resumesplus.net
www.resumesplus.net

One of only a handful of resume writers nationwide to earn both CPRW and NCRW credentials, Bea has been writing resumes in all industries—entry level to executive—since 1992.

Tina Harlan, CPRW
Words That Work Communications
1309 Morningside Dr.
Charlotte, NC 28205
Phone: (704) 372-7167
E-mail: charlan@carolina.rr.com
www.wordsthatworkcom.com

I write every resume as if it were my own.

Beverly Harvey, CPRW, JCTC, CCM, CCMC, MRW, CPBS
Beverly Harvey Resume & Career Services
P.O. Box 750
Pierson, FL 32180
Phone: (386) 749-3111
Toll-free: (888) 775-0916
E-mail: beverly@harveycareers.com
www.harveycareers.com

Branded resumes, career coaching, career transition, career management, and leadership coaching for Chief Officer-level and Senior-level executives. 16 years of experience.

Makini Theresa Harvey, CPRW, JCTC, CEIP, CCMC
Career Abundance
405 El Camino Real, #601
Menlo Park, CA 94025
Phone: (650) 630-7610
E-mail: makini@careerabundance.com

Over 20 years of providing excellent quality career-managment services and products, helping clients live their purpose, passion, place, vision, and value to others.

Maria E. Hebda, CCMC, CPRW
Career Solutions, LLC
4580 Dolores Dr.
Trenton, MI 48183
Phone: (734) 676-9170
E-mail: maria@writingresumes.com
www.WritingResumes.com

Quality and professional resume-development and job search coaching services, leading each client to career success!

Terri W. Henderson, CPRW, NRW
The Executive Level, Inc.
1025 Northpark Dr., Ste. C
Ridgeland, MS 39157
Phone: (601) 956-5002
E-mail: thenderson@excecutivelevel.net
http://executivelevel.net

Take it to the next level with The Executive Level. We are committed to designing, writing, and producing quality resumes. Visit our Web site for testimonials or call us when you are ready to begin your project.

Susan Hoopes, CJCTC, CJST, CWDP
Cuyahoga Valley Career Center
8001 Brecksville Rd.
Cleveland, OH 44141
Phone: (440) 746-8260 or (440) 543-1506
E-mail: shoopes@cvccworks.com or sjhoo@aol.com
www.cvccworks.com

20+ years' experience in job search training, human resources, public and proprietary technical education, and sales. Experience working with high-school students and adults.

Phyllis Houston
The Resume Expert
Upper Marlboro, MD 20772
Phone: (301) 574-3956 or (202) 361-0847
E-mail: phyllis_houston@msn.com

Mobile service, free consultation, portfolio showcase, multi-years' experience, federal employees/transitioning military specialist, database input, KSAS.

Gayle Howard, CCM, MCD, CERW, CPRW, CWPP, CRMS, CPRW
Top Margin
P.O. Box 74
Chirnside Park, Victoria 3116
Australia
Phone: +613 9726 6694
E-mail: getinterviews@topmargin.com
www.topmargin.com

Multi-award winning resume writer (9 TORI Awards) published in 20 career books internationally. Providing strategic, creative, and technically accomplished career-marketing solutions that propel the careers of people at all levels.

Karen Hughes, CPRW
Jewish Family Services
1070 College Ave.
Columbus, OH 43147
Phone: (614) 599-0177
E-mail: khughes@jfscolumbus.org
http://jfscolumbus.org/JobSeeker.asp

My focus is on professional, executive resumes. I stress the importance of branding, testimonials, and tag lines to strengthen a client's candidacy.

Diane Irwin
Dynamic Resumes
Cherry Hill, NJ 08002
Phone: (856) 321-0092
E-mail: dynamicresumes@comcast.net
http://dynamicresumesofNJ.com

Resumes that get results! As a former recruiter, I know what employers look for in a resume. I can help jumpstart a job search by helping with job hunting, interviewing, networking, recruiter connections, and career-site postings.

Kim Isaacs, NCRW, CPRW
Advanced Career Systems, Inc.
4695 Watson Dr.
Doylestown, PA 18902
Phone: (215) 794-9527
Toll-free: (800) 203-0551
E-mail: info@resumepower.com
www.resumepower.com
www.execresumes.com
www.resumesystems.com

Advanced Career Systems is one of the most respected resume writing companies in the U.S. Kim Isaacs has been trusted to serve as monster.com's resume expert since 1999.

Caroline M. Jagot, CPRW
A Better Resume
513-A Ingleside Ave.
Tallahassee, FL 32303-6335
Phone: (850) 425-1175
E-mail: caroline@getabetterresume.com
www.getabetterresume.com

A Better Resume positions local and long-distance clients to be prepared for opportunity with effective resumes, executive bios, curriculum vitae, and letters in a career market where "runner up" isn't good enough.

Deborah James, CPRW, CCMC
Leading-Edge Resumes and Career Services
1010 Schreier Rd.
Rossford, OH 43460
Phone: (419) 666-4518
E-mail: djames@leadingedgeresumes.com
www.leadingedgeresumes.com

Deborah helps clients take command of their career and become architects of their lives with professional resume development, cover letters, and career-marketing strategies.

La-Dana Renee Jenkins, MA
LRJ Consulting Services LLC
P.O. Box 40483
Staten Island, NY 10304
Phone: (718) 448-5825 or (917) 328-2550
E-mail: info@lrjconsulting.net
www.lrjconsulting.net

La-Dana Renee Jenkins, Personal Career Developer™, is the founder and CEO of LRJ Consulting Services LLC. Her passion is helping her clients prepare for a career, not a job.

Jerry D. Johnson, B.A., M.S.
Execu-Image Writing Services
921 N. Tyus
Groesbeck, TX 76642
Phone: (254) 729-3144
E-mail: jerryjohnson@execuimageresume.com
www.execuimageresume.com

Emphasis is on creating a unique resume and cover letter for each client based on specific needs. Close collaboration with each client ensures accuracy and a sense of client "ownership" in the completed documents.

Suzette Jolly, CPRW, CDS, BA, BS, MS
Willimantic CT Works
1320 Main St.
Willimantic, CT 06226
Phone: (860) 465-2128 or (860) 465-2120
E-mail: suzette.jolly@ct.gov

Certified resume writer offering a wide range of experience from entry-level, clerical, students, and professionals, including gaps in employment.

Angela Jones, CPRW
Haute Resume & Career Services
3201 S. 33rd St., Ste. G
Lincoln, NE 68506
Toll-free: (866) 695-9318
E-mail: angie@anewresume.com
http://anewresume.com

Is just any job good enough, or are you looking to receive the pay you deserve? We work to create a resume that highlights a job seeker's unique skills and experience.

Denette Jones
Jones Career Specialties
P.O. Box 2317
Pahoa, HI 96778
Phone: (808) 430-1177
E-mail: dj@jonescareerspecialties.com
www.jonescareerspecialties.com

More than 10 years' experience providing professional resume services tailored to meet individual, unique needs. Featured in several resume and job search software products and books.

Billie P. Jordan
Advantage Resumes and Career Services
2362 Belgrade Swansboro Rd.
Maysville, NC 28555
Phone: (910) 743-3641 or (910) 389-7087
E-mail: bjordan1@ec.rr.com
www.advantageresumes4you.com

While a resume is a personal marketing tool, it must have ingredients appreciated by a hiring executive. My background provides this vantage point. You'll get great service from a professional resume writer.

Karen P. Katz, M.Ed.
Career Acceleration Network
2865 S. Eagle Rd., #369
Newtown, PA 18940
Phone: (215) 378-6685 or (215) 860-6869
E-mail: karen@careeracceleration.net
www.careeracceleration.net

"Together We CAN" is more than a tagline—it describes the energetic, cutting-edge, and collaborative style of the Career Acceleration Network (CAN). CAN teaches clients to take control of their careers.

Wally C. Keenan, CARW, CPRW, JCTC, CPBA, BA
The Resume Connection, Ltd
1020 Park Ave., Ste. 106
Cranston, RI 2910
Phone: (401) 461-8899
E-mail: wallykeenan@the-resume-connection.com
www.the-resume-connection.com

Custom-written resumes and cover letters, resume distribution, authorized career assessment center, career coaching services, interview training.

Fran Kelley, MA, CPRW, SPHR, JCTC
The Resume Works
P.O. Box 262
Waldwick, NJ 07463
Phone: (201) 670-9643
Toll-free: (800) 551-6150
E-mail: FranKelley@optonline.net
www.careermuse.com

Exceptional resume-writing skills and extensive corporate human resources and outplacement career coaching experience.

Gillian Kelly, CARW
Career Edge
147 Redland Bay Rd.
Brisbane, Queensland 4161
Australia
Phone: +61 73824 5200
E-mail: jill@careeredge.com.au
www.careeredge.com.au

International award-winning and certified resume writer with more than 15 years' experience in the development of professional career marketing documentation. Experience writing for US, Australia, Europe, Asia, and Middle East.

Pat Kendall, NCRW, JCTC
Advanced Resume Concepts
14928 SW 109th Ave.
Tigard, OR 97224
Phone: (503) 639-6098
Toll-free: (800) 591-9143
E-mail: pat@reslady.com
www.reslady.com
www.careerfolios.com

Recognized job search expert, industry leader, and career author with more than 25 years' experience in resume writing and job search consulting. Expert knowledge of traditional, electronic, and online resumes.

Erin Kennedy, CPRW
Professional Resume Services
Lapeer, MI 48446
Toll-free: (866) 793-9224
E-mail: ekennedy@proreswriters.com
www.proreswriters.com
www.professionalresumeservices.com

Full service resume writing/personal marketing company partners you with a writer that will customize a dynamic, "must-read" resume marketing package to your specifications. Get results FAST!

Kathy Keshemberg, NCRW
A Career Advantage
1210 George St.
Appleton, WI 54915
Phone: (920) 731-5167
E-mail: kk@acareeradvantage.com
www.acareeradvantage.com

Our team of Nationally Certified Resume Writers has the training, experience, and knowledge of industry trends to write interview-winning resumes.

Jeanne Knight, JCTC, CCMC
P.O. Box 760828
Melrose, MA 02176
Phone: (617) 968-7747
E-mail: jeanne@careerdesigns.biz
www.careerdesigns.biz

With a 20-year background as an HR executive, Jeanne has interviewed and hired hundreds of employees in companies ranging from small start-ups to Fortune 500 corporations.

Myriam-Rose Kohn, CPRW, CEIP, IJCTC, CCM, CCMC, CPBS, Accredited Translator
JEDA Enterprises
27201 Tourney Rd., Ste. 201
Valencia, CA 91355
Phone: (661) 253-0801
Toll-free: (800) 600-JEDA
E-mail: myriam-rose@jedaenterprises.com
www.jedaenterprises.com

Your passport to international career success. Career management professional assisting clients to manage their careers in U.S. and abroad.

Cindy Kraft, CPBS, CCMC, CCM, CPRW, JCTC
The CFO-Coach, a division of Executive Essentials
P.O. Box 336
Valrico, FL 33595
Phone: (813) 655-0658
E-mail: cindy@cfo-coach.com
www.cfo-coach.com
www.cfo-career-forum.com

America's leading Career and Personal Brand Strategist for corporate finance and banking executives.

Frost Krist, CPRW
Datatype Inc.
15 Pendleton Dr.
Hebron, CT 06248
Phone: (860) 228-3542 or (860) 989-6301
E-mail: frost@datatypeinc.com
www.datatypeinc.com

Providing assistance across a wide range of needs, including recent grads, home-to-work, career changers; skilled, professional, executive levels.

Bonnie Kurka, CPRW, CCMC, CPBS, FJST, JCTC

Executive Career Suite
Tulsa, OK 74133
Phone: (918) 494-4630
Toll-free: (877) 570-2573
E-mail: bonnie@executivecareersuite.com
www.executivecareersuite.com
www.resumesuite.com

Ready to move up in your career? Our "Own Your Success" program gives you the tools, objectivity, and accountability to envision success and take action. We offer unique programs for unique individuals.

Louise Kursmark, MRW, CCM, JCTC, CEIP

Best Impression Career Services, Inc.
Reading, MA 01867
Phone: (781) 944-2471
Toll-free: (888) 792-0030
E-mail: LK@yourbestimpression.com
www.yourbestimpression.com

Expert resume and career services for senior executives. My passion is helping you communicate your value and "tell your story" in a way that is compelling, memorable, and relevant.

Laura Labovich, CARW, CFRW

A & E Consulting, LLC
Potomac Falls, VA 20165
Phone: (703) 725-5878
E-mail: lauramichelle@gmail.com
www.aspire-empower.com

Our career-coaching methodology arms you with tools to make even a daunting job search fun! Our resourceful, compassionate, client-focused professionals help you create a career you love.

Malloy Lacktman, BBA

Sage Resumes
9427 W. Olympic Blvd.
Beverly Hills, CA 90212
Phone: (213) 503-9663
E-mail: Malloy@SageResumes.com
www.SageResumes.com

Sage Resumes is the #1 user-rated resume service in Los Angeles. Malloy Lacktman creates exceptional resumes for clients across the United States, working with them by phone and e-mail.

Alia Lawlor, M.Ed., PC, CCMC
BluSpark Careers
Cleveland, OH
Phone: (216) 401-8731
E-mail: alialawlor@sbcglobal.net

Why choose between a life and a career? We specialize in helping people uncover their purpose, focus their intentions, and express their authentic selves.

Lorie Lebert, CPRW, JCTC, CCMC
The Loriel Group/Resumes For Results
P.O. Box 91
Brighton, MI 48116
Phone: (810) 229-6811
Toll-free: (800) 870-9059
E-mail: Lorie@CoachingROI.com
www.CoachingROI.com
www.ResumeROI.com
www.DoMyResume.com

I help people write the next chapter of their career with a blend of elite career coaching, resume writing, interview training, and personal branding.

Linsey Levine, MS, Career Development, MCDP, LMHC
CareerCounsel
9 Redway Rd.
Ossining, NY 10562
Phone: (914) 923-9233
Toll-free: (888) 747-1870
E-mail: LinZlev@aol.com
www.4careercounsel.com

I help clients get clear, get focused, *and* get moving *with conscious career guidance, effective strategies, and powerful materials that work to open doors.*

Sandra Lim, CPRW, CECC
A Better Impression
Toronto, Ontario
Canada
Phone: (887) 559-1193 (access code: 063376531)
E-mail: newcareer@abetterimpression.com
www.abetterimpression.com

A Better Impression's vision/mission is to provide high-quality, personalized resume and career counseling services to help job seekers believe in themselves and empower them to discover and attain their life's calling.

Abby Locke, CARW, CPBS
Premier Writing Solutions, LLC
3289 Hardin Place NE
Washington, DC 20018
Phone: (202) 635-2197
E-mail: info@premierwriting.com
www.premierwriting.com

We create highly customized, branded executive resumes and career marketing document that capture the best of who you are on paper. When first impression counts, our resumes tell your story.

Lynda Lucas, CPRW
Resumes By Tammy
3332 Wedgewood E-2
El Paso, TX 79925
Phone: (915) 590-7885
E-mail: resumesbytammy@sbcglobal.net
http://resumesbytammy.com

Since 1990, Professional Certified Resume Writers and Professional Certified Federal Resume Writer.

Tamelynda Lux
Lux & Associates
785 Wonderland Rd. S.
P.O. Box 29064
London, Ontario N6K 4L9
Canada
Phone: (519) 670-5219
www.resumewordwiz.com

Lost for words? Template not enough? Custom written resumes and so on. 18+ years experience. Specializing in complex employment histories, career transitions, and re-careering.

Murray A. Mann, CCM, CPBS
Global Diversity Solutions Group
5651 N. Mozart St., Ste. B
Chicago, IL 60659-4822
Phone: (312) 404-3108
Toll-free: (877) 825-6566
E-mail: murray@globaldiversitysolutions.com
http://GlobalDiversitySolutions.com
http://JobSearchGuideforLatinos.com

Global Diversity Solutions Group, an award-winning multicultural career management practice, has helped thousands of job seekers and professionals reach their career goals.

Irene Marshall, MBA, PhD, CPRW, CEIP, CPCC
Tools for Transition
38750 Paseo Padre Parkway #C-11
Fremont, CA 94536
Phone: (510) 790-9005
Toll-free: (800) 332-7996
E-mail: irene@toolsfortransition.com
www.toolsfortransition.com

Irene Marshall has 40 years of business background in accounting, finance, sales and marketing, and recruiting. Her team provides resume writing, career coaching, and interview coaching for people making changes in their careers.

Maureen McCann
ProMotion Career Solutions
Ottawa, Ontario K2H 5N9
Canada
Phone: (613) 721-8646
E-mail: maureen@mypromotion.ca
www.mypromotion.ca

We market tomorrow's leaders. Choose ProMotion Career Solutions. "It's your move."

Sharon McCormick, MCC, NCCC, NCC, CPRW
Sharon McCormick Career Counseling and Consulting Services
Durham, NC 27713
Phone: (919) 424-1244 or (727) 824-7805
E-mail: careertreasure@gmail.com

Hire the career counselor who gets hired! 15+ years experience. I have personally interviewed for hundreds of jobs over the years—and received hot job offers from top companies.

Debbie McMahan, CPRW
MyResumeHelp.com
Collinsville, OK
Toll-free: (877) 800-6742
E-mail: support@MyResumeHelp.com
http://MyResumeHelp.com

At MyResumeHelp.com, our mission is to provide the highest-quality customized job search tools and resume services at an affordable price.

Jan Melnik, MRW, CCM, CPRW
Absolute Advantage
P.O. Box 718
Durham, CT 06422
Phone: (860) 349-0256
E-mail: CompSPJan@aol.com
www.janmelnik.com

Be inspired. It's your career. It's your life. That's Jan Melnik's slogan, and it describes the focus and energy she has brought to clients coast to coast since founding her resume-writing and job-search coaching practice in 1983.

Marti Miller
Bridge to Success
10263 Northlake Circle
Olathe, KS 66061
Phone: (913) 780-6399 or (913) 707-6399
E-mail: millermea@comcast.net

Specialize in assisting young people—college graduates and 1st-time job seekers—assess skills and focus on a career that fits their personality and values. Design a resume that effectively targets the desired goal.

Cheryl Minnick, M.Ed.
University of MT-Missoula
Campus Dr.
Missoula, MT 59812
Phone: (406) 243-4614
E-mail: cminnick@mso.umt.edu
www.umt.edu/career/

A career counselor with over 25 years' experience in higher education, teaching workshops, and working with students on academic and career decision-making, internship placement, job development, and resume writing.

Meg Montford, MCCC, CMF, CPRW
Abilities Enhanced
P.O. Box 11823
Kansas City, MO 64138
Phone: (816) 767-1196
E-mail: meg@abilitiesenhanced.com
www.abilitiesenhanced.com

Guiding careers since 1986: helping executives embrace change, stand out, and achieve success with award-winning resumes and professional coaching.

Doug Morrison, CPRW
Career Power
5200 Park Rd., Ste. 231
Charlotte, NC 28209-3651
Phone: (704) 527-5556
Toll-free: (800) 711-0773
E-mail: dmpwresume@aol.com
www.careerpowerresume.com

Documents that sell your unique value and position you above the competition. All work prepared by an award-winning writer, who has contributed to 12 resume and cover letter books.

Joan Murrin, JCTC, CPRW
University of Iowa
411 Gilmore Hall
Iowa City, Iowa 52242-1320
Phone: (319) 353-3791
E-mail: joan-murrin@uiowa.edu
www.uiowa.edu/~dcn

Joan Murrin is the founder/director of the University of Iowa's Dual Career Network, which assists the accompanying partner of a new faculty or staff member in locating and securing employment.

Carol Nason, MA, CPRW
Career Advantage
95 Flavell Rd.
Groton, MA 01450
Phone: (978) 448-3319
E-mail: nason1046@aol.com
http://acareeradvantageresume.com

Create resumes that get results for all occupations and positions. Particular expertise working with clients who are changing careers or are age-advantaged.

Patricia Navin, CPRW, JCTC
Accent Resume Design
Langhorne, PA 19047
Phone: (215) 860-5345
E-mail: careerdesigner@aol.com

Ten years as a resume writer and job coach, with experience as a sales recruiter, job placement coordinator for a college career program, and caseworker for welfare-to-work program.

Beverley Neil, CERW CRW
d'Scriptive Words
Queensland
Australia
Phone: 61 7 3820 8051
E-mail: d_scriptive@optusnet.com.au

I view each resume with the ethos that this is not just a job! This is how you pay the bills, go on holidays, care for your children. I never lose sight of the importance to the individual.

Sari Neudorf
SDN Consulting
St. Louis, MO 63141
Phone: (314) 283-6876
E-mail: sari@sdnconsulting.biz
http://sdnconsulting.biz

Increase your career possibilities.

Katie Newton
Choice Business Services
2525 E. Paris SE, Ste. 100
Grand Rapids, MI 49546
Phone: (616) 975-0100
E-mail: resume@choicebiz.com
www.choicebiz.com

JoAnn Nix, CPRW, JCTC, CCMC, CEIP, CPBS
A Great Resume Service, Inc.
Van Buren, AR
Phone: (479) 410-3101
Toll-free: (800) 265-6901
E-mail: info@agreatresume.com
www.agreatresume.com
www.1executiveresume.com

Talented in exploring the careers of clients to uncover their value, talents, and brand, and facilitate conversations between clients and businesses.

Samantha Nolan, MS, CPRW
Ladybug Design
4200 Regent St., Ste. 200
Columbus, OH 43219
Phone: (614) 570-3442
Toll-free: (888) 9-LADYBUG
E-mail: admin@ladybug-design.com
www.ladybug-design.com
www.dearsamonline.com

Samantha also authors a nationally syndicated job search advice column where she responds to readers' questions with the caring and intuitive approach she offers her clients.

John M. O'Connor, MFA, CCM, CPRW, CRW, MRW
Career Pro Inc.
3700 National Dr., Ste. 215
Raleigh, NC 27612
Phone: (919) 787-2400
Toll-free: (866) 447-9599
E-mail: john@careerproinc.com
www.careerproinc.com
www.careerproresumes.com

For the serious job seeker. Your best choice for outstanding personal branding, resume writing, federal resume writing, and full executive outplacement/career management search knowledge and tools.

Debra O'Reilly, CPRW, JCTC, CEIP, FRWC
A First Impression Resume Service
Brandon, FL 33510
Phone: (813) 651-0408
Toll-free: (800) 340-5570
E-mail: debra@resumewriter.com
www.resumewriter.com

"If I isolated what your value added, it was your energy and ability to restart my [executive] search with new hope." ~ S. Alvo, VP (telecom). Resumes for professionals since 1991.

Don Orlando, MBA, CPRW, JCTC, CCMC, CCM
The McLean Group
640 S. McDonough St.
Montgomery, AL 36104
Phone: (334) 264-2020
E-mail: yourcareercoach@charterinternet.com

Don Orlando helps senior and very senior executives win the careers they deserve, get paid what they are worth, and even have fun in the process. He welcomes your calls or e-mails any hour of any day or night.

Ethan Pang
Tinyplaces International Pte. Ltd.
Rm2104C, 21/F, Admiralty Centre Tower 1
18 Harcourt Rd.
Hong Kong
Hong Kong Admiralty
Phone: +852 2157-1770
E-mail: career@tinyplaces.com
www.tinyplaces.com

Committed to helping youths and young professionals discover their design, capabilities, and passions. We prepare our clients for life, not just a career. And we help them to live a fulfilling, great adventure now!

Tracy M. Parish, CPRW
CareerPlan, Inc.
P.O. Box 957
Kewanee, IL 61443
Toll-free: (888) 522-6121
E-mail: Resume@CareerPlan.org
www.CareerPlan.org
www.ExecutiveCareerSolutions.com
www.ResumesForSuccess.com

When you really want the job! We position you as the ONLY clear choice over your competitors, so we're the only clear choice for you! Popular Portfolio and PowerPoint resumes.

Stephanie Peacocke, MA, CCM, CPRW, PMP
SRP Consulting Career Transition Services
Gig Harbor, WA 98335
Phone: (253) 853-7571
E-mail: speacocke@comcast.net
www.srpcareertransitions.com

Providing action-oriented solutions to help people transcend challenges, call forth new possibilities, and bring extraordinary value to the world through their work.

Sharon Pierce-Williams, BSBA, M.Ed., CPRW
JobRockit
609 Lincolnshire Lane
Findlay, OH 45840
Phone: (419) 422-0228
E-mail: Sharon@JobRockit.com

If you want to showcase who you are in a unique format that is "jaw dropping" (according to one executive who hired me), and sets you apart from neck-in-neck competition, I'm your writer! Eight national awards.

Kris Plantrich, CPRW, CEIP
ResumeWonders Writing and Career Coaching Services
Ortonville, MI 48462
Phone: (248) 627-2624
Toll-free: (888) 789-2081
E-mail: info@resumewonders.com
http://ResumeWonders.com

Discover your winning advantage, unlock your potential, and control your future working with a certified professional resume writer and career coach.

Judit Price, MA, IJCTC, CPRW, CMI, CDFI
Berke & Price Associates
6 Newtowne Way
Chelmsford, MA 01824
Phone: (978) 256-0482
E-mail: jprice@careercampaign.com
www.careercampaign.com

Judit counsels individuals in career direction and job search strategies from entry- and mid-level professionals to senior management. She is a speaker, resume writer, and workshop leader for various Boston-area organizations.

Robert Prock, CEIP
A "Preferred" Career & Resume Service
2704 E. North St.
Greenville, SC 29615
Phone: (864) 292-5288
Toll-free: (800) 350-0993
E-mail: expertresume@yahoo.com
http://expertresume.com

Winner of "Most Unique Resume" award from the Professional Association of Resume Writers. Guest expert on NBC Television affiliate. Former "Career Talk" radio show host. Professional resume writer for 20+ years.

Julie Rains, CPRW, BSBA
Executive Correspondents
6319 Cook Ave.
P.O. Box 495
Clemmons, NC 27012
Phone: (336) 712-2390
E-mail: jr@workingtolive.com
www.WorkingToLive.com

Great listener who asks probing questions to gather all relevant information and gain insight into your unique qualifications.

Michelle Mastruserio Reitz, CPRW
Printed Pages
3985 Race Rd., Ste. 6
Cincinnati, OH 45211
Phone: (513) 598-9100
E-mail: michelle@printedpages.com
www.printedpages.com

Consultation, writing, expert design. Electronic resumes, cover letters, military conversions. Friendly, professional guidance for every step of your job search.

Edie Rische, NCRW, ACCC, CPBS, JCTC
Write Away Resume & Career Coaching
5908 73rd St.
Lubbock, TX 79424
Phone: (806) 798-0881
E-mail: earische@suddenlink.net
www.writeawayresume.com

Helping college graduates step out with confidence.

Camille Carboneau Roberts, CFRW/C, CARW, CPRW, CEIP
CC Computer Services
P.O. Box 50655
Idaho Falls, ID 83405
Phone: (208) 522-4455
E-mail: camille@superiorResumes.com
www.superiorResumes.com

Specializing in federal applications—SES-level federal resumes, ECQs, TQs, KSAs, Resumix, interview coaching, federal job search assistance, and transitioning military.

Martha Rockwell, CPRW
A+ Resumes and Career Coaching
8651 E. Royal Palm Rd. #236
Scottsdale, AZ 85258
Phone: (480) 663-0681 or (602) 499-3138
E-mail: prostrategies@cox.net
www.confidencebuilder.net

A+ Resumes and Career Coaching is a full-service company that offers assistance in all *areas of the search process: resume development, networking, interview/salary negotiation coaching, and career assessment.*

Barbara Romano, MBA
BJR Career Services
22 Teak Rd.
Wayne, NJ 07470
Phone: (973) 595-0331
E-mail: bjromano@careersummary.com
www.careersummary.com

With more than 30 years of combined corporate and entrepreneurial experience, Barbara is qualified to work with all levels of management as well as professionals in various fields.

Jane Roqueplot, CPBA, CWDP, CECC
JaneCo's Sensible Solutions
194 N. Oakland Ave.
Sharon, PA 16146
Phone: (724) 342-0100
Toll-free: (888) JaneCos (526-3267)
E-mail: client@janecos.com
www.janecos.com

JaneCo will design your professional resume that highlights your skills, accomplishments and personality, empowering you to focus your unique strengths on creating a rewarding future.

Teena Rose, CPRW, CEIP
Resume to Referral
1824 Rebert Pike
Springfield, OH 45506
Phone: (937) 325-2149
E-mail: admin@resumetoreferral.com
www.resumebycprw.com
http://teenarose.com

Personable ... professional ... skilled. Resume writer Teena Rose is a columnist, personal branding expert, public speaker, and executive resume writer.

Nancy Rozum
Moon River Writing and Resumes
3728 Thomas Ct.
Commerce Twp., MI 48382-1867
Phone: (248) 360-7113
E-mail: nrozum@sbcglobal.net

By asking the right questions during a client interview, I am able to craft a document that strategically markets the client to potential employers. 500+ resumes written in past 10 years for clients in a wide variety of careers.

Jennifer Rushton, CARW, CEIC, CWPP
Keraijen, Certified Resume Writer
Level 14, 309 Kent St.
Sydney, NSW 2000
Australia
Phone: 612 9994 8050 or 61 4 1498 1062
E-mail: info@keraijen.com.au
www.keraijen.com.au

Keraijen specializes in highlighting clients' skills and accomplishments into dynamic marketing documents that secure interviews and lead to job search success. Published in 13 books; consecutive winner of prestigious TORI Awards.

Lori Russel, MBA
Executive Careers, Inc.
680 Brent St.
Manchester, NH 3103
Toll-free: (866) 626-8120 or (800) 234-8817
E-mail: lori@execareers.com
www.execareers.com

Career advancement reinvented! Full-service executive career firm. Your own stellar team—your success is our goal! In today's job market, you will need every advantage to maintain a competitive edge.

Barbara Safani, MA, NCRW, CPRW, CERW, CCM
Career Solvers
470 Park Ave. S., 10th Floor
New York, NY 10016
Phone: (212) 579-7230
Toll-free: (866) 333-1800
E-mail: info@careersolvers.com
www.careersolvers.com

Ms. Safani partners with both Fortune 100 companies and individuals to deliver targeted programs focusing on resume development, job search strategies, networking, interviewing, and salary negotiation skills.

Evelyn U. Salvador, NCRW, JCTC
Creative Image Builders.com
8 Marla Dr.
Coram, NY 11727
Phone: (631) 698-7777
E-mail: CareerCatapult@aol.com `
www.careercatapult.com
www.creativeimagebuilders.com

Groundbreaking resume and career products and services that put your best foot forward—Creative Image Builders will craft your interview-generating resume or provide you with exceptional resources to do it yourself

Robin Schlinger, CARW, CFRW
Robin's Resumes
860 Peachtree St. NE #2206
Atlanta, GA 30308
Phone: (404) 875-2688
Toll-free: (888) 278-8149
E-mail: robinschlinger@robinresumes.com
http://robinresumes.com
http://federalresumepros.com

Our mission: Develop the best resume package to show how you add value. Our record: Our certified writers have many years of success writing civilian and federal resume packages.

Linda Schnabel, PCC, CRS, CIS, JCTC
CareerWorks
1455 Lakeshore Rd., Ste. 204 S.
Burlington, Ontario L7T 1K6
Canada
Phone: (905) 523-4281
E-mail: linda@careerworks.biz
www.careerworks.biz

Served as certification committee chair for the development of Canada's CRS (Certified Resume Strategist) certification program.

Kimberly Schneiderman
City Career Services
53rd St. and Lexington
New York City, NY 10022
Phone: (917) 584-3022
E-mail: kimberly@citycareerservices.com
www.citycareerservices.com

Achieve your professional goals with City Career Services' personalized services.

Joellyn Wittenstein Schwerdlin, CCMC, CPRW, JCTC
A-1 Quality Resumes & Career Services, Inc.
40 Chippewa Rd.
Worcester, MA 01602
Phone: (508) 459-2854
Mobile: (847) 331-4489
E-mail: joellyn@a-1qualityresumes.com
www.a-1qualityresumes.com

I provide resumes as part of a career coaching package, which includes uncovering "key success factors" that drive a client's overall career campaign.

Nancy H. Segal, CFRW
Solutions for the Workplace
404 Greenwood St., Ste. 2
Evanston, IL 60201
Phone: (847) 866-6675
E-mail: nancy@solutions-workplace.com

Expert in assisting clients with their federal career search.

Phyllis B. Shabad, MS, NCRW, JCTC, CPBS
CareerMasters
95 Woods Brooke Circle
Ossining, NY 10562
Phone: (914) 944-9577
Toll-free: (800) 330-1356
E-mail: target@CareerIQ.com
http://CareerIQ.com

Phyllis Shabad takes you into the executive suite and boardroom. She has helped thousands of senior executives break through with CEO career coaching and board director services.

Debbie Shalom, M.A.T.
Amazing Resumes and Coaching Services
Baltimore, MD 21209
Phone: (410) 653-7679 or (443) 326-8427
E-mail: debbie@amazingresumesmd.com
www.amazingresumesmd.com

Invest in your success! We help you discover your unique assets and move your career forward through career assessments, personal branding, interview and job coaching, and resume preparation services.

Harriet Shea, CPRW, LSW
Jewish Family Services
1070 College Ave.
Columbus, OH 43209
Phone: (614) 559-0120
E-mail: hshea@jfscolumbus.org
http://jfscolumbus.org/JobSeeker.asp

As a social worker, I have the ability to work with a wide range of clients from entry-level to professional. I create a resume at my desk, face to face with a client as well as via phone or e-mail.

Janice M. Shepherd, CPRW, JCTC, CEIP
Write On Career Keys
Top of Alabama Hill
Bellingham, WA 98226-4260
Phone: (360) 738-7958
E-mail: janice@writeoncareerkeys.com
www.writeoncareerkeys.com

Located in the Pacific Northwest, I write a variety of resumes: career transition, blue collar, return to work, new graduates, public service, nurses, and teachers, to name a few.

Igor Shpudejko, CPRW, JCTC, BSIE, MBA
Career Focus
23 Parsons Ct.
Mahwah, NJ 07430
Phone: (201) 825-2865
E-mail: Ishpudejko@aol.com
http://Careerinfocus.com

With more than 20 years' experience in sales and marketing, I know how to get the attention of a prospective buyer. Let me create for you a professional resume that tells what you did, how well you did it, and where you are going.

Karen M. Silins, CMRS, CARW, CCMC, CECC, CEIP, CTAC, CCA, CPC
A+ Career and Resume, LLC
9719 Woodland Ln.
Kansas City, MO 64131
Phone: (816) 942-3019
E-mail: karen@careerandresume.com
www.careerandresume.com

On the cutting edge of career and business coaching techniques and resume development trends, Karen is committed to individual, personalized service and provides a realistic approach to clients' goals.

Kelley Smith, CPRW
Resume GhostWriter
Sugar Land, TX
Toll-free: (877) 478-4999
E-mail: ksmith@resumeghostwriter.com
www.ResumeGhostWriter.com

Specializing in resumes for senior finance executives in all industries and career changers transitioning into or out of the retail industry.

Laurie J. Smith, CPRW, JCTC
Creative Keystrokes Executive Resume Service
Gastonia, NC
Phone: (704) 853-3153
Toll-free: (800) 817-2779
E-mail: ljsmith@creativekeystrokes.com
www.creativekeystrokes.com
www.executive-resumes.com

The executive's one-stop resource for career management and personal branding, headed by 30-year career transition industry veteran Laurie Smith.

William (Bill) Smith, BA
The Resume Professional
4151 Emerald St.
Oakland, CA 94609
Phone: (510) 652-5912
E-mail: resume_pro@consultant.com

Your resume will be developed so that employers will see a match between you and the position they are trying to fill within 30-seconds—guaranteed. I know first hand what employers look for in a resume.

Chris Starkey, CPRW, CEIP
KeyRidge Resume Services
22 Olympic Dr.
Mount Pearl, Newfoundland A1N 4K3
Canada
Phone: (709) 368-1902
Toll-free: (877) 968-1902
E-mail: resume@resumechoice.com
www.resumechoice.com

Communicate your value and potential to prospective employers. Ensure professionalized presentation in both your resume and interviewing skills.

Beth W. Stefani, MBA, Ed.M., JCTC, CPRW
Orison Professional Services, Inc.
265 Union St., Ste. 101
Hamburg, NY 14075
Phone: (716) 649-0094
E-mail: Beth@OrisonServices.com
www.OrisonServices.com

"Inspire ... illuminate ... ignite!" Beth Stefani is a career strategist providing a full range of career coaching, personal branding, and resume writing services to executives in the U.S. and abroad.

Ann Stewart, CPRW
Advantage Services
P.O. Box 525
Roanoke, TX 76262
Phone: (817) 424-1448
Toll-free: (800) 424-1448
E-mail: asresume@charter.net

I offer a strong understanding of employer requirements and recruiting in a corporate environment. I enjoy using that experience and knowledge to help my clients sell their skills in today's highly competitive employment market.

Denise Stewart, CPRW
Dynamic Resume Design
893 HCR 4333
Milford, TX 76670
Phone: (254) 580-1026
Toll-free: (800) 713-7331
E-mail: dynamicrd@yahoo.com

Professional and personal experiences have given me a unique perspective on "other-abled" individuals and what they have to offer employers. As a resume writer, I can best represent those abilities and skills on paper.

Marilyn Stollon
400 29th St., Ste. 102
Oakland, CA 94609
Phone: (510) 987-7271 or (510) 301-6118
E-mail: ms@findworkNow.org
www.findworkNow.org

Twenty years' experience providing high-quality employment counseling services, including resume and cover letter prep, to individuals from many careers. Reputation for quality work, getting interviews, and getting a job offer.

Billie R. Sucher, MS, CTMS, CTSB, JCTC
Billie Sucher & Associates
7177 Hickman Rd., Ste. 10
Urbandale, IA 50322
Phone: (515) 276-0061
E-mail: billie@billiesucher.com
www.billiesucher.com

Trusted by professionals and executives to "deliver superb career management services with compassion, creativity, competence, and consistency." Published resume writer.

Lonnie L. Swanson, CPRW, CDF, IJCTC
A Career Advantage
21590 Clear Creek Rd. NW
Poulsbo, WA 98370
Phone: (360) 779-2877
E-mail: resumes@nwinet.com

Your success is *my business! 15 years of experience in entry-level to CEO resume development. Federal resume and military conversion specialist.*

Kathy Sweeney, NCRW, CPRW, CEIC, CCM
The Write Resume
Phoenix, AZ
Phone: (480) 726-9052
Toll-free: (866) 726-9052
E-mail: info@awriteresume.com
www.awriteresume.com

Twenty years' experience preparing effective resumes and job search materials to win the interview for more than 10,000 entry-level to executive-level clients.

Tanya Taylor, CRS, CHRP
TNT Human Resources Management
190 Clark Blvd. Unit 205
Brampton, Ontario L6T 4A8
Canada
Phone: (416) 887-5819
E-mail: tnt_hr@rogers.com

Tanya imparts "insider knowledge" to give her clients the upper edge. She is skilled at crafting portfolios that result in interviews, which lead to lucrative employment offers.

Wendy J. Terwelp, CCMC, JCTC, CEIP, CPBS
Opportunity Knocks of Wisconsin LLC
11431 N. Port Washington Rd., Ste. 101
Mequon, WI 53092
Phone: (262) 241-4655
E-mail: consultant@knocks.com
www.knocks.com

Are you ready for your next big gig? Be a rock star in your career. Our experience in recruiting and journalism helps you get hired faster.

Kevin Tucker, CCM
C~Cubed Career Consulting & Coaching
891 E. Warner Rd., Ste. 100-103
Gilbert, AZ 85296
Phone: (480) 892-9204
Toll-free: (888) 522-8233
E-mail: info@CCubedCareer.com
www.CCubedCareer.com

Offers comprehensive career enhancing programs featuring career assessment, resume preparation, interview and negotiation coaching. Licensed by state.

Edward Turilli, MA, CPRW
AccuWriter Resume and Writng Services
28363 Hidden Lake Dr.
Bonita Springs, FL 34134
Phone: (401) 268-3020
E-mail: edtur@cox.net
http://resumes4-u.com

Because each client is unique, our written documents command a like uniqueness to powerfully and accurately portray each client's values, strengths, and objectives.

Christine Tutor, CPRW, MS
CareerStep Resumes
Cary, NC 27511
Phone: (919) 616-3801
E-mail: info@tutorresumes.com
www.tutorresumes.com

CPRW leveraging a counseling background to brand clients' unique strengths and create targeted resumes and cover letters that land interviews.

Claudine Vainrub, MBA, CPRW, CPBS
EduPlan, LLC
21205 NE 37th Ave., Ste. 2105
Aventura, FL 33180
Phone: (305) 936-8159
Toll-free: (888) 661-8234
E-mail: info@eduplan.us
www.eduplan.us

Claudine uses career-strategy savvy, inventiveness, and a high dose of energy to inspire professionals to reach their maximum potential. She has advanced oral and written skills in English and Spanish.

Ilona Vanderwoude, CPRW, CCMC, CEIP, CJST
Career Branches
P.O. Box 330
Riverdale, NY 10471
Phone: (718) 884 2213
E-mail: ilona@CareerBranches.com
www.CareerBranches.com

Vivian VanLier, CPRW, JCTC, CEIP, CCMC, CPRC
Advantage Resume & Career Services
6701 Murietta Ave.
Los Angeles, CA 91405
Phone: (818) 994-6655
E-mail: VivianVanLier@aol.com
www.CuttingEdgeResumes.com
www.CareerCoach4U.com

Vivian combines more than 15 years of resume writing and career coaching with a B.S.B.A. from the prestigous Haas School of Business at U.C. Berkeley and past corporate experience, to give her clients a competitive advantage.

Chris Van Petten
YourPro.com
8502 E. Via de los Libros
Scottsdale, AZ 85258-3553
Phone: (480) 367-1315
E-mail: chris@yourpro.com
www.YourPro.com

A complete resume service, including cover letters, references, thank-you letters, and applications for executives, career re-entry, new grads, sales and marketing, engineering and technology, hospitality, and administrative.

Ellie Vargo, CCMC, CPRW, CFRWC, CCMC
Noteworthy Resume Services
11906 Manchester Rd., Ste. 112
St. Louis, MO 63131
Phone: (314) 965-9362
Toll-free: (866) 965-9362
E-mail: ev@noteworthyresume.com
www.noteworthyresume.com

Clear, concise, credible resumes with bottom-line impact to take your career to the next level. Areas of special expertise include educational administration, information technology, and executive.

Roleta Fowler Vasquez, CPRW, CEIP
Wordbusters Resume and Writing Services
433 Quail Ct.
Fillmore, CA 93015-1137
Phone: (805) 524-3493
E-mail: resumes@wbresumes.com
www.wbresumes.com
www.bestchoiceresumes.com

Wordbusters markets you at your best by writing hard-hitting, targeted resumes that showcase your unique qualifications and answer the needs of your intended employer.

Judith Vince, CPRW
DeAnjo Career Services, LLC
P.O. Box 284
Oakland, NJ 07436
Phone: (201) 337-8803
Toll-free: (888) 703-3370
E-mail: deanjo@optonline.net

"Gain the competitive edge." Hiring authority 25+ years. Vice president four-plus years. Executive recruiter seven years. Healthcare 17 years. Start-ups through Fortune 50.

Debra M. Vinikour, CPRW
Vinikour Career Consulting
1067 Stearns Ave.
Boulder, CO 80303
Phone: (303) 494-5846
E-mail: debra@vinikourcareerconsulting.com
www.vinikourcareerconsulting.com

With experience as an outplacement consultant and a recruiter, Debra understands how to craft resumes and other documents that provide the edge in today's challenging market.

Kathy Voska, Career Management Fellow
Right Management
7300 W. 110th, Ste. 800
Overland Park, KS 66210
Phone: (913) 323-2309 or (816) 942-0588
E-mail: kathy.voska@right.com
www.right.com

Kathy provides personalized career transition consulting, interacting at all organizational levels to merge human resources with business initiatives.

James Walker, MS
Army Career and Alumni Center
Bldg. 210, Rm 006, Custer Ave.
Fort Riley, KS 66442
Phone: (785) 239-2278 or (785) 239-2248
E-mail: jwalker8199@yahoo.com

Retired army colonel with 28 years of service; human resource director; job assistance counselor. Member of three professional resume writer organizations and author of 10 resumes nationally published in resume books.

Julie Walraven, CPRW
Design Resumes
1202 Elm St.
Wausau, WI 54401
Phone: (715) 574-5263
E-mail: design@dwave.net
www.designresumes.com

Develop resumes using an interactive client/writer method. Provide 20 business day guarantee as a no-fault resume revision, rewrite, and reprint for free, allowing client to review resume and maximize client satisfaction.

Jill Walser
"I Got the Job!"
SE Allen Rd.
Bellevue, WA 98006
Phone: (425) 241-8689
E-mail: jill@igotthejob.us
www.igotthejob.us

Corporate recruiter providing professional resume writing, interview coaching, and job finding strategy assistance.

Kendra Walters
Great Expectations Resume Writing Service, LLC
Wauwatosa, WI 53213
Toll-free: (866) 251-5622
E-mail: kwalters@geresume.com
www.geresume.com

Judy Ware, BA
Resumes for Careers
23515 NE 9th St.
Camas, WA 98607
Phone: (360) 834-4720
E-mail: resumes4careers@iinet.com

A resume that defines you and impresses others.

Kathy Warwick, NCRW, CCMC, CPBS
Confident Careers LLC
Collingswood, NJ
Toll-free: (877) 295-8600
E-mail: krwarwick@comcast.net
www.aconfidentcareer.com

Leveraging a business and management background to deliver no-nonsense career management services to executives moving up to the next level.

Martin Weitzman, NCRW, CPRW, IJCTC, CPBS
Gilbert Resumes
Croydon Court
Englishtown, NJ 07726
Phone: (732) 536-0158
Toll-free: (800) 967 3846
E-mail: resumepro@gmail.com
http://executiveresumewriter.com
http://resumepro.com

Your experience, translated into unparalleled value, equals profitable opportunities. Marty writes executive career documents that take you to the top of the candidate short list—small investment, big returns.

Kathleen Weston, CRS
A Resume To Remember
19973 Bathurst St.
Holland Landing, Ontario L9N 1N3
Canada
Phone: (416) 677-4635
E-mail: resumesplus.msn.com
www.resumesplus.org

Objective: Empower the job seeker.

Michael B. Wetherington
Knockout Resumes
Florida
E-mail: customercare@knockoutresumes.com
www.knockoutresumes.com

Resumes with a marketing twist geared for today's competitive job market. Knock out the competition!

Susan Britton Whitcomb, MRW, NCRW, CCMC, CCM
Career Coach Academy
757 E. Hampton Way
Fresno, CA 93704
Phone: (559) 222-7474
E-mail: susan@careercoachacademy.com
www.CareerCoachAcademy.com
www.CareerAndLifeCoach.com
www.CareerWriter.com

Author of Resume Magic, Interview Magic, Job Search Magic, 30-Day Job Promotion *(JIST Publishing), and* eResumes *(McGraw-Hill).*

Pearl White, CPRW, JCTC, CEIP
A 1st Impression Resume and Career Coaching Services
41 Tangerine
Irvine, CA 92618
Phone: (949) 651-1068
E-mail: pearlwhite1@cox.net
www.a1stimpression.com

A winning combination of quality workmanship, commitment to excellence, and personalized service differentiate my business, as confirmed by testimonials from clients who are quickly invited to interviews that lead to job offers.

Amy Whitmer, CPRW
Virginia
E-mail: amyxyz@gmail.com

Betty H. Williams, NCRW, CPRW
BW Custom Resumes
Richmond, VA 23225
Phone: (804) 330-9277
E-mail: bwresumes@comcast.net
http://customresumes.net

Betty has 25+ years of experience and provides top-level professional and personalized resume development. All resumes are written from scratch in a way that best highlights the skills and experience of each client.

Beth Woodworth, M.S., RPC, JCTC, CWDP, CAC
Career Innovations
California
Phone: (530) 604-4347
E-mail: bethwoodworth@sbcglobal.net
www.career-innovations.org

I work with professionals who feel stuck in their careers. I help them find direction, reorganize, and take action to renew their energy.

Janice Worthington, MA, CPRW, JCTC, CEIP
Worthington Career Services
6636 Belleshire St.
Columbus, OH 43229
Phone: (614) 890-1645
Toll-free: (877) 9Resume
E-mail: Janice@WorthingtonResumes.com
www.worthingtonresumes.com

Jeremy Worthington, CARW
Buckeye Resumes
2092 Atterbury
Columbus, OH 43229
Phone: (614) 861-6606
Toll-free: (877) 973-7863
E-mail: Jeremy@BuckeyeResumes.com
www.buckeyeresumes.com

Certified Advanced Resume Writer offers design/development of successful marketing tools for mid-level professionals and support personnel. Interview coaching offered.

Daisy Wright, CDP
The Wright Career Solution
Brampton, Ontario L6Z 4V6
Canada
Phone: (905) 840-7039
E-mail: careercoach@thewrightcareer.com
www.thewrightcareer.com
www.nocanadianexperience-eh.com

Winner of a prestigious "Outstanding Canadian Career Leader" award, published author, and a verifiable track record of supporting clients in their job search and careers.

Angela P. Zimmer, AAS
All Write Resumes
12 Thompson Bridge Rd.
Jackson, NJ 08527
Phone: (732) 833-8870 or (732) 600-9734
E-mail: allwriteresumes@earthlink.net
www.allwriteresumes.net

Professional writing, competively priced since 1993. Conveniently available weekdays, evenings, and weekends, specializing in a variety resumes and cover letters, including entry-level to executive.

PART 3

Resume Samples from the Pros

What better way to judge a resume writer's skill than to examine his or her work? In this section, you will find 46 sample resumes that represent the very best efforts of some of the writers featured in this book.

Each resume is identified by specialty area, but don't limit yourself to the resumes from your field. Browse the samples to find strategies, formats, and approaches you like, and add those writers to your "possibles" list. Most of the writers work in multiple specialty areas, and many of the sample resumes could fit into more than one category. For example, the resume for Jenna Thompson, written by Jan Melnik, is featured under the Sales and Marketing specialty area. However, this sample could just as easily fit within "Managers and Executives" or even within "Healthcare," because it was written for a marketing executive whose career has been with various medical-device companies.

Not every specialty area is represented in these samples, but they certainly give you a glimpse of the diversity of styles you will find among professional resume writers. Now, your challenge is finding the one whose style best fits your needs. With the guidelines, questions, and resources included in this book, you're ready to get started.

Good luck with your resume, your current career challenge, and your lifelong career!

1

Specialty Area: Blue Collar/Trades
Writer: Debbie Shalom

JOHN DERRY

5306 Tarragon Rd.
Owings Mills, MD 21117

Home: (443) 253-8390
johnder2007@verizon.net

Conscientious, reliable **Maintenance Supervisor** with 12 years' experience in facility maintenance. Highly efficient manager with strong mechanical, administrative, and time-management skills. Possess CFC / EPA Universal license (Type I, Type II, and Type III) and A+ Computer certification. Consistently honored by management with **Outstanding Service** awards (2000–2006). Significant knowledge and expertise in:

Facility Operations	**Supervision & Training**	**Equipment Maintenance**
Tenant Relations	**Preventive Maintenance**	**Carpentry & Plumbing**
Records Management	**Service Scheduling**	**Grounds Maintenance**

PROFESSIONAL EXPERIENCE

J& B APARTMENT AGENCY, Reisterstown, MD 1995–Present
Maintenance Supervisor (1999–present)
Maintenance Technician (1995–1999)

Manage property consisting of 600 apartments and 20 acres of land. Oversee and supervise five maintenance technicians, two carpenters, and seven groundskeepers to ensure smooth operation and upkeep of premises and systems.

- Improved turnaround time on rental unit service tickets by 25%.
  - Process and complete approximately 50 service tickets daily.
  - Collaborate with office manager to schedule and implement repairs for 20 newly leased apartments per month.
  - Allocate work assignments based on employee skill sets and strengths; lead monthly training workshops on preventive maintenance and repair techniques.
  - Maintain up-to-date, accurate, and detailed maintenance records for each rental unit.
- Regularly examine facilities, equipment, and systems; use tools, specialized equipment, and electronic testing devices to troubleshoot and accurately diagnose problems; replace or repair malfunctioning materials.
- In 2006, reduced capital improvement expenses 43% by calculating replacement versus repair costs.
- In 2005, reduced cost of outsourced repairs 11% by evaluating vendor work performance levels and calculating cost effectiveness.
- Supervise and evaluate employee work performance through personal observations and daily assignment logs.

PROFESSIONAL DEVELOPMENT

THE COMMUNITY COLLEGE OF BALTIMORE COUNTY, Essex, MD

Associate of Applied Science Degree in Construction Management

Certificate of Completion in A+ Certification – PC Repair Technician program

2

Specialty Area: Creative Professions
Writer: Samantha Nolan

Graphic Artist

"...been one of the go-to people when we've needed someone we can count on to do a good job and do it right, no matter how creative and complicated..."

Recognized for strengths including:

Creativity & Design

Planning & Organizing Skills

Deadline Management

Work Coordination

Client / Associate Contacts

Acceptance of Change & Responsibility

Work Judgment

Quality of Work

Effectiveness

Initiative

JENNIFER BAKER

5235 Heil Street | Columbus, OH 43215
h: 734.447.7161 | m: 734.585.1441 | e: jbaker@email.com

PROFILE

Noted as "Exceeding Expectations" on performance reviews, receiving such comments as:

"Produces high-quality work and designs in a timely manner...minuscule error rate while maintaining a high level of productivity...demonstrates a positive attitude...great team player...will drop everything to help with emergency projects for both layout and production...was requested or assigned to meeting with several customers that required special attention..."

DESIGN EXPERIENCE

NEWS PUBLICATION, Columbus, OH
Graphic Artist (1995–Present)

Conceptualize, design, and finalize artwork and layouts for diverse clients, working closely with sales team to define client needs, understand target market, and translate into highly effective designs. Produce design and copywriting concepts to present to prospective and existing clients, yielding key account wins for the organization. Maintain cutting-edge technical skills spanning Photoshop, Illustrator, and QuarkXPress. Manage competing priorities on a daily basis, utilizing excellent communication, time-management, and multitasking skills to beat deadlines in a high-volume, high-pressure environment. Offer design expertise to various departments throughout the organization, volunteering to produce emergency exit maps for the plant and affiliate buildings. Serve as an avid supporter of company-sponsored community initiatives.

Technologies Used: Adobe Creative Suite, Adobe Photoshop CS, Adobe Illustrator CS, Adobe InDesign, Macromedia Freehand, QuarkXPress 4.11, Adobe Acrobat 5.0, MAC OS 9 & X

Key Results:

- Demonstrated the ability to exceed productivity and creativity goals, coupled with the self-motivation and initiative required to excel while working independently. Honors include:
  - → **Employee of the Year Award** – 1998
  - → **Customer Service Awards** – *Focus on teamwork; Exceptional creativity* – Numerous
  - → **Commitment to Excellence Award** – *Initiative and creativity* – 2006
    - ✓ Upon reviewing ad that generated above award, Sales Rep wrote: "WOW!!! Great work...you nailed this one...you certainly have a knack for understanding what being creative is all about...thanks so much for all of your hard work."
  - → **Company Attendance Awards** – *Attendance and timeliness* – Annually
- Developed in-depth knowledge of publishing and graphic art prepress production, concept design, copywriting, image manipulation, typography, scanning, and digital output.
- Created dynamic designs and layouts for clients including Home Fireplace (12-page special section), Local Growers, Windows Inc., Closets Inc., New Homes Inc., Floors Inc., Local Homebuilder, New Home Builder, and ABC Stitching.
- Serve as a member of the Ad Clinic Committee, assisting in coordinating an annual weeklong event promoting professional development and rewarding exceptional performance.
- Assigned to projects requiring extraordinary creativity, a keen understanding of production processes, and the ability to translate needs into dynamic layouts. Key projects included:
  - → Played a key role in the comprehensive redesign of *Weekly Pub*, producing numerous conceptual layouts to increase publication awareness and bolster advertising results.
  - → Selected by management to create interoffice promotional pieces to motivate staff and maintain focus on the massive redesign of *Weekly Pub*.

(continued)

(continued)

JENNIFER BAKER
CONTINUED

NEWS PUBLICATION – continued

Key Projects...

- Appointed main designer in producing cover designs for the monthly *Savings Package,* working with Custom Publications and Special Sections from design through output.
- Teamed with Marketing to develop a presentation of conceptual advertisements, utilizing special placement to better reach intended target market.
- Managed entire design lifecycle from concept to print for the Columbus High School football championship tab and accompanying tribute pages.
- Worked with the City Auto Dealer Association and Classified Advertising Automotive Manager to develop a shell for weekly editorial advertisements.
- Charged with creating the *News Publication's* weekly Celebrations page.

Early career experiences include serving within a sales role with QSM ('94–'95), and as a Graphic Artist with *The Local Standard* ('93–'94).

ACADEMIC BACKGROUND

PITTSBURGH TECHNICAL INSTITUTE, Pittsburgh, PA
Associate's Degree in Specialized Technology (1993)

- Major in Graphic Design

[PORTFOLIO AVAILABLE FOR REVIEW]

3

Specialty Area: Finance and Accounting
Writer: Cliff Flamer

TIM SEETHER, CPA

11 Radcliffe Road, Medford, MA 02155
Home: 617.530.0962, tseether@aol.com

CONTROLLER / CFO

Analytical Review ~ Feasibility Studies ~ Strategic Planning ~ Financial Forecasting ~ Cash Management
International & Domestic Taxes ~ Internal Controls ~ Training & Mentoring ~ Software Purchasing

CAREER HIGHLIGHTS

Served as financial backbone for multinational development firm as well as iconic hotel franchises Sheraton and Britania, facilitating business development in U.S., Mexico, Europe, and the Caribbean.

- Joined leadership team in planning the construction of firm's premium resorts, LeStage du Soleil and San Ysidro Ranch, including extensive forecasting and financial modeling.
- Launched $26 million resort's only private golf club, attracting 500+ six-figure salaried clientele.
- Reduced receivables backlog $3.3 million, lowered catering fees 3%, and cut payroll $200,000 annually, as Controller for 600-room Sheraton hotel.
- Implemented operational/accounting cost-reduction initiatives for all employers, within the areas of vendor negotiation, SOPs, telecom, product development, and facilities maintenance.
- Groomed and motivated teams of up to 40 controllers, accountants, and support personnel.

PROFESSIONAL EXPERIENCE

CONTROLLER: LESTAGE DU SOLEIL, EASTHAM, MA — **08/2001 TO PRESENT**

Charged with streamlining operations for this 52-room Cape Cod resort. Tripled revenue to $26 million through P&L management, customer service initiatives, and staff development programs.

TEAM LEADERSHIP: *Incentive Programs...Trainings...Restructurings...Litigation Prevention*

- Implemented multi-tiered commission structure for reservation staff to drive sales and boost customer service—a program that has subsequently been rolled out at affiliate resorts.
- Developed financial management acumen in select supervisory staff to facilitate operations-related decision making. Oversaw full-time staff of 7 financial personnel.
- Reduced workers' compensation liabilities 10%–20% each year by preparing comprehensive, accurate audit reports linked to W2s. Maintained 0% challenge rate for four consecutive years.
- Built out infrastructure to accommodate increased headcount by redesigning back-office work areas at nominal expense.

OPERATIONS & ACCOUNTING: *Service Audits...Vendor Negotiation...IT Expenses...Product Development*

- Salvaged $270K loss per annum by identifying and eliminating inefficiencies in food-service line, thus maximizing table turnover rate.
- Renegotiated mortgage from conventional program to "labor swap," with long-term rates.
- Dropped telecom expenses $45K by switching telephone system from analog to digital service.
- Prevented costly initiatives by reviewing pricing structure of product lines as related to budget. Served integral role in the approval process of all tariffs and menu pricing.
- Lowered uniform maintenance fees 25% by negotiating cleaning contract with new vendor.

(continued)

(continued)

TIM SEETHER, CPA

Home: 617.530.0962, tseether@aol.com
Page 2 of 2

DIRECTOR OF ACCOUNTING / FINANCE: LESTAGE RESORTS, LLC, EASTHAM, MA **10/1995 TO 08/2001**
Managed variable costs and expenses in alignment with company goals mandating extensive financial and operational reviews to improve productivity, performance, perception, and profitability. As head of the centralized office, supervised 6 direct reports, 2 controllers and 4 property accountants.

DEVELOPMENT PROJECTS: *Strategic Planning...International Tax...Territory Expansion... Hiring & Training*

- Developed strategic plan to construct LeStage du Soleil and San Ysidro Ranch, LeStage's premiere resorts offering top-tier products and impeccable customer service to high-end clientele.
- Championed LeStage's only private-membership golf resort, with 45 rooms and 500+ active memberships valued at over $100,000 each. Funded debt service from membership revenue.
- Developed accounting structure and international tax protocols and hired and trained controller to oversee Mexico-based Vallejo Resort & Spa, featuring 50 hotel rooms, 80 fractional 2-, 3-, and 4-bedroom units, and 6 whole-ownership condos.

OPERATIONS & ACCOUNTING: *Software Purchases...Report Generation...Best Practices...Labor Standards*

- Managed PMS selection process including drafting a 600-item RFP, negotiating purchase price down from $3.6 million to $1.4 million, and arranging license to be held by management company with costs allocated to 11 resorts.
- Researched and purchased $25,000 accounting system to expedite internal procedures such as end-of-month closing. Designed reports around cash flow and variance analysis functions.
- Centralized Accounting in 2001 to support 3 existing resorts, 2 management contracts, and 6 new development projects in Cabo San Lucas, Glen Ellen, Calistoga, Cordoval, and Palmetto Bluff.

CONTROLLER: SHERATON HOTEL, BOSTON, MA **08/1986 TO 10/1995**
Supervised staff of 38 Finance and Accounting professionals to maximize profits and productivity for this renowned 600-room hotel with 4 restaurants, 2 bars, and 52,000 square feet of designated catering space.

OPERATIONS & ACCOUNTING: *A/R...Payroll...Debt Reconciliation...Pay Scales...Internal Controls*

- Reduced convention-billing backlog from 90 days to 10 days, thereby lowering receivables from $5.6 million to $2.3 million and dropping outstanding debts from $125,000 to $10,000.
- Cut payroll overhead $200,000 by reorganizing Accounting including 26% workforce reduction.
- Decreased Food & Beverage costs 3.2% and 2.5% respectively via Receiving & Inventory controls.
- Minimized payroll expenses $188K via staffing levels for Rooms division.

PREVIOUS EXPERIENCE

Group Controller: Britania Hotels, Inc. ($5 million annual sales), Boston, MA
Senior Auditor / Auditor: Georges, Knorr, Bruster, & Company, Boston, MA

EDUCATION

BS Accounting, New York University, New York, NY
CPA in Commonwealth of Massachusetts since 1995

4

Specialty Area: Human Resources
Writer: Julianne Franke

JENNIFER P. MOORE, PHR

63682 SW Westin Drive
Phoenix, Arizona 85254
928-264-8451
jpmoore845@hotmail.com

SENIOR-LEVEL HUMAN RESOURCES MANAGER

Building consensus to achieve organizational excellence through training, quality, teamwork, and reengineering.

Results-oriented manager with 20+ years of HR generalist experience in dynamic manufacturing, nonprofit, and private-sector environments. Recognized as a *change agent* for taking the initiative to implement innovative HR programs that maintained competitive edge and contributed to bottom-line improvements. Articulate communicator and skilled negotiator; record of integrity, dependability and service. Areas of expertise include:

- Training Needs Assessment / Matrix Design
- Competency-Based Training Design
- Manufacturing Industry Certification
- Quality: ISO9000, QS9000, TS16949
- Project Management / Technology Conversions
- Cost Effective Compensation & Benefit Programs
- Outcome-Based Organizational Change Initiatives
- Labor Relations / Collective Bargaining
- Safety / OSHA Compliance / Workers' Compensation
- Performance Management Systems

Career Achievements

Training & Development: *Improving workforce competencies*

- Secured grant funding and developed a career path training system, in collaboration with NIMS industry consultants, that significantly improved technical skills of production workers, contributing to improved quality and productivity (75% of workers achieved professional certification; 10% less parts rejection; 10% reduction in production time; 5% increase in press-room utilization; 8.3% increase in press efficiency).

Benefits: *Reducing costs while expanding employee healthcare options*

- Proactively addressed rising healthcare costs by developing and implementing diversified benefit programs for all employee classifications (Union, Hourly, Salaried) including the following:
  - Shared healthcare option with savings of 15% on monthly premiums
  - Pre-taxed and flexible spending accounts with 25%–30% savings on reimbursed charges
  - Three-tiered medical and dental options with various costs and benefits targeting families
- Introduced HMO plan to complement existing PPO program with an 8% savings on annual premiums.
- Spearheaded employee health initiatives including annual on-site health screenings and flu shots.

Organizational Development & Change Initiatives: *Maximizing employee retention*

- Led strategic planning, execution, and workforce transition involving a major plant consolidation that affected more than 500 employees. Collaborated with union representatives and successfully communicated outcomes and benefits, retaining 80% of existing employees and maintaining high employee morale.

Technology / System Conversions: *Optimizing reporting capabilities*

- Served as Project Manager for three payroll system conversions that automated and enhanced reporting capabilities, reduced benefits administration costs $12,000 annually, and streamlined tax filing and compliance reporting.
- Member of ADP payroll conversion team that transitioned 401K data for hourly, salary, and union workers with various levels of contribution and payroll cycles to proprietary mainframe system.

Performance Management: *Quantifying productivity*

- Led initiative to reevaluate and upgrade the existing performance appraisal system to a behavior-based system that identified specific behaviors with objective measures to assess and quantify performance.
- Initiated company-wide job analysis and classification process that developed a task matrix across all categories and established benchmarks to measure job competencies and identify training needs.

Employee Relations: *Mitigating corporate risk*

- Successfully resolved five EEOC claims over an 11-year period resulting in all allegations being dismissed by the Arizona Department of Human Rights.

Workplace Safety: *Ensuring a safe environment*

- Implemented a comprehensive disability management plan in response to the increasing cost of workers' compensation claims that significantly reduced workplace injuries and lost days from 11.49% per 100 employees in 2003 to 22% in 2006, a 56% improvement over the period.

(continued)

(continued)

JENNIFER P. MOORE, PHR

Page Two

PROFESSIONAL EXPERIENCE:

MASON INTERNATIONAL, Phoenix, AZ – *Confidential* Nov '96 – Present
(TS-Certified manufacturer of metal stampings and assemblies for the auto industry. Recognized as the industry leader and named as one of the "Top 50 Progressive Manufacturers" for 2007 by Managing Automation)

Summary: Fast-track advancement based on demonstrated leadership in developing cost-effective HR programs that enhanced employee satisfaction of 517 union and non-union employees at two manufacturing facilities.

Human Resources Manager / Training Manager – *Reporting to Executive VP/CFO* (12/97 – Present)
Training Manager (9/97 – 12/97)
Human Resources Administrator (11/96 – 9/97)
Senior Human Resources Manager providing strategic direction to senior management with responsibility for organizational planning, benefits & compensation, training & development, staffing & recruitment, payroll (executive, salaried, hourly, union), employee relations, labor relations, safety/health, and employee services. Collaborate with union officials, legal counsel, insurance brokers, OSHA inspectors, employment agencies, and local university systems. Direct administrative team of two. Manage training budget and grant funding.

- Recruited to establish HR infrastructure and implement systems to capture real-time data for payroll and benefits administration. Designed and implemented new-hire orientation program.
- Built alliances with industry resources and developed training and quality objectives to recruit and maintain a competent workforce of highly skilled hourly, salaried, and union workers.
- Researched industry trends and workforce demographics and developed models to measure performance, identify training needs, and support QS/TS Certification.
- Initiated and developed grant proposals totaling $60,000 including a single company grant for $19,372 from the Arizona Department of Commerce & Economic Opportunity.
- Recognized with *Employer Training Award,* 2004

NORTHERN, INC., Phoenix, AZ Jan '90 – Nov '96
(Privately held graphic arts industrial manufacturer)

Human Resources Manager (2/93 – 11/96)
Human Resources Assistant (1/90 – 2/93)
Promoted from HR Assistant to manage all HR functions servicing 120 non-union employees company-wide.

- Established HR function including administrative infrastructure, policies/procedures, payroll, workers' compensation, insurance, and company handbook.
- Spearheaded on-campus recruitment program for internships and job placement.

PROFESSIONAL DEVELOPMENT / CERTIFICATION / AFFILIATIONS:

Human Resources Certification Institute, Society for Human Resources Management
  Professional in Human Resources (PHR) National Certification, 2006 – 2009
Society of Human Resources Management (SHRM)
Tooling & Manufacturing Association, Job Board Advisory Committee
Precision Metalforming Association Educational Foundation, University Task Group
National Institute for Metalworking Skills, 2003

TECHNICAL PROFICIENCIES:

Computer Software: Microsoft Word, Excel, PowerPoint, Outlook, proprietary payroll software, ADP, Ceridian, RSM McGladrey, customized manufacturing software (Symix, Syteline, Intra.doc, Stellent)

5

Specialty Area: Human Resources
Writer: Kathleen Weston

KELLY DORU

303 McKeon Avenue
Toronto, Ontario M4J 2K7

Home: 416.431.1445
Cellular: 416.663.5965

SENIOR HUMAN RESOURCES EXECUTIVE

Optimizing Performance through Organizational Change & Proactive Business Leadership
Broad Industry Experience
CHRP Designation, Green Belt Certified Six-Sigma Professional

Energetic leader with 13 years' experience directing complete HR operations for start-up, turnaround, and fast-growth companies. Recognized for innovative leadership and counsel in transitioning organizations into top producers and providing guidance through accelerated growth and global market expansion. Decisive, energetic and focused. Superior communication skills and in-depth awareness of multicultural issues. Demonstrated interpersonal relations, mentoring, negotiation, and mediation skills. Keen presentation, problem-solving, and conflict-management skills. Talented team leader, team player, and project manager.

Strategic HR leader with expert qualifications in all generalist HR affairs. Particular success in:

- Recruitment & Employment Management
- HR Policy and Procedure Development
- Labour Law & Regulations
- Employee & Management Retention
- Employment Equity
- Benefits & Compensation Design
- Performance & Productivity Improvement
- Consulting & Customer Service Delivery
- Training & Development Leadership
- Employee Reward & Recognition Programs
- Internal Change & Reorganization
- Merger & Acquisition Integration
- Organization Design & Development
- Professional Presentations
- Advanced HRIS Systems & Technologies
- Vision, Mission & Shared Values Statements

PROFESSIONAL EXPERIENCE:

Global Foods Inc., Toronto, Ontario — 2004 to Present
Senior Human Resources Manager – Corporate

Corporate Office and Senior HR Manager for multimillion-dollar high-growth global food processor and exporter with approximately 23,000 employees. Strategic partner to the corporation, consistently successful driving broad organization change, aligning with corporate goals, and achieving critical improvement and cost-saving initiatives. Tasked with creating a formal HR infrastructure to support continued growth, standardize operations, create structure and control, and strengthen financial performance.

Hold strategic planning, leadership, and operating management responsibility for HR and OD affairs including employment/recruitment, compensation, benefits, employee relations, training & development, quality, organization effectiveness, and HRIS management. Respond to management and employee questions on HR matters, provide counsel to employees, and conduct investigations as needed to resolve employee relations or legal issues. Direct a staff of five HR professionals. Guide business and HR vision.

Selected Achievements:

- Administer the RFE, Total Rewards, and Base Pay Programs.
- Translate corporate mission statements into a coherent set of performance measures using the Balanced Scorecard system.
- Successfully implemented Six Sigma methodology, resulting in cultural transformation towards a fact-based, accountable organization.
- Developed successful Leadership Hiring program, saving an estimated $14 million in costs.
- Key member of the Merger and Acquisition transition team, including employee data (resumes, compensation, agreements, etc.), planning and scheduling, sensitive corporate communication flow, employee offers and transfers, transition training, termination and outplacement, negotiating, and smooth information between Global Foods and Schneider's.
- Key player of the Senior HR Leadership Share Group.
- Successfully applied Talent Room strategy in recruitment and retention of management, saving $1.5 million.

(continued)

Kelly Doru, CHRP **page 2**

Link Up Employment Services for Persons with Disabilities 2003 to 2004
Senior Human Resources Manager (Contract)

Developed and implemented policy. Provided leadership in all areas of personnel relations, training, and HR practices. Consulted with the Executive Director, managerial staff, and supervisors to ensure policy compliance with established procedures and regulations. Coordinated complete employment services to a diverse client base throughout the area. Maintained staff training programs, including diversity-training programs for external clients.

Selected Achievements

- Conducted a formal needs assessment on current HR practices versus desired HR practices.
- Determined skill gaps and training requirements to centralize the HR department.
- Executed job analysis and redesign.
- Effectively designed and deployed knowledge-transfer plan obtaining buy-in and assigning accountability.
- Developed and implemented Employee Engagement Survey and Annual Employee Survey.

Bank of Montreal 2000 to 2003
EMFYSIS Technology & Solutions
Senior Resource Manager

Led and managed the Human Resources department, including strategic planning and processes, organizational effectiveness, management/employee development, communication, compensation, training and development, and resource management. Directed a staff of four Resource Managers and two Recruitment Consultants.

Selected Achievements

- Administered a "*Total Rewards*" annual compensation program of approximately $2.2 million.
- Initiated, developed, and implemented specific training to address changing corporate objectives. Monitored the training plans and budget of approximately $3 million.
- Conducted a Business Process Reengineering needs analysis, including process mapping, design, and transformation.
- Developed a minority group-hiring plan, specifically in aboriginal and disability recruitment and retention planning.

Royal Bank – Employment Resource Centre 1998 to 2000
Manager of Recruitment

Directed recruitment activities and supervised support personnel in daily activities. Conceptualized, developed, and implemented highly effective marketing campaigns. Designed and implemented programs to reach specialized target groups. Developed and controlled annual operating budgets.

EDUCATION:

- *Foundations of Leadership:* **School of Business Management, 2005**
- *Advanced Program in Human Resource Management:* **University of Toronto, J.L. Rotman School of Business, 2001**
- *Certified Human Resources Professional:* **Human Resources Professional Association of Ontario (HPRAO), 2000**
- *B.A. in English and Physiology:* **University of Ottawa, 1990**

PROFESSIONAL CREDENTIALS AND AFFILIATIONS:

- CHRP Designation
- PMP – LII
- RPR (Registered Professional Recruiter)
- Green Belt Six Sigma Professional
- Predictive Index Certification
- Member Human Resources Association of Ontario

COMPUTER SKILLS:

- Microsoft Office Suite
- HRIS
- Hyperion
- Netegrity
- Gelco
- Adobe

COMMUNITY INVOLVEMENT:

- Skills for Change – Teach Behavioral-Based Interviewing Current
- Link Up, The Employment Consulting Group for Persons with Disabilities – Board Chair 1998–2004

6

Specialty Area: Advertising, Public Relations, Sales and Marketing, and Business Development
Writer: Roleta Fowler Vasquez

ZACHARY A. TUNICZEK
In-Tun Entertainment, Inc. – 5000 Wilshire Blvd., Ste #300 – Westwood, CA 90024
Tel: (310) 555-5550 — Fax: (310) 555-5551 — E-mail: zack@slavic.org

PROFESSIONAL SUMMARY

Professional Marketing / Public Relations Consultant with exceptional business planning, development, financial management, and corporate administration skills. Ardent communicator and negotiator with strong closing ability. Additional success as a **Fundraiser** with experience in **Non-Profit** starts. Impressive contributors list.

PROFESSIONAL EXPERIENCE

PRESIDENT / CO-FOUNDER **2002–PRESENT**
IN-TUN ENTERTAINMENT, INC. – WESTWOOD, CA

In-Tun is a public relations agency specializing in music industry talent marketing and management.

Designed and produced high-impact communications strategies (print media, concerts, parties, special events, and fundraisers) to market musical artists and non-profit agencies or to diffuse negative press. Identified and built partnerships within the music industry and outlying communities. Administered company programs such as workers' compensation, payroll, and insurance for up to 12 employees.

- Collaborated with the City of Los Angeles on the first annual Slavic-American Festival in 2005.
  - Entertainment industry background allowed recruitment of show-business luminaries and corporate giants for participation in media events, lectures, and festivals.

PRESIDENT / FOUNDER **1999–PRESENT**
SLAVIC-AMERICAN FOUNDATION, INC. – WESTWOOD, CA

The Slavic-American Foundation is a non-profit community educational and research organization dedicated to spreading Eastern European cultural and HIV/AIDS awareness while combating negative stereotypes.

Established the Slavic-American Foundation. Engineered the initial program budget and internal controls. Wrote and executed the organization's marketing plan and operating manual, defining its purpose, responsibilities, and structure. Recruited key management and financial officers and steered the selection of the first Board of Directors. Acted as liaison between the Board, local service organizations, and the public.

- Conceived and coordinated national and regional AIDS awareness and community outreach campaigns through media publication, professional networking, and public broadcasting.
  - Consistently maintained administrative costs below 22%, qualifying us as a Combined Federal Campaign (CFC) preferred charity.
  - Raised over $2 million yearly through grants, corporate and private donors, and fundraising events.
  - Channeled nearly $1.5 million annually into health and socioeconomic improvement programs.

EDUCATION

University of California, Santa Barbara, CA — Bachelor of Arts in Communications — 1999

7

Specialty Area: Advertising, Public Relations, Sales and Marketing, and Business Development
Writer: Malloy Lacktman

MADELINE JACOBS

132 Bay Boulevard ▪ Santa Monica, CA 90020
323-932-8340 ▪ MadelineJacobs@earthlink.net

OBJECTIVE

Proven and dedicated Advertising Executive seeks Chief Operating Officer Position with mid-size, Wisconsin-based agency.

QUALIFICATIONS TESTIMONIAL

"Madeline has the instincts and experience to bring an advertising agency to its fullest potential. She exhibits a number of traits that I have found to be rare in this industry. She is a ***natural leader***, mentor, and teacher for her staff and takes great pains to ensure that the work environment is close-knit, positive and open. Madeline is a ***relationship builder***. I have never met anyone who works as hard and effectively at forging deep relationships with both her clients and colleagues, engendering unprecedented loyalty. She is a ***skilled strategist*** with a gift for sorting through information and discerning the best strategy for a brand, product, or campaign. She is a ***loyal partner*** who commits herself completely to her work and colleagues. I could always depend on her for handling our daily operations. She will be a major asset to the next organization she chooses to join."

– Hugh Duncan, Chairman and CEO, Duncan & Associates

EXPERIENCE

Duncan & Associates ▪ Los Angeles, CA 1996–2007
Chief Operating Officer

VALUE-ADDED EXAMPLE

Challenge: Albertsons' brand was undefined, causing consumers to choose other grocery stores, which were perceived has having either lower prices or higher quality.
Action: Developed "Patricia Heaton" campaign, which defined the Albertsons brand in a way that appealed to its target market.
Result: Albertsons' market share rose 9% in the 6-month period following campaign launch, while the market share fell for its main competitors, Kroger and Safeway. The campaign achieved an 87% awareness rating from its target market after 5 months on the air. The campaign won numerous "Platinum" awards, including the Mobius, Telly, and Aurora.

OVERVIEW

▪ Helped build a full-service advertising agency from launch to its current position as the second-largest independent agency in Southern California, billing $170M annually by consistently helping clients grow their businesses.
▪ Recruited and managed 55+ employees in 4 regional offices. Empowered employees, achieving strong productivity with little attrition.
▪ Managed all areas of operation, including account planning and management, research initiatives, and creative affairs.

HIGHLIGHTS

▪ Developed and implemented a successful grassroots Latino marketing plan in 11 states, including a customized advertising campaign.
▪ Initiated and launched a quarterly consumer trends publication, *D&A Trend Watch*, for all clients.
▪ Organized and led annual strategic planning retreats to brainstorm and create marketing plans.
▪ Built a functional, coherent employee team that produced (3,500+ annually) and trafficked (35,000+ annually) original retail spots.

MADELINE JACOBS

132 Bay Boulevard ▪ Santa Monica, CA 90020
323-932-8340 ▪ MadelineJacobs@earthlink.net

EXPERIENCE (cont.)

Leo Burnett ▪ Chicago, IL 1987–1996
Vice President

VALUE-ADDED EXAMPLE

Challenge: Sales of Rice Krispies were suffering due to increased saturation in cereal market.
Action: Developed and introduced Rice Krispie Treat Bars, which allowed the cereal brand to profit in new markets.
Result: Rice Krispie Treat Bars became the #1 selling vending machine product in less than a year, increasing overall sales for the brand by 48%.

OVERVIEW

▪ Managed $125M+ advertising budget for Kellogg's, Burnett's largest account.
▪ Developed strategies, campaigns, and marketing plans that consistently grew cereal brands, including Corn Flakes, Rice Krispies, Frosted Flakes, Frosted Mini-Wheats, and Special K.

HIGHLIGHTS

▪ Led strategy, creation, and implementation of 4 new consumer targets for key brands including the use of new media vehicles and promotional food.
▪ First female Account Director on the Kellogg's account, which had been with Burnett 45+ years.
▪ Developed and implemented *Copy College* for account and client personnel, which covered strategy, positioning, and media planning.
▪ Recruited 20+ MBAs annually.

Hallmark Cards, Inc. ▪ Kansas City, MO 1983–1987
Product Manager

VALUE-ADDED EXAMPLE

Challenge: Hallmark was losing greeting-card sales to competitors who offered cards in addition to other products (*e.g.*, gift stores, car washes, grocery stores).
Action: Helped develop a line of gifts unique to Hallmark, including Rodney Reindeer family toys.
Result: Rodney Reindeer family became the #1 product in Hallmark's history. It increased traffic into stores and thereby increased sales of greeting cards.

OVERVIEW

▪ Managed integrated marketing programs that incorporated products, store décor, premiums, themes, and national advertising.

HIGHLIGHTS

▪ Managed the development and implementation of strategic business plans for the Sticker, Plush, Figurine, and Impulse product lines.
▪ Consistently exceeded profit and quality requirements.

EDUCATION

Indiana University ▪ Bloomington, IN Bachelor of Arts, Journalism, 1983

INTERESTS

Green Bay Packer football, cancer charities, reading, and cooking.

8

Specialty Area: Advertising, Public Relations, Sales and Marketing, and Business Development
Writer: Norine Dagliano

SANDRA D. NEWHOUSE

278 East Hillcrest Avenue, Adamstown, MD 21710
Home: 301.555.1234 • Mobile: 301.555.1234 • sdn@comcast.net

SALES AND MARKETING MANAGER

Problem Solver...Money Maker

Top-producing sales and marketing professional charged with ambition, energy, and self-discipline. Designer and executor of innovative marketing strategies that motivate, educate, and create demand. Mentor and coach committed to transforming novice account reps into rainmakers. Unequaled professional who embraces change and thrives on challenge.

TRACK RECORD OF SUCCESS

E-Business Development: Launched and continue to develop a unique B2B and B2C electronic shopping mall, capturing the small-business market and blazing new inroads to non-traditional advertising.

Advertising Production: Conceived, designed, and published a quarterly advertiser-funded, lifestyle and leisure magazine promoting a quad-county area of southern PA. Circulation—20,000/month.

Territory Development: Exploded Cellular One presence in the Frederick/Urbana business community. Propelled lowest-producing B-mall to top producer, with sales averaging over 300 phones/month. Orchestrated opening of two new in-line stores.

Market Penetration: Delivered an impressive first-year TV advertising sales growth from $40K to $380K by capturing the untapped auto dealership market.

Brand R & D: Forged alliance with an auto dealership to create and launch a market brand that continues to outshine the competition. Proved skills in creating and implementing campaign budgets that work.

Leadership and Mentoring: Pioneered an in-the-trenches training ground for new sales personnel in the nuances of television advertising. Motivated staff to attain third-year sales revenues approaching $190K over first-year sales.

CAREER EXPERIENCE

TELEVISION/NBC AFFILIATE, Frederick, MD — 2004 to Present

Area's Best Shopping Sales Manager (2006 to Present)

- Recruited to lead a unique Internet/television advertising partnership, from initial concept to full implementation. Manage a $300K+ annual operating budget. Hire, train, and direct sales activities of three account executives. Train and mentor 11 television sales reps.
- Strategically drove first-quarter profits to $8K; project year-end to $127K; second-year profits expected to top $200K with $1.9M in sales. Indirectly impacted television-advertising revenues by $262K+ in less than three years.

Account Executive (2004 to 2006)

- Grew Frederick County business accounts more than 900% by identifying and capturing untapped business markets.

ENTREPRENEURIAL ENDEAVORS, Middletown, MD — 1995 to Present

Concepts Unlimited (1998 to Present)

- Co-founded an advertising consulting firm targeting local businesses with limited advertising knowledge, skills, and experience. Provide a comprehensive analysis of advertising needs and resources and big-picture management strategies to maximize ROI while trimming the fat.

Key projects:

- Formulated two-year multi-faceted marketing and advertising campaign that propelled sales for a single-family home construction firm from $140K price range to a multimillion-dollar development with home sales averaging $350K.
- Expanded market reach and doubled profits in one year with a strategically designed advertising and merchandising campaign promoting an indoor/outdoor furniture retail operation.

SANDRA D. NEWHOUSE Mobile: 301.555.1234 • sdn@comcast.net **Page 2**

ENTREPRENEURIAL ENDEAVORS *(Continued)*

I Do Magazine (1995 to 1998)

- Conceived, designed, and published a monthly, advertiser-supported wedding-planning magazine. Implemented creative marketing/distribution strategies that placed the publication into the hands of approximately 1,000 newly engaged couples each month.

CABLE ADVERTISING, Chambersburg, PA 2000 to 2001

Account Executive

- Penetrated Gettysburg business community unaccustomed to cable advertising, and drove sales from zero to $120K in one year. Received numerous Sales Excellence Awards for consistently exceeding monthly sales goals.

WIRELESS COMMUNICATIONS/RETAIL, Ellicott City, MD 1997 to1999

Sales Manager

- Within first three months of hire as Outside Sales Executive, earned corporate Giant Step Award for greatest percentage increase in sales—promoted to Sales Manager. Tasked with oversight for mall kiosk and four sales personnel.
- Grew low-producing mall kiosk to an in-line mall store; expanded market reach by establishing a second in-line store in a neighboring community. Grew sales staff to seven; managed $1.2M operating budget, inventory, promotions, and advertising for both locations.
- Developed internal communication channel, linking sales and management personnel in 25 locations across seven territories to ensure full staff coverage and networked resources for resolving operational issues and concerns.
- Created mentoring and job-shadowing relationship between Sales Managers and top sales performers to provide career advancement opportunities.

PC & WIRELESS COMMUNICATION SAVVY

PowerPoint, Excel, Word, Access, PrintShop, Publisher, FrontPage, Adobe Acrobat, Internet, E-mail; Blackberry

PROFESSIONAL DEVELOPMENT

Stephen Covey, *First Things First* • Zig Ziglar, *See You At The Top* • *How to Supervise People: Managing For The 90's And Beyond* • *Influence Management Skills* • *Purchasing Basics for the New Buyer* • Tom Peters, *WOW!* Seminar • *The Networking Seminar* • *Interpersonal Skills* • Jim Doyle Training

9

Specialty Area: Advertising, Public Relations, Sales and Marketing, and Business Development
Writer: Jan Melnik

Jenna L. Thompson

617-525-5515 | 76 Claremont Street, Boston, MA 02117 | jthompson4@comcast.net

Senior Marketing Executive: Vice President / Director

Marketing Leadership: *Upstream Marketing, Strategic Product Definition & Planning …*
Understanding / Translating Customer Requirements & Business / Market Needs …
Product Positioning & Launch … Domestic & Global Expansion

Strategic, hands-on leader in medical devices industry with 15+ years of professional experience and a consistent record of overachievement augmented by an exceptional background in clinical medicine and technology. Distinguished as U.S. Patent Holder. Record reflects consistent success in quickly bringing new products to market, driving profitability and business growth.

- **Technological expertise:** industrial design/prototypes, wireless and disruptive technologies, and product development (hardware/software). **Clinical background:** intravascular ultrasound, ECG interpretation, pacing/programmer technology, pharmacology, pathophysiology, and therapy delivery.
- Demonstrated expertise bringing vision and proactive thinking to wide spectrum of business issues; talent for identifying untapped marketing opportunities and adding value throughout product development/design process, including reengineering, by leveraging core strengths.
- Outstanding presentation skills; extensive multicultural understanding; experienced global business traveler.

Leadership Strengths …

- Marketing Strategy & Execution
- Innovative Product Definition / Design
- Relationship Management
- Profit & Performance Improvement
- Team Leadership / Motivation
- Brand Development & Strengthening

Experience & Accomplishments

CENTRIUM CORPORATION • Waltham, MA 2004–Present
Associate Director of Marketing (2005–Present) • **Senior Product Manager** (2004–2005)

Medical device company with broad suite of intravascular ultrasound (IVUS) and functional measurement products used in next-generation diagnosis/treatment of vascular and structural heart disease. Company has experienced 30% growth rates for the past 3 years in a market estimated to be $320 million (CTRM on NASD).

Recruited to commercialize Virtual Histology software (VH IVUS) and drive Centrium to a position of profitability. Manage product development, launch, and marketing for next-generation s5 hardware platform/ancillary products. IVUS represents 89% of Centrium's revenues. Spearhead business development and upstream marketing initiatives for IVUS hardware and software products, including commercialization of VH IVUS software technology poised to revolutionize treatment of atherosclerosis.

Directly manage 2 product managers and work closely with R&D team (80 engineers); maintain signature authority over all IVUS product development. ***Select accomplishments:***

- In 2006, managed a high-performance team that **successfully brought 5 new products to market** allowing head to head competition for market leadership. To date, 400 new-generation s5 systems have been placed worldwide with more than 1200 IVUS units targeted for hardware upgrade globally.
- Key contributor of team positioning Centrium for successful IPO (went public in 2006); company ranked as **#1 Performing Medical IPO** and the **#5 IPO Overall** (2006).
- Strategic launch of new products fueled market expansion into Japan.
- Instrumental to Centrium's exceptional growth track: from $60M (2004) to $120M (2007).
- Recipient, **Centrium 100 Award 2006** (conferred by Global Sales Management Team). *… continued*

Jenna L. Thompson Page Two

Experience & Accomplishments

CENTRIUM CORPORATION • *Select Accomplishments …* *continued*

- Conducted field research of IVUS use that identified key hurdles related to difficulty of use: heavy equipment, awkward and complicated user interface, unfriendly controls, images that were difficult to interpret, and poor reimbursement model. Worked with engineers to improve system design; reduced weight from 400 to 95 pounds for the portable unit; developed an integrated version that allows for incorporation into cath lab, and enhanced user interface (improved controls and navigation) that follows the typical user's work flow. **Candidate, Medical Design Excellence Award**. Enabled Centrium's first new product releases in more than 3 years.

JOHNSON & JOHNSON • New Brunswick, NJ 1992–2003
Senior Product Planning Manager – CRM (1999–2003)

Multibillion-dollar global company and world leader in medical technology providing lifelong solutions for 5 million people with chronic disease; instruments used in treatment of diabetes, heart disease, neurological disorders, and vascular illnesses (JNJ on NYSE).

Recruited to bring medical background and marketing talent to the next generation of pacemaker technology development. Played pivotal role in identifying market trends and needs from patient/physician perspectives; conducted extensive market research to pinpoint enhancements resulting in directed product development. Helped company transform the Cardiac Rhythm Management field through development of premium pacing system products with expandable platforms featuring integrated technology. ***Primary achievements:***

- **Led team in successful effort to devise $240M product development strategy for XE ProgrammerPlus.** Collaborated with regulatory, clinical, and multidisciplinary experts on cross-functional team to create branding, taglines, and collateral materials for XE. Wrote business analysis, conducted product planning, and managed implementation and launch for worldwide market release in 2002.
- Partnered with creative talent of IDEO (world-renowned company specializing in the strategic value of design, innovation, and design practice) to most effectively achieve breakthrough product design of the **XE ProgrammerPlus**.
- Identified global customer needs and defined completely automatic pacemaker **EnPulse**—a premium pacemaker featuring then new-to-industry device-lead standard connection that enabled simpler arrhythmia management by clinicians.
- Established highly successful **Patients Travel website,** providing patient and physician access and information about **XE ProgrammerPlus** from anywhere in the world; with Johnson & Johnson programmers used in 50% of the world's pacing devices, this capability was tremendous.
- Recipient, **1999 Customer Focused Quality Award** (recognizing achievements in customer requirement identification for new generation of programmer system; established robust database identifying key customer market segments throughout North America, Europe, and Japan).

Product Marketing Manager (1995–1999)

Headed up development and planning of incorporating **The Assessor,** a lead implant testing instrument, into the **XE Programmer**. Managed product planning for **The Connector,** accurately projected to be the clinical management tool of the future. ***Select accomplishments:***

- Planned and launched **The Assessor**, an instrument that improved efficiency of implant procedures.
- Developed strategy to reduce cycle time at pacemaker system implant and follow-up.
- Focused on new hardware, software, and system integration capabilities; coordinated product management worldwide for Johnson & Johnson.
- Researched and identified customer needs for clinical management tools.

… continued

(continued)

(continued)

Jenna L. Thompson Page Three

Experience & Accomplishments

JOHNSON & JOHNSON • Product Marketing Manager (cont'd.)

- Recipient, **1998 Customer Focused Quality Award** (Connector Customer Requirements Team).

Customer Education Program Manager (1994–1995)

Managed redesign of New Jersey-based customer education programs focusing on curriculum addressing key marketing objectives, adaptability to customer needs, and outcome-based education. Communicated regularly with U.S. and international sales force. ***Key achievements:***

- Co-wrote the **Customer Education Strategic Plan,** which streamlined process of delivering quality customer education.
- Managed 500+ customer visits and programs.
- Named **Contributor of the Quarter** (recognizing Customer Education & Planning Team).
- Promoted from Product Education Specialist, a position held from 1992–1994.

Earlier Career Background includes more than ten years as a Professional Nursing Practice Standards Consultant, University Nursing Instructor, Nurse-Administrator, and Critical Care Nurse at institutions throughout Connecticut and Kentucky. Select career highlights include:

- Selection as **Kentucky Colonel**
- Honored as member of **Sigma Theta Tau, International**
- Named to **Who's Who** (both in American Education and American Nursing)
- Publications include **Initiating Temporary Transvenous Dual-Chamber Pacing** (*Nursing94,* May 1994: 48-50)

Education

MSN **UNIVERSITY OF MASSACHUSETTS HEALTH SCIENCE CENTER • Amherst, MA**

BSN **UNIVERSITY OF CONNECTICUT • Storrs, CT**

CONTINUING PROFESSIONAL DEVELOPMENT ...

- Broad range of **professional development training** in such disciplines as marketing, product management, Internet, technology decision making, team building, and presentation skills (multiple week-long executive programs at such schools as Wharton, UCLA, and the University of Chicago)
- **CV Nurse Specialist** (Hartford Hospital, Hartford, CT)

10

Specialty Area: Technology, Science, and Engineering
Writer: Marilyn A. Feldstein

DAVID M. FRANKLIN

7721 Happy Feet Trail
Macon, GA 31210

(478) 357-6987
dfranklin@bellsouth.net

SUMMARY

Innovative IT Professional with more than 15 years' experience in diverse business environments. Key strengths in design, development, implementation, production, and problem analysis. A focused, self-motivated team member who takes pride in solving complex problems.

TECHNICAL SKILLS

Databases	Operating Systems, Languages, and Utilities
Microsoft Visual Basic/SQL Server 7.0/2000/Access/Sun Java Programming	Microsoft NT/XP, T-SQL, DTS
ORACLE V4 - V8	UNIX Shell, SQL*Plus, PL/SQL

PROFESSIONAL EXPERIENCE

Quality Information Systems, Atlanta, GA 1990 – 2007

Staff Consultant/Contractor, Health Systems, Atlanta, GA 2002 – 2007

Scheduled daily production of reports, processes, and data transfers from internal and external systems for IT hardware and software and Project Administration.

- Developed and implemented the database components of an IT Project Administration system that automated time, labor, and other costs as they related to programs, projects, and plans. The system greatly reduced manual documentation, saved administrative costs, and improved the timeliness of the project costs and status information.
- Developed and implemented the database components of an IT Assets Management system to track more than $40 million in hardware and software, identifying location, status, usability, and configuration and significantly improving accountability and delivery of information services.

Staff Consultant, Health Foundations of South Florida, Miami, FL 1997 – 2002

Worked with systems analyst to design and implement database components that supported the Coordination of Benefits business requirements.

- Designed and implemented the database and related components to create the Coordination of Benefits system, saving administrative time and reducing cost of claims.

Senior Programmer/Analyst, ISP Health Systems, Tampa, FL 1990 – 1997

Developed databases for the upgrade expansion of pre-paid calling cards to handle all the functional aspects of the cards, which included managing production schedules and execution, tracking customer accounts, providing essential details for new product offerings, and generating management reports.

- Implemented replication and partition options (dual-master sites) that increased the volume of phone cards from 10 million to 40 million while maintaining responsiveness and reliability.

EDUCATION

B.S., Information Technology, University of Texas at Austin, Austin, TX 1990

11

Specialty Area: Technology, Science, and Engineering
Writer: Karen P. Katz

Doreen Mo

601 Parkway Road, #45
Pittsburgh, PA 15146

Email: doreenmo@xmail.com
Phone: (555) 567-9876

PROFILE

HANDS-ON BUSINESS ANALYST with extensive experience in
DATABASE DEVELOPMENT, ANALYSIS, and **WEBSITE DEVLOPMENT**

Demonstrated ability to integrate and apply background in
COMPUTER SCIENCES and **CHEMISTRY**

Contributor to web-based database solutions; solved administrative challenges in
HEALTHCARE, ACADEMIC, and **ENGINEERING SETTINGS:**

- Increased patient recruitment and completion rate
- Integrated data from multiple sources
- Eliminated error data
- Initiated and completed major website projects

DATABASES	WEB DEVELOPMENT	PROGRAMMING LANGUAGES	OTHER
ACCESS	JSP	JAVA	DREAMWAVER, MS .NET, JBUILDER
SQL	ASP/VISUAL BASIC	C++	ADOBE PHOTOSHOP, MS PUBLISHER
MYSQL	COLDFUSION		SPSS, EXCEL
ORACLE	HTML, CSS, JAVASCRIPT		APACHE/TOMCAT, IIS

CAREER HISTORY / ACCOMPLISHMENTS

FOUR+ YEARS' USA WORK EXPERIENCE WITH RESEARCH-BASED ORGANIZATIONS

UNIVERSITY OF PENNSYLVANIA, PHILADELPHIA, PA 2004–2006

DATA ANALYST, DEPARTMENT OF PSYCHIATRY
Developed and implemented web-based programs as part of IT team working with multidisciplinary psychiatry faculties and staffs; trained end-users on applications.

- Electronic Patient Interview System: HTML interface; MySQL back-end; SQL code, JavaScript functions
- Medical Record Tracking System: MS Access

Created statistical reports for faculties and research assistants using SPSS, Excel, and Access.

Conducted and implemented data integrity procedures.

Designed and developed project website using ASP, Visual Basic, HTML and SQL Server 2000.
http://psych.unotavail.edu/copedweb/index.asp

WEB DEVELOPER, MEDICAL CENTER, NUTRITION AND FOOD SERVICES
Coordinated with non-technical staff to identify and implement Internet strategy. Translated business requirements and implemented designs; trained staff members to update and maintain site.

- Designed website interfaces, layout, and content using HTML and Photoshop.
- Set site standards and templates using CSS and JavaScript.

http://nutrition.notavailmedicalcenter.org

Doreen Mo

601 Parkway Road, #45
Pittsburgh, PA 15146

Email: doreenmo@xmail.com
Phone: (555) 567-9876

CAREER HISTORY / ACCOMPLISHMENTS (CONT):

VILLANOVA UNIVERSITY, PHILADELPHIA, PA 2003–2004

WEB DEVELOPER, LAW SCHOOL/IT SERVICE

Integral member of Law School Web Service team. Developed Web/database interactive applications, designed web pages, coded new programs, and provided support.

- Developed web-database applications with Cold Fusion 5.0, JavaScript, and MS Access and SQL.
- Designed web GUIs using HTML, Dreamweaver, CSS, and PhotoShop.
- Maintained and enhanced PHP, Perl Scripts, and CSS of Penn Law and Penn Law Goat website.

http://www.law.notavail.edu, http://goat.law.notavail.edu

THOMAS JEFFERSON UNIVERSITY HOSPITAL, PHILADELPHIA, PA 2002–2003

ASSISTANT BUSINESS ADMINISTRATOR/CARDIOLOGY DEPARTMENT

Participated in managing medical records; implemented procedure codes to expedite billing.

CHINA SUNSHINE INTERNATIONAL CORPORATION, BEIJING, CHINA 1995–1999

PROJECT MANAGER

Managed international trade of chemical products; supervised staff of four.

EDUCATION

M.S., COMPUTER AND INFORMATION SCIENCE DECEMBER 2003
College of Science and Technology, Villanova University
Philadelphia, Pennsylvania, USA

B. E., PHYSICAL CHEMISTRY JULY 1995
University of Science and Technology
Beijing, China

Core courses: Advanced Mathematics; Linear Algebra; Probability & Statistics; Mechanics; Thermal Physics; Electromagnetics; Optics; Atomic and Nuclear Physics; Inorganic Chemistry; Organic Chemistry; Analytical Chemistry; Physical Chemistry; Electrical & Electronic Technology; Metallography & Heat Treatment; Metallurgical Thermodynamics; Metallurgical Kinetics

Permanent Resident – U.S.A.

12

Specialty Area: Technology, Science, and Engineering
Writer: Barbara Safani

JANE SIMMONS

200 West 45th Street, 10G • New York, NY 10019 • H: 212-555-5667 • M: 646-682-2387 • jane_simmons@gmail.com

TECHNOLOGY BUSINESS STRATEGIST • IT Enterprise Roll-Outs • Financial Consolidation Systems • Sarbanes-Oxley Implementation • Post-Merger Integrations • Risk Assessment and Mitigation • International Business/Alliance Development

Over 15 years' experience managing technology needs for international client base with ten of those years working directly with Fortune 500 firms. Expertise implementing financial consolidation systems in conjunction with change-management initiatives, corporate acquisitions, and departmental start-ups. Proven ability to deliver solutions that reduce operating expenses by millions of dollars, improve departmental efficiencies exponentially, and significantly diminish firm's exposure to risk. Big-picture thinker with knack for explaining technical information in a way that inspires user confidence and cross-functional collaboration.

AREAS OF EXPERTISE

Technology Driven Transformation

- Corporate, business unit & enterprise technology
- Competitive & impact analysis of technology products
- Systems integration program assessments
- Enterprise data-management strategy
- Merger integration planning /due diligence
- Network security, information assurance & digital risk

Operation Model Strategy & Design

- Sarbanes-Oxley applications
- Consolidation systems
- Procurement sourcing tools
- PeopleSoft conversions
- Tax-document management systems
- Document storage systems

PROFESSIONAL EXPERIENCE

BBC., New York, NY **1998 to Present**

IT Director, New York and London (2003 to Present)
Provide applications systems support for six-department corporate division. Oversee management of close to 40 applications and lead team of developers in New York and London. Project Scope: $180K to $5M; Staff: 8

Led multimillion-dollar Sarbanes-Oxley application keeping all phases of project on time and under budget.

- Trimmed $170K off phase one alone by effectively managing resources and eliminating need for additional consultants.
- Spearheaded due diligence process; audited ten different applications and developed prototype before launching project.
- Oversaw 16-person senior task force comprising 8 corporate divisions to define requirements and develop proposal.
- Mitigated risk and corporate liability by developing robust security documentation process in compliance with SOX.
- Act as "go to person" and sounding board for Information Security Senior Manager regarding all SOX issues.

Shaved millions of dollars off systems costs and eliminated need to replace corporate accounting shared server system by recommending and implementing migration to more robust PeopleSoft.

- Decommissioned redundant servers and reduced number of personnel needed to maintain systems.
- Created opportunity to outsource process and improve efficiencies.

Trimmed time spent locating and managing corporate tax department documentation by hundreds of hours annually by launching company's inaugural Treasury Workstation documentation management system.

- Improved firm's ability to source crucial tax breaks by installing a state and local planning system to identify regional tax structures and associated perks.
- Bolstered integrity and tracking of audit data by developing corporate division's first-ever internal audit tracking tool.
- Eliminated potential risk factors associated with mandatory auditing processes by developing guidelines for and reviewing meticulous documentation system designed to protect firm from potential misappropriation of funds.

Saved millions of dollars for firm by implementing enterprise-wide procurement application to consolidate purchases and improve tracking mechanisms.

- Installed cost-saving features including an e-auction tool, shared contracts, and supplier analysis reporting features.

Elevated expectations for team accountability and project management resulting in virtually no occurrences of projects going over time or budget constraints.

- Streamlined communications between New York and London by developing monthly project reporting tool and promoting the corporate resources group in London to their New York counterparts.
- Saved significant time and eliminated document retrieval issues by creating a shared U.S./UK document storage system.
- Maximized communications across groups despite six-hour time difference; instilled project autonomy while giving developers increased lead time on projects and implementing systematic documentation guidelines.

JANE SIMMONS

Page Two

IT Manager, New York, NY (2000 to 2003)
Managed all financial applications for multiple corporate departments including financial reporting and accounting policy, financial consolidation, budgeting and forecasting, purchasing, tax, treasury, real estate, corporate accounting, internal audit, and print shop. Support included process management, security issue management, application support, stress testing, and systems auditing. Additionally tasked with managing vendor relationships and liaising with internal IT groups for implementation, upgrades, and maintenance. Project Scope: 100K; Staff: 5

- Partnered with IT team of recently acquired company to streamline and consolidate financial reporting tools in preparation for BTC/BBC merger; advised BBC on their rollout of consolidation tool, including centralized access for remote offices.
- Appointed acting VP for six-month period with responsibilities for a 13-person team, department budget, and internal/external customer relationship management.
- Slashed close time for corporate UK Treasury and Tax by five days by consolidating financial reporting systems.
- Improved functionality of financial reporting systems for eight unique divisions; automated procedures, created seamless interface, customized solutions, centralizing systems, and developed training manuals and platform training program for 120 users; new standardized processes became the template for future consolidation efforts.
- Significantly improved document storage and tracking capabilities related to Sarbanes-Oxley documentation by co-developing enterprise-wide e-Room document storage and management tools that converted email correspondence to a more sophisticated shared tracking database for 260 users.

Senior Applications Consultant, New York, NY (1998 to 2000)
Recruited from Intershare Inc. to become BBC's sole applications consultant for the financial consolidation systems.

- Tested and rolled-out Y2K version of consolidation tool (first mission-critical application to pass Y2K testing).
- Developed new Excel-based front-end for consolidation tool.
- Provided all documentation for consolidation systems including user manual, IT manual, relevant install and support documentation, and systems development life-cycle documentation for upgrades.
- Trained users on implementation and usage of applications across divisions, created area on corporate Internet for consolidation application, and rolled out enterprise-wide portal allowing select access to CITRIX consolidation tool.

INTERSHARE INC., London, UK **1990 to 1998**

Senior Applications Consultant, New York, NY (1997 to 1998)
Selected for U.S. consulting position working on consolidation systems for Fortune 500 companies. Provided general application support for AIG, Dover Corporation, Texaco, Time Inc., Time Warner Inc., and Toshiba American Consumer Products.

Project Leader, Management Support Systems, Paris, France (1993 to 1997)
Recruited for assignment with Corenet Inc. to provide front-line support for the corporate consolidation system.

- Created training database, documentation, user manual, and training program delivered to 150 users worldwide.
- Implemented General Ledger interface; U.S. with J.D. Edwards, Switzerland with SAP and Abacus.

International Product Support Consultant, London, UK (1990 to 1993)
International support for retail and financial consolidation software products.

EDUCATION AND ONGOING PROFESSIONAL DEVELOPMENT

Certified Information Security Manager (CISM), New York, NY, 2006

BBC Leadership Development Program, London, UK, 2003

Management Skills for IT Professionals, New Horizons Computer Learning Center, New York, NY, 2000

B.A., Social Science, Middlesex Polytechnic, Middlesex, UK, 1990

TECHNOLOGY

Client, server, and mainframe operating systems, Microsoft Professional Office Suite, Microsoft FrontPage, Excel VBA, HTML, Adobe Acrobat, Visio, Hyperion Financial Products, J.D. Edwards FASTR, Citrix Metaframe and NFuse, peregrine and remedy call logging and change management programs, RIM Blackberry implementation.

13

Specialty Area: Technology, Science, and Engineering
Writer: Ellie Vargo

MATTHEW J. OLDHAM

13344 Meadowbrook Circle • St. Louis, MO 63017 • 555.421.8239 • mjoldham@yahoo.com

INFRASTRUCTURE PLANNING • NETWORK ARCHITECTURE/SYSTEMS INTEGRATION
Standards • Performance Monitoring • Technical Support

Accomplished Network Engineer with uncommon technical expertise and proven results in interpreting, organizing, and executing complex enterprise Internet/e-commerce business solutions requiring end-to-end data flow management. Knowledgeable in basic security trading, order flow, market data technology, and market data vendors. Critical thinker. Clear communicator; adept at bridging the gap between business users and technology partners. Thorough and comprehensive, but flexible, planner.

Hands-on, energetic project manager; adept at juggling rapidly changing business priorities to deliver accurate, value-added solutions on deadline. Intuitive problem solver. Empowering, supportive and respectful team leader, trainer, and facilitator. Engaging rapport builder; skilled in building positive working relationships based on sincerity, professionalism, and trust. Collaborative change manager with a strong work ethic, a reputation for integrity, and a passion for getting the job done right the first time.

▸ Strengths

Analysis	e-Commerce	Purchasing/RFPs	Team Building/Training
Compliance	Implementation	Risk Management	Telephony
Configuration	Installation	Security	Testing
Connectivity	Integration	Solution Design	Troubleshooting
Data Flow Management	Load Balancing	Standards/Practices	Vendor Management
Disaster Recovery	Packet Analysis	Strategic Planning	Vendor Sourcing
Documentation	Performance Monitoring	Technical Support	Voice/Data Technologies

▸ Technical Expertise

Technologies	VoIP Telephony, Ethernet 802.3, KVM switches
Telecom/Topologies	CTI, CMAPI, AES, VDN, Intuity, vectoring, CMS, ACD, HSSI, IPmedpro cards, CLAN, VPN, BRI/ISDN, POTS, frame relay, trunk ports, DS0/1/3, OC12/48 and other layer 2 and 3 devices, Dialogic telephony cards, DWDM, ATM, SONET, FDDI
Network Equipment	Avaya; Cisco Catalyst series 6500 and 2900 switches; Cisco series 7600, 7200, 3800, and 2821 routers; MFSC; Sup720; SSL modules; CSS; CSM
Protocols	TCP/IP, OSPF, MPLS, BGP, IPX/SPX, SNA, HSRP, PPP, DHCP, DNS, SNMP, EIGRP, RDP
WAN Devices	CSU/DSU, modems, V.35
Security	ACLs, Cisco FWSM, Cisco Riverhead DDOS, Cisco IDS, CrossBeam X-Series, IPSEC
Load Balancing	Cisco CSS/CSM, F5 BIG-IP global traffic manager (GSLB)
Monitoring Tools	Mercury Siteseer/Sitescope, Keynote, Gomez, CA Spectrum, Cisco Works, Ethereal, Network Instruments Observer
Standards	IEEE, IETF, IANA, ANSI, OSI model

▸ EXPERIENCE

BASCOMB CAPITAL MARKETS, St. Louis, MO 1994–2006

Installed, configured, integrated, and customized voice and data network technologies and equipment to meet increasingly sophisticated customer expectations and changing regulatory requirements while accommodating dynamic business growth in a fiercely competitive securities trading marketplace.

Network Services Manager (3/05–8/06)
Managed voice and data systems in a heavily technology-dependent financial services company with nearly $2 billion in annual revenue. Played an integral role in enterprise infrastructure planning and change management. Analyzed business needs; researched leading-edge technologies, vendors, and equipment to develop sophisticated yet practical business solutions to enhance business agility and competitive advantage.

MATTHEW J. OLDHAM page 2

Coordinated strategic and tactical direction for voice and data infrastructure in close collaboration with the Network Services team and 4 infrastructure colleagues. Authored LAN/WAN standards and procedures; established common monitoring practices and activities. Conducted periodic performance/configuration reviews; identified potential risk. Presented findings and improvement/upgrade recommendations to executive IS management.

Managed relationships with strategic vendors and business partners. Helped estimate equipment requirements and implement solutions. Assisted project, operations, quality assurance, and infrastructure managers with staffing issues and status updates. Performed quality testing; held final approval on test processes and migration. Documented voice and data systems architecture and integration.

Resolved network planning, architecture, implementation, maintenance, security, and support issues. Managed enterprise network issues involving 900 servers, 3000 branches, and 1,800 employees; imaging and COLD systems; multifunctional Avaya (voice) systems and services; customer order flow; market-maker interfaces; market data feeds; and regulatory interfaces to SEC, NASDAQ, OATS, DTC, and OCC; as well as systems/applications technical support.

Directed troubleshooting of production networking issues related to bridging loops, WAN connectivity, network slowness, and server connectivity issues. Provided single point-of-contact for all major voice/data outages requiring Avaya and/or Cisco TAC escalation. Managed an 8-member technical team.

- Designed state-of-the-art core and edge network for multimillion-dollar, 20,000+-sq.-ft. data center.
- Developed DWDM/Ethernet solution incorporating AT&T UVN for geographically diverse MAN connecting 3-building campus and remote disaster-recovery site.
- Helped develop new Internet hosting architecture to accommodate fault tolerance using F5 BIG-IP global traffic manager (GSLB) to distribute end-user application requests according to business policies and network conditions, ensuring highest possible availability between geographically diverse data centers.
- Partnered with AT&T to design 270+ MPLS branch network and plan migration path from PRN to MPLS.
- Designed and implemented "NICE" centralized auto recording solution enterprise-wide, working in conjunction with Avaya equipment, VoIP and CMAPI technologies, and eliminating the need for dedicated recording servers in each branch office.
- Maintained and supported a network of ±270 Cisco routers and switches and VPN concentrators.
- Designed, coordinated, and supervised installation of fiber and copper cabling schemes at remote branch locations. Installed and supported various Avaya phone systems including Partner and Definity, G250, G350, and G650. Coordinated remote office data network/voice equipment installations and relocations (including WAN provisioning) with MCI and Verizon telecom vendors.
- Audited the Network Services team's adherence to policies and procedures.
- Created logical maps of new network designs/layout in Visio for ease of troubleshooting.

Network Engineer II/Team Lead (6/00–3/05); **Network Engineer I** (10/94–5/00)
Planned, designed, and managed enterprise-wide voice and data network; monitored performance and performed statistical capacity reviews to assure seamless transitions when new components, systems, or locations were added. Provided escalated technical support for headquarters data communication hardware and software. Oversaw tier-1 and tier-2 issue resolution with respect to routers and switches. Managed 4 network technicians/administrators.

- Installed new wiring in the headquarters data center and offices, enabling PC LAN/WAN communication to 300 employees and 40 branches nationwide.
- Migrated Inter-Tel telecom switch to Avaya Definity G3Si switch and Intuity voicemail, 1999.

▶ PROFESSIONAL TRAINING/EDUCATION

Avaya Definity Call Vectoring Programming • Avaya Definity Administration

B. S., Computer Science, Emphasis: Information Management
Washington University, St. Louis, MO

14

Specialty Area: Technology, Science, and Engineering
Writer: Stephanie Clark

Robert de Groot

161 Rosewood Blvd. · Cambridge, ON N1T 8J5 · 519.622.8122 · degroot@yahoo.ca

Innovative Mechanical Designer

CAD/CAM software	Quality & Continuous Improvement	Project Management
Unigraphics, Solid Works, Solid Edge, AutoCAD, VisiCAD, MasterCAM, Machining Strategist	Six Sigma Greenbelt, FMEA, Kaizen, SIPOC, Statistical Evaluation, Root Cause Analysis	WBS, Project & Communication Planning, Network Diagrams, Earned Value Concepts, Risk Management

Strengths

- Honours graduate with 10+ years' progressive and diverse experience in Mechanical Design.
- Advanced knowledge of Microsoft Office and CAD/CAM software: Solid Works (6000+ hours); Unigraphics (6000+ hours); excel in learning new CAD applications.
- Demonstrated skills in identifying problems and finding appropriate solutions; knowledge of analytical techniques, such as FEA. *"Robert continues to challenge himself with difficult projects…he makes improvements where others have not."* – Team Leader
- True team player who works without friction with diverse people. *"Robert is without ego or arrogance…respects the core values at Hercules and reflects how people should act."* – Team Leader
- Enrolled in Project Management Professional Development Program through McMaster University with expected completion in 2008.

Professional Experience

HERCULES INJECTION MOLDING SYSTEMS, Cobourg, ON 2004–present

Hercules is the world's market leader of injection-molding equipment and services to the plastics industry (80% share of global PET preform market), with 2006 sales approaching $1 billion US.

Tooling Designer

Design PET molds ranging from single-cavity prototypes to 144-cavity production molds; work closely with engineering team and machine and hot-runner designers; deliver continuous process improvement strategies; work on PDM equivalent software (Teamcenter), and MRP equivalent software (Baan).

Selected Accomplishments:

- Liaising between teams, developed an easy-to-use standardized process in the form of an Excel tool that reduced scrap and saved $200,000 in its first year
- Led team of 12 in a 6-month project to produce a project management and training tool – a mold design manual – that standardized drawings and processes; this initiative shaved 10% from project timelines and improved product quality more than 25%.
- Charged with scheduling project designs and stepping into roles of Production Engineer and Team Leader, as necessary.
- Completed Greenbelt training, which has significantly improved my ability to evaluate data and make recommendations as to an idea's viability.

▶

Robert de Groot

Page 2

BENNETT PRECISION TOOLING Pty Ltd., Sydney, Australia 2003–2004
Established in 1981, now a leading designer and manufacturer of injection molds, blow molds, special purpose machines, gauges, precision machining and grinding.

Mechanical Designer / Product Designer – Prepared engineering drawings for the manufacture of injection, blow, and vacuum mold tools and designed electrodes for use in their manufacture.

Selected Accomplishments:

- Initially hired on a 3-month working holiday visa; based on superior work produced, this business sponsored me on a temporary business visa allowing me to remain with the company for the duration of my wife's post-secondary Australian schooling.
- Designed innovative "one-time-use" injection-molded medical devices.

ATS AUTOMATION TOOLING SYSTEMS, Cambridge, ON 2000–2003
A global manufacturer of automation technology for micro-electronic and telecommunications industries.

Senior Product Designer – Developed working drawings for prototypes and for customer proposals; designed prototype tooling and fixtures for manufacturing and inspection.

Selected Accomplishments:

- As the only senior designer, produced drawings for experimental prototypes.
- Member of team that produced 3 winning micro-electronic products: heat sink, plastic heat-sink clip, and compact server fan; customers include Intel, Dell, and Hewlett Packard. Further, participated in product certification for export, implementing foreign safety requirements; clip is now patent pending.

ULTRATECH TOOL AND GAUGE, Cambridge, ON 1999–2000
Relative newcomer dedicated to quality, innovation, and the use of advanced technologies.

Mechanical Designer/Draftsperson – Designed inspection gauges for stamped metal/plastic molded parts; assisted in product and process reviews.

- Received training on Solid Edge advanced software.

TECHNICAN PACIFIC INDUSTRIES, Brantford, ON 1996–1999
In business for over twenty years manufacturing quality custom swimming pool products.

Mechanical Designer – Designed custom pool liners; prepared engineering drawings.

- Secured this position upon completion of schooling and on my instructor's recommendation to Technican's Production Manager, who had been a previous student.
- Began as the junior member of a 3-person team; given progressively senior responsibilities such as use of the advanced CAD and 3D engineering drawings.
- Offered position of Team Leader as incentive to remain with company.

Education & Training

Project Management Professional Development Program – Master Certificate
Expected completion in 2008 – first course achieved over 90%
McMaster University/CDI

Mechanical Engineering Technician – Honours Graduate
Conestoga College

Metal Machining & Manufacturing Techniques – Graduated top of class
Mohawk College

EXCELLENT REFERENCES AVAILABLE

15

Specialty Area: Managers and Executives
Writer: Linda Schnabel

TED WILSON, M.Sc. Management

283 Main Wood Drive ▪ Mississauga, Ontario ▪ LK1 1JL
Phone: 905.123.4567 ▪ tedw@sympatico.ca

BUSINESS, INFORMATION & ORGANIZATION CHANGE STRATEGIST

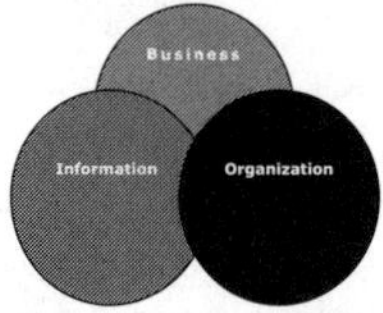

Optimizing results by aligning business processes, information technology, and organizational structure.

High-performing professional with an innate ability to align business, information, and organizational requirements to overall strategic goals. Energetic and visionary contributor who inspires teams, balances stakeholder needs, and integrates collective expertise to develop winning outcomes for manufacturing and high-tech industries. International experience and global perspective adds strength to overall profile.

Key Competencies:

- Performance & Process Revitalization
- Strategic Vision & Planning
- Project & Change Management
- "Intrepreneurial" Leadership
- Team Training & Coaching
- Knowledge Management
- Organizational Learning
- Employee Research
- Global Perspective
- Business Analysis

NOTEWORTHY CAREER HIGHLIGHTS

- **Acted** as EBM's project liaison to successfully support the implementation of a key customer's Automated Line Control System.
- **Assigned** by EBM's senior management to oversee two diverse teams for a three-month customer support project. In spite of cultural complexities related to Japanese parent, exceeded expectations.
- **Demonstrated** solid problem-solving skills to avert a major lean manufacturing challenge on customer assembly line; led troubleshooting team to analyze, define, and resolve acute equipment issues.
- **Coached** manufacturing sales representatives throughout Ontario in marketing and sales situations. Facilitated increased consultative marketing and sales for EBM.
- **Architected** decision-making framework to clarify "build or buy" options for client's systems requirements. Conducted complete application requirements analysis and systems audit that led to implementation of ERP.
- **Utilized** "Seven Tools of Management" to engage client stakeholder group, leading to successful process optimization that supported exponential acquisition growth.
- **Managed** the roll-out of a new ERP process for international company that included development and implementation of project plan for all sales and marketing activities globally.
- **Conducted** manufacturing plant audit of business, information, and organization. Streamlined operations, reduced inventory, and developed project plan that led to Class "A" certification.
- **Wrote** thesis in conjunction with extensive research project, which clearly defined components of a learning organization. Granted M.Sc. Management degree, augmenting practical hands-on B.I.O. expertise.

Continued page 2...

TED WILSON, M.Sc., B.Sc. Page Two ▪ 905.123.4567 ▪ tedw@sympatico.ca

CAREER CHRONOLOGY

Ted Wilson Associates International – Mississauga, ON **2006–Present**

INDEPENDENT BIO CONSULTANT

- Provide BIO change strategies that optimize processes for small and medium-sized businesses in GTA.

Professional Sabbatical, Great Britian **2003–2005**

- Designed and launched two-year sabbatical to include postgraduate studies at Liverpool Hope University. Awarded M.Sc. Management degree.

EBM Canada Ltd – Toronto, ON **1997–2003**

The province's largest provider of IT services, hardware, and software, EBM develops innovative solutions for an impressive client list across 10 industries.

MAJOR ACCOUNT MANAGEMENT, MARKETING & SALES

Accountable for major OEM in the automotive manufacturing sector. Quarterbacked all communication and touch points within EBM for major clients. Managed bugets of up to $5M and cross-functional teams of up to 40 players.

MANUFACTURING INDUSTRY MENTOR

Responsible for analysis of BIO processes; coached EBM account representatives to fully identify and address clients' operational challenges.

APPLICATIONS MARKETING & SALES MANAGER

Responsible for marketing and sales of a third-party product (online purchasing system) for EBM.

Wilco International – Mississauga, ON **1995–1997**

One of the largest ERP software vendors with head office in Germany.

INTERNATIONAL MARKETING MANAGER

Co-led the international roll-out of Wilco V Process, a new ERP application, for the process industry. Accountable for project plan for marketing and sales, including all elements required to launch new application: market analysis, education and training, image building, distribution, and support.

Contact Equipment Corporation of Canada – Toronto, ON **1986–1994**

One of the largest information technolgy systems organizations in the world.

NATIONAL ACCOUNT MANAGER

Responsible to quarterback all sales efforts for Canadian accounts. Led national sales representatives.

EDUCATION & PROFESSIONAL DEVELOPMENT

- **Management Studies** ▪ Liverpool University – Liverpool, England
- **Computer Science** ▪ York University – Toronto, Ontario
- **Adult Teaching & Training** ▪ Durham College – Oshawa, Ontario
- **Operational Management** ▪ Durham College – Oshawa, Ontario

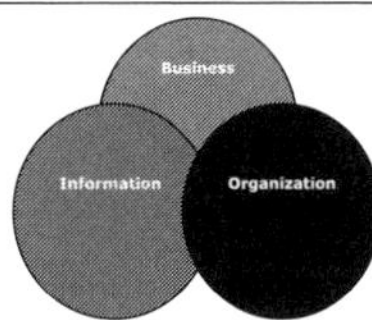

Optimizing results by aligning business processes, information technology, and organizational structure.

16

Specialty Area: Managers and Executives
Writer: Susan Guarneri

SHARON C. CLEMENTS
2721 Abernathy Drive, Columbia, MD 21044
(410) 997-7521 Home ▪ (703) 771-8113 Mobile ▪ sharonclem@newmedia.com

Operations Management Executive
Area Director / Regional Director ▪ General Manager ▪ Operations Manager

General/Operations Management professional with creative vision and flawless execution. Proven expertise in expanding product/program lines, increasing revenue streams, and capturing market share in highly competitive Health and Fitness industry. Leadership role in health and fitness clubs expansion (15 greenfields and 10 acquisitions). Key contributor to market dominance on East Coast.

Hands-on P&L role in strategic planning and initiative management, multi-site operations, recruitment and training (60 management and 1000 line staff), team building, and project management. Met or exceeded revenue/development expectations for 20+ years. Experienced in:

- ☑ Revenue & Market Expansion
- ☑ Staff & Management Development
- ☑ Budget & Financial Performance
- ☑ Change Management
- ☑ Sales & Marketing
- ☑ HR Management
- ☑ Start-ups & Acquisitions
- ☑ Business Development
- ☑ Branding & Technology

PROFESSIONAL EXPERIENCE

FITNESS CLUBS INTERNATIONAL, Washington, DC (corporate headquarters) 1985–2007
Leader in Health & Fitness Industry, ranked 2nd in U.S. and 7th worldwide (based on revenues) with 365,000 members at 132 clubs and 7,200 employees.

General Manager – Columbia Fitness Club (CFC), Columbia, MD (2004-2007)
Full P&L responsibility for sports club ranked 1st in suburban-DC market. Managed 20,000 SF club with 2000 members, and supervised 40 management and line staff. Key player in strategic planning, business development, operations, sales and marketing, brand building, PR and community relations, customer service/retention, human resources, administration, and technology performance.

ACCOMPLISHMENTS

Challenged in company restructure and brand-building initiative to deliver smooth-running, profitable operations and sales in high-profile fitness club facility. By 2006 Voted "Best Health Club" in DC-Metro area. Introduced new product and service lines, negotiated cost reductions (from 10% to cost of item) with vendors, collaborated in succession planning and team building, and led major revenue and profitability increases (demonstrated by financial metrics below):

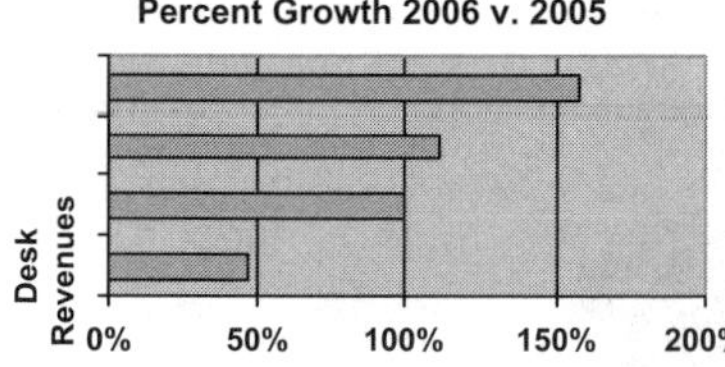

2006 v. 2005

PT Revenues: $509,136 v. $197,225
Gross Revenues: $1,863,790 v. $881,506
Membership Income: $1,544,748 v. $768,564
Desk Revenues: $27,541 v. $18,774

SHARON C. CLEMENTS Page 2
(410) 997-7521 Home ▪ (703) 771-8113 Mobile ▪ sharonclem@newmedia.com

Area Manager – CFC, Columbia, MD (1999–2003)
Oversaw operations and explosive growth of suburban-DC clubs. Full P&L responsibility for sales and marketing, systems, finance, SOP, customer service, multi-unit management, HR, initiative management, succession planning, recruitment, training, and management development.

- **Start-up and Acquisition Leader.** Delivered strong revenues and development results in soft market: spearheaded growth from 1 club with 500 members (starting revenues of $1.4M) to 6 clubs with 13,200 members and annual revenues of $14.5M (2003). Clubs ranged in size from 20,000 SF to 200,000 SF on 23 acres. Managed and motivated team that grew to 550 employees. Chosen as member of Washington DC Mayor's Health & Fitness Council Committee in 2003.
- **Technology Improvements.** Played key team role in 2002–2003 rollout of Club Networks, integrated enterprise software solution for sales reporting with online point-of-sale/real-time sales, tracking, financial, and reporting capability. In 2000 successfully launched automated Fitness Database, as well as online direct payroll processing IT system (Kronos).

General Manager – Washington, DC, Fitness Club (DCFC), Washington, DC (1990–1999)
Directed operations of largest sports club in DC market (8 locations), with full P&L responsibility. Supervised 30–60 management and line staff, including recruitment, training, and staff development.

- **Acquisitions and Revitalization.** Designated Lead Management Trainer for new Manager Orientation, including Senior Management. Initiated Employee Cross-Training Programs, New Employee and Customer Service seminars, monthly performance incentives, and SOP guidelines for training, operations, maintenance, tracking, and production. Negotiated cost-saving contracts with outside vendors. Oversaw multimillion-dollar club renovations.
- **New Technology and Products.** In 1997, transitioned club from manual to computerized system for sales tracking (Sales, Leads and Management System software), increasing accuracy and turnaround time for sales reporting. First to introduce electronic funds transfer.

Previous FCI Career History:
Progressive promotions from Sales Consultant through Sales Supervisor to Area Membership Supervisor (supervised 36) as company grew from 3 to 9 locations. Set year-over-year (YOY) sales records, pre-sold and assisted in opening 7 clubs, and initiated performance improvement processes.

EDUCATION & AWARDS

Bachelor's Degree Program, University of Maryland, College Park, MD
Certificate, Managing Performance, American Management Association (AMA), 1999
Certificate, The Manager's Role in Professional Management, AMA, 1998
International Racquet Sports Association (IRSA) Conventions & Seminars, 1986–1998

Fitness Clubs International (FCI) Management & Sales Awards
Service Recognition Award for Outstanding Achievement in Sales & Marketing, 1999
Certificate of Achievement "Employee Primer" Award, 1997
Certificate of Achievement for "greatest drop in cancellation percentage," 1996

17

Specialty Area: Managers and Executives
Writer: Sharon Pierce-Williams

ABIGAIL LAURENT

1304 Durango Drive ▪ Denver, CO 80537
Phone: 970.348.0434 ▪ Mobile: 970.722.5081
Email: alaurent@another.com

* SENIOR OPERATIONS EXECUTIVE *

Drive Exceptional Business Performance through a Tenacious Quality Focus and a Devotion to Manufacturing Operations Excellence

Professional integrity, a big-picture focus, and a history of driving significant gains in profitability are the cornerstones of a career distinguished by sustained accomplishments. Respected as intuitive start-up and turnaround strategist and record-breaking implementation leader. **Possess global manufacturing perspective** with 15 years' experience in the international arena with partners, suppliers, and contract manufacturers, including 5 years' residence in China. **Conversational Mandarin.**

- **Identified as top-performing manager** and handpicked to tackle the toughest assignments; rocketed through positions of increased responsibility at ABC. Formulate performance metrics, strategic plans, and sustainable processes **enabling companies to achieve unparalleled success.**
- **Grew Shanghai manufacturing site output 942% in 5 years—site 37+% of business group's total revenue.** Final production output represented a $1M per-day business revenue generator.
- **Experienced in acquisition integration,** including multicultural manufacturing and distribution processes. Planned and realigned organizational initiatives to position company for high growth.
- **Supported and ramped to volume 30+ new product introductions** across different markets and technologies.
- **Lead by influence,** as well as authority, to build strong collaborative organizations among competing resources while **developing top-notch multidisciplinary teams that reliably deliver.**

CAREER HIGHLIGHTS IN U.S. & GLOBAL MANUFACTURING MARKETS

XYZ TECHNOLOGIES, INC., Palo Alto, CA 1998–2005

XYZ specializes in tools and technologies that drive productivity across the communications, electronics, life sciences, and biotech industries with 28K+ employees worldwide and $10B+ in annual revenue (a spin-off of ABC, Inc.)

Manufacturing Senior Manager, Shanghai, China – 2000–2005

Challenge Build a world-class manufacturing entity out of a state-owned enterprise and integrate the organization into the global order-fulfillment business.

Management Overview Negotiated, agreed, and executed cooperation among 3 sites for 5-year strategic product transfer. Steered operational efficiency improvements and provided growth engine for operations.

Goal To become the XYZ site of choice through exceptional performance.

SHANGHAI, CHINA SNAPSHOT

Total organization – 250 employees

Manufacturing size – 150 employees

$350M in legal revenue from a 10K square meter distribution center

$136M+ annual material procurement

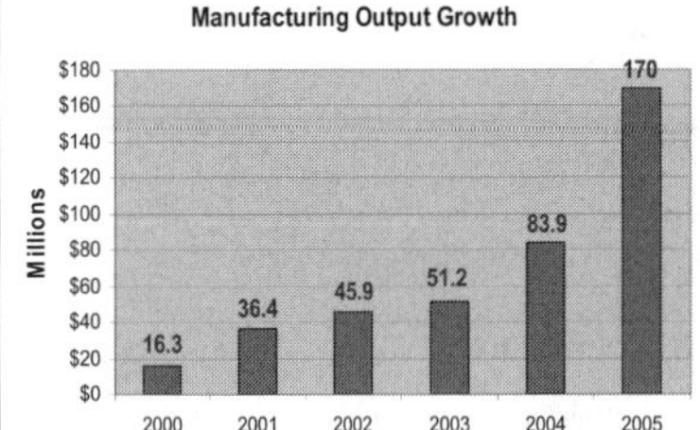

— PERFORMANCE BENCHMARKS & MILESTONES —

- Reduced overall headcount from 176 to 142 and decreased inventory days of supply from 120 to 51.
- Completed 47 product transfer projects on time, under budget, and with improved product quality.
- Improved material cost reductions from 1% to 5%, meeting an 8.7% reduction that reduced cost of sales 1.2% in 2005.
- **Skills development process and format became site standard in all departments.**
- China Manufacturing recognized at Board of Directors' meeting as competitive advantage for the critical China market efforts.

ABIGAIL LAURENT

1304 Durango Drive ▪ Denver, CO 80537
Phone: 970.348.0434 ▪ Mobile: 970.722.5081
Email: **alaurent@another.com**
Page 2

CAREER HIGHLIGHTS IN U.S. & GLOBAL MANUFACTURING MARKETS (continued)...

XYZ TECHNOLOGIES, INC., Palo Alto, CA 1998–2005

Materials Manager, Denver, CO – 1998–2000

Challenge Revitalize stagnant team while delivering critical business result — **material cost reduction of 3%.** Team supported new product and production materials for 15 distinct business units within ABC.

Management Overview Introduced 7 new products with no materials–related delays, while managing 13 additional products in process and on schedule.

Goals To empower teams to focus on core issues — new products, cost reduction, assurance of supply — and to identify outsourcing companies for context products and processes.

— PERFORMANCE BENCHMARKS & MILESTONES —

- **Delivered 5.37% total cost reduction to 4 major business units and *at least* the required 3% to the remaining 11 minor units.**
- Improved overall assurance of supply to lines from 63% to 90+%.
- **Developed cohesive, proud team that delivered; celebrated early results and wins.**
- Established outsource plan with Mexico and Singapore for 7 products, generating excellent results.

"Abby expects the best from those around her and, by example, gets it. We were given a seemingly impossible task, and she brought together a team that met and exceeded expectations. She expects and respects disagreements and manages to turn these into team-building opportunities." — Senior Buyer, XYZ Technologies, Inc.

ABC, INC., Palo Alto, CA 1984–1998

ABC is the world's largest IT company with operations in 170 countries, a team of 150K employees, and sales of $80B.

Production Manager, Denver, CO – 1997–1998
Manufacturing Development Engineer – 1995–1997
PhotoIntel Division, formerly Silver Springs Home Imaging Division

Challenge Design, justify, install, and implement a new factory for photo scanner launch. **First engineer hired** when product design was mere sketches on paper.

Management Overview Negotiated for available floor space to develop a Greenfield operation. Collaborated with R&D to fully understand product design; and with Marketing to establish product launch date, expected ramp rates, stable volumes, and sales distribution forecasts.

Goals Ensure stability and to maintain high quality standards at strong delivery volumes.

FACTORY EXPECTATIONS

Ramp product from $0 to $500M in less than 9 months.

Produce a good unit every 15 seconds for 2 shifts working at full capacity within 70 days.

Design criteria for factory delivered to total factory team – simple, flexible, and modular to accommodate critical optical alignment tools in a class 10000 clean room.

— PERFORMANCE BENCHMARKS & MILESTONES —

- **Total factory installation and capital costs less than $7M vs. target of $12M.**
- Achieved target productivity on all shifts within 60 days.
- **Day 1 product turn-on rate 78% vs. expected target of 40%.**
- **Long-term turn-on rate, 97.5%; previous best average for similar product, 47%.**
- **First product roll after 11 months;** easily integrated into manufacturing floor allowing for dual production and ease of introduction.

"This was the best manufacturing effort I have ever seen from any team in my 27 years." — Lead Design Product Engineer, ABC, Inc.

(continued)

(continued)

ABIGAIL LAURENT

1304 Durango Drive ▪ Denver, CO 80537
Phone: 970.348.0434 ▪ Mobile: 970.722.5081
Email: **alaurent@another.com**
Page 3

PREVIOUS POSITIONS WITHIN ABC, INC., Palo Alto, CA

Manufacturing Development Engineer
Denver Hardcopy Division Flatbed Scanners – 1994–1995
Fresco Printer Division Disc Drives and Surface Mount Center – 1992–1994

Industrial Engineer – 1990–1992
Silver Springs Industrial Division, Multi-Meters, Custom Test Systems

Manufacturing Process Engineer – 1984–1990
Colorado Springs Division, Logic Analyzers, Test Systems

— EDUCATION & PROFESSIONAL DEVELOPMENT —

Bachelor of Science, Industrial and Systems Engineering
University of Florida, Gainesville, FL

Master of Science, Manufacturing Management
National Technology University

******

PROFESSIONAL & MANAGEMENT TRAINING

(ABC and XYZ Technologies)
Value Chain: Managing the Cost of the Supply Chain
Six Sigma Training ▪ Lean Manufacturing
TQC Instructor

"Climbing Your Own Everest" Leadership ▪ Optima Performance Coaching
Fundamentals for Leaders ▪ 7 Habits of Highly Effective People
Decker's Effective Communication ▪ Conflict Management
Dialogue Training ▪ Covey Leadership

******

PROFESSIONAL ASSOCIATIONS

Institute of Industrial Engineers (IIE)
Institute for Supply Chain Management (SCM)
International Who's Who of Business

******

KEYNOTE SPEAKER

"Start–Up Business Challenges," Technical Women's Conference, Ft. Collins, CO – 1996

BUSINESS PHILOSOPHY ...

As an influential leader with a record of initiating change, I consistently deliver results in reduced costs, increased quality, and increased profitability. My passion for working in manufacturing provides a resolute energy that springs from raising levels of performance through goal-oriented teams with unmatched loyalty. I am intrigued by the unique qualities of individuals and recognize that the secret to great teams is casting by individual strengths. A strong discipline and the diffusion of innovative solutions through actionable knowledge lead to solid performances even in the midst of economic turndowns.

— Abigail Laurent

18

Specialty Area: Managers and Executives
Writer: Meg Guiseppi

Robert Alden

Mobile: (999) 212-9314 ■ Email: Bob@toprealestate.com
234 Westfield Road ■ Parsippany, New Jersey 07004

Real Estate — Sales, Marketing & Operations Executive

Start-Up & Turnaround . . . Business Development & Rapid Growth . . . Multiple Site Operations
New Products & Services Launch . . . Recruitment & Training of Top-Producing Teams

Strategic leader with strong track record of advancing businesses through start-up and expansion to tremendous growth. Powerful combination of sales acumen and vision-branding to position new enterprises ahead of well-established competitors. Deep expertise in operations, marketing, budget management, financial affairs, and banking relationships. Entrepreneurial passion and talent for recruiting quality sales teams and instilling corporate vision. MBA in Finance. Willing to relocate.

Professional Experience

Founder/President
Top Real Estate Consultants, LLC, Parsippany, NJ 2000 to 2007

Conceptualized, rapidly grew, and sold nontraditional real estate firm with one centralized processing/ telecommunications center and over 100 virtual sales professionals positioned throughout northern New Jersey. Systematized and directed entire operation including marketing, training, key corporate account development, communications, human resources, risk reduction, outside vendor negotiations, legal affairs, financial/accounting functions, and website development.

- Created turnkey marketing and processing system earning associates substantially higher commissions than with previous real estate firms and a close ratio 3–4 times higher.
- Showed nice profit within first year and grew company dramatically each year, despite frequent downturns in local real estate market. Achieved sales volume of $237 million in 2006.
- On a limited budget, branded a quality company image through high-impact advertising and marketing campaigns — newspapers, magazines, direct mail, outdoor advertising, video, and website.
- Achieved customer satisfaction score of at least 95% for 5 years.
- Engaged and motivated sales associates to achieve maximum potential. Encouraged a culture of integrity and mutual respect.
- CEO and Operations Manager were confident enough of firm's continued growth to purchase operation in 2007.

Vice President (1994–2000), **General Manager** (1987–1994)
National Realtors, Parsippany, NJ, and Heritage Real Estate, Summit, NJ 1985 to 2000

Rapidly promoted at Heritage from Sales Associate through several management positions to General Manager. Singlehandedly led this small family business through tremendous growth, from one office with 4 sales associates to 12 sales offices and 2 administrative offices with over 200 sales associates. In 1992, transitioned Heritage through merger with National (a 30-office regional firm) and a 23% leap in sales volume within the first 6 months. Held full P&L responsibility, all strategic and business planning functions, budgeting, marketing, human resources, and administrative affairs. Benchmarked National as a strong competitor against larger regional firms, while branding its personalized sales approach.

(continued)

(continued)

Page 2

Robert Alden Mobile: (999) 212-9314

National Realtors, continued

Sales and Operations Management

- Increased market share and profitability by more than 300% over 7 years.
- Increased operating efficiency 30% within 4 months of merger.
- Cut advertising and marketing expense 15% within one year of merger while increasing revenue.
- Critical revenue-producing contributions included:
  - An ancillary mortgage company delivering 39% of pre-tax profits within 3 years.
  - A bank foreclosure department and expanded relocation department that gained dominant market share and national recognition.
  - A state-licensed and accredited real estate school that clearly branded the company's vision, enhanced its reputation, and accessed high-potential sales associates.

Recruitment and Human Resource Development

- Deeply involved with recruiting and interviewing new sales associates to identify high-quality, top-producing professionals.
- Advanced company's brand through the creation of specialized training for new associates along with numerous ongoing business-enhancing seminars, ranging from basic selling skills to company culture. Training models are still in use today at National.
- Followed up initial training with mentoring strategy that coupled experienced sales professionals with new associates, resulting in more immediate sales results.
- Pioneered incentive program offering more lucrative compensation packages.

Marketing

- Created all advertising and marketing strategies including newspaper, magazines, billboards, comprehensive presentation manual, and public/community relations. Designed and systematized a high-response direct mail campaign.
- Produced and distributed three annual marketing promotional magazines.
- Continuously updated business plan and marketing strategies to adjust to ever-changing market conditions.

Previous Real Estate Sales experience (6 years) includes **Sales Associate** for Green Valley Realtors and Morristown Real Estate in Morris County, New Jersey.

- Earned Multimillion-Dollar Sales Award each year with both firms.

Education

MBA, Finance, Fordham University (1989)
BA, Marketing, New York University (1984)

19

Specialty Area: Managers and Executives
Writer: Louise Garver

DAVID SOMERS

133 Reymore Drive • Croton, NY 10438

SALES & MARKETING EXECUTIVE

914.555.6653 • dsommers@best.net

PROFILE ***Executing tactical sales and marketing plans that delivered $75+MM in new business throughout career.***
Creating and seizing new business opportunities by penetrating untapped vertical markets.
Pioneering innovative product/application development and market launch.

Expert in building, motivating and leading top-tier sales teams from the ground up … defining sales strategy … identifying profitable market trends and product categories … forging productive business partnerships/alliances/networks—to achieve strong and sustainable revenue and profit growth in start-up to multibillion-dollar enterprises.

Exceptional at developing, cultivating, and managing long-standing high-level customer/account relationships through consultative-selling strengths. Talent for building trust as well as bringing together, aligning, and leading groups to work in concert to achieve successful results.

PROFESSIONAL EXPERIENCE & ACCOMPLISHMENTS

Executive Vice President – Sales & Marketing Advanced Technologies LLC, Croton, NY • 2001 to 2004

Recruited to spearhead the marketing, launch, and sales throughout the Americas of an innovative technology that creates virtual private networks requiring no administration, end-user training, installation, or configuration. Recruited and trained independent sales force; managed $1.5MM product-development budget. Instrumental in attracting investors and establishing strategic business partnerships; secured 2 rounds of financing through private equity and VC firms.

Refocused company and repositioned the software technology as a product that allows large corporations to build customer relationships at reduced costs through a private mass-marketing Internet application—and as an affordable business tool sold to small businesses through mass-market retailers. Directed development of product packaging, marketing materials, advertising, and website.

- Developed concept and delivered more than $1MM in opening product orders of the world's first user-friendly private network—marketed through select major retailers. Launched product into 4000 distributors throughout the Americas.
- Led product sales efforts at major US companies and numerous advertising, marketing and promotion agencies. Sold pilot programs to 2 corporations, resulting in $1.5MM in contract value.
- Built core business sales to ISPs and telecom companies by landing a pivotal contract with an extremely difficult-to-penetrate company—the largest telecom in Latin America with US holdings.
  —First-year revenues projected at $750K and $2MM annually, thereafter. Contract provides private network capability to 500,000 large and small businesses in Mexico.

Rescued Company from post-dot-bomb-bust liquidity crisis by persuading investors to change the business model to develop and sell product directly to end-users. Teamed with major suppliers such as Hitachi Data Systems, bandwidth suppliers, and retailers to embrace the new model. Negotiated with Hitachi to provide all infrastructure requirements at no cost and to use the Hitachi brand logo to inspire customer confidence.

- Attracted the necessary new investors, retailers, and distributors by tapping personal network of contacts to draw attention of the world's most influential technology columnist for the *Wall Street Journal.* Garnered excellent media coverage through the *WSJ* and *CRN* magazine.
- Successfully penetrated target retailers and distribution partners by sourcing a key independent manufacturer's rep firm that had launched major players' product lines into mass-market retail.

Led organization through post-9/11 slump by designing a new business model for retailers and distributor partners, affording them high margins and recurring revenue.

- Developed subscription-based service model with gross margin of 80% that could be sold through 2- or 3-step distribution providing partners with 15% to 50% margins with recurring revenue opportunities.

(continued)

(continued)

DAVID SOMERS **PAGE 2**

Vice President, Cross Sales & Corporate Marketing Intertech Corp., White Plains, NY • 1996 to 2001

Developed and executed sales plans that integrated cross sales and improved sales efficiency between 5 operating units of a $150MM domestic and international supplier of merchandising and marketing services. Directed the software development business, as well, which included new e-training applications among the first to be launched using browser-based technology. Managed 5 Sales VPs and a sales team of 60 indirect reports; revenue accountability of $9MM–$12MM.

Captured $14MM in cross-selling opportunities within first 12 months by opening communication channels and building trust between the operating units and corporate headquarters. Created a corporate brand to replace individual operating units' local or regional focus. Designed compensation program that rewarded sales team for cross selling without double-counting revenue.

- Dramatically increased overall sales, reduced high turnover, and improved morale at an underperforming operating company by creating a centralized outbound call center—freeing outside sales force to pursue larger, more lucrative contracts. Results: $1MM in new contracts monthly since implementation.
- Improved communication flow and service satisfaction between operating companies and their customers through implementation of enterprise-wide contact management software.

Took charge of a flagging, behind-schedule online training application development project in the Internet division. Delivered product in just 3 months to the "rave reviews" of customers and $3MM in annual sales.

Account Manager Sandburst Inc., Chicago, IL • 1989 to 1996

Recruited by $1.5B global leader in integrated performance improvement, incentive travel, and marketing research services to develop new business for 5 holding companies in the metro New York area. Managed all aspects of client relationships with several Fortune 500 accounts—from initial sales to follow-up and service, including P&L responsibility for client portfolios. Supervised 4 account executives on the account team.

During tenure achieved annual sales growth from $3MM in year one to $24MM, with gross margins above 40%, in the most competitive region in US. Consistently ranked among top 5% of 300 Account Managers nationwide. 4-time winner of the Company's "Master Award" as a top producer (at least $1.5MM annually) and 2-time Standards of Excellence Award winner.

- Within first 60 days of hire, captured a $3.3MM telecom contract, which Sandburst had never been able to penetrate, through exceptional relationship building and knowledge of prospect's marketplace, industry, and future needs.

  —Expanded contract to service 22+ different organizations over 6 years, producing $6+MM at gross margins above 45%.

  —Awarded for landing the account—only the 3rd account manager in Company's 25-year history to earn award.
- Promoted to manage long-standing $50MM account and succeeded in retaining the historically difficult client on the verge of severing ties with Sandburst.

  —Led team that increased account sales in consumer incentives by more than $11MM over 4 years.

  —Rescued the account—after client decided to rely on in-house sales department—by expanding relationship to client's other departments. Increased sales more than 25% in one year despite lost consumer incentives revenues.

  —Managed largest trade promotion in the account's history, which included an Emmy-winning launch video, and guided brand groups to create 2 successful consumer promotions, one of which was an award winner.

EDUCATION & PROFESSIONAL AFFILIATIONS

Bachelor of Science in Business Management
Fordham University, New York, NY

American Marketing Association

20

Specialty Area: Practice Limited to Executives
Writer: Abby Locke

TROY PATTERSON

20810 Hazelnut Grove
Waldorf, MD 20603
Email: tpatterson@aol.com
Residence: 301-555-7454
Cellular: 301-625-9856

SENIOR OPERATIONS & MANAGEMENT EXECUTIVE

US & International Markets – High-Growth Companies – Executive Consulting

Exude high level of personal integrity and professionalism that raises the standards on organizational leadership and executive management

EXECUTIVE PROFILE

- Consummate leader able to seamlessly bring together diverse, multicultural groups to one accord; unique talent for encouraging true collaboration and cohesiveness. Fluent in Spanish.
- Innovative visionary, focused on practical problem solving and delivering positive results. Prominent career marked with consistent record of top work performance and organizational achievements.
- Articulate communicator with demonstrated ability to effectively navigate organizations through highly sensitive or politically charged situations.
- Ideal leader to direct and promote sound business principles and incorporate new vision to move organizations forward. Sought to head priority initiatives and originate new programs.
- Hold Sensitive Compartmentalized Information (SCI) and Top Secret (TS) security clearances.
- Possess access to influential corporate and government executives and international security networks.

CORE EXECUTIVE QUALIFICATIONS

• Strategic / Tactical Planning	• Staff Development	• Crisis Management / Security Operations
• EEO / Affirmative Action	• Media & Public Relations	• Change & Turnaround Management
• Financial Management	• Succession Planning	• Budget Planning, Development & Control
• Diversity Training	• Emergency Preparedness	• Problem & Conflict Resolution
• Team Building	• Recruiting, Staffing & Training	• Program Development / Implementation
• Organizational Leadership	• Interagency Relations	• Strategic Alliances & Partnerships
• Relationship Management	• Influencing Decision-Makers	• Government & International Relations
• Policy Formulation	• Investigations Management	• Process & Productivity Improvement

CAREER ACHIEVEMENTS & PERFORMANCE HIGHLIGHTS

Over 25 years of career leadership experience with the United States Drug Enforcement Administration (DEA) marked with steady promotions to lead challenging drug operations in the United States and Latin America. Scope of responsibilities included divisional and regional leadership, operations management, human resource administration, financial management, and public affairs.

Recognized for exceptional work performance and outstanding contributions to agency's growth and operational success while efficiently meeting unique political, economic, and organizational challenges. Key executive management assignments, both foreign and domestic:

DEA ASSISTANT SPECIAL AGENT-IN-CHARGE, Washington, DC (2005 to present)

Provide pivotal leadership at the Washington Division heading federal drug operations in Washington DC, Maryland, northern Virginia, and West Virginia. Direct Division administration, allocate budgets, and oversee high-profile programs including recruitment, personnel training, demand reduction, and division special projects. **Created and developed "first-ever" division leadership program providing mid-level personnel with mentoring and regular exposure to executive management activities.**

▪ **Human Resource Management:** Pioneered complete turnaround in office morale and division productivity by instituting year-long training in financial management and general administration; encouraged ongoing collaboration and teamwork that resulted in increased financial performance, better qualified personnel, and improved employee commitment.

(continued)

(continued)

TROY PATTERSON **Page Two of Three**

CAREER DEVELOPMENT & PERFORMANCE HIGHLIGHTS ***continued***

ASSISTANT SPECIAL AGENT-IN-CHARGE ***continued***

- **Program Management:** Revitalized recruitment program by assessing program effectiveness and creating increased momentum for achieving annual goals. Program has exceeded expectations and is acknowledged as "best-of-its-kind" nationwide.
- **Program Development:** Conceived and coordinated new leadership program to advance leadership opportunities for senior-level employees. Groundbreaking program, still in pilot stage, has received overwhelming endorsement from upper management and may be adopted agency-wide.

COUNTRY ATTACHÉ / ASSISTANT REGIONAL DIRECTOR, Lima, Peru (2002 to 2005)

Recruited to manage program efficiency and ensure operational productivity and personal safety for 60+ employees for fifth-largest DEA foreign office. Supported development of US foreign drug policy initiatives; served as top advisor to US Ambassador and senior representatives of Embassy Country Team. **Forged global partnerships and promoted cohesive strategies to support international and regional counter-narcotics programs in South America.**

- **Executive Management:** Directed counter-drug operations in Peru and Andean Region.
- **Budget Administration:** Administered $2 million operational budget with expanded oversight for federally funded programs exceeding $12 million.
- **Management Training:** Improved staff efficiency in budget controls and financial planning by incorporating training (financial management, budget planning, operational spending) for mid-level and executive-level managers assigned to foreign agency offices.
- **Consensus Building:** Employed continuous coalition and multi-agency coordination that resulted in improved police and government relations and significant achievements in program operations, joint strategies, and policy goals.

SENIOR EXECUTIVE STAFF MEMBER / CHIEF SPOKESMAN, Washington, DC (1999 to 2002)

Piloted all facets of public affairs program for the Office of Congressional & Public Affairs. Provided media guidance to senior executive staff on press briefings, network events, movies, and other related public information matters. Member of Administrator's Executive Staff and served as Chief Spokesman for agency. **Actively promoted public awareness programs to bring national and international attention and recognition to agency's mission and accomplishments.**

- **Public & Media Relations**: Liaised with national and international media representatives, scheduled live television and radio interviews, planned press conferences and appearances, and developed press releases.
- **Public Appearances**: Appeared on CNN, Court TV, C-Span, Univision, Telemundo, the History Channel, and Discovery Channel to profile and highlight agency's investigative successes, ongoing program development, and special events.
- **Process Improvements**: Led design and implementation of computerized tracking / retrieval system to store public information and media contacts. Database became "practical management tool" allowing division to effectively review media activities.
- **Project Management**: Conferred with museum design experts and Smithsonian Institute specialists for final design and planning phases of DEA Museum. Museum has been noted as "renowned cornerstone of public awareness on the history of drug abuse and federal law enforcement in America."

GROUP SUPERVISOR, Miami, FL (1996 to 1999)

Mobilized and guided team of specially trained Special Agents to arrest and immobilize violent drug offenders operating in rural and urban communities throughout Florida. Worked in concert with local and state law enforcement agencies and Department of Defense to review and approve counter-drug initiatives and programs.

- **Strategic Alliances**: Tapped into expansive pool of leaders from police forces, local government, community organizations, federal agencies, and state offices to synchronize enforcement activities to meet investigative and operational challenges.

TROY PATTERSON **Page Three of Three**

CAREER DEVELOPMENT & PERFORMANCE HIGHLIGHTS ***continued***

COUNTRY ATTACHÉ, Bogota, Colombia (1990 to 1996)
Directed and oversaw counter-drug and intelligence operations for six-year international tour in South America. Supervised Special Agents and administrative and foreign-national support personnel.

- **Strategic & Tactical Planning**: Established strategic vision and long-range planning for enforcement operations; set standards for staff recruiting and training; directed key international investigations; and supported institution-building initiatives according to US policy objectives.
- **Team Coordination**: Collaborated extensively with CIA Chiefs of Station and Departments of State and Defense on joint intelligence plan to accomplish established US drug and foreign policy objectives. Forged powerful coalitions and alliances with foreign police counterparts.

DEA SPECIAL AGENT / CRIMINAL INVESTIGATOR (1985 to 1990)
Began career after extensive specialized training at the DEA Academy. Assigned to the Boston Division and Rhode Island offices and honed investigative leadership skills including drug and money laundering crimes, undercover operability, surveillance techniques, and legal brief preparation. Responsible for the arrests, federal prosecution, and conviction of hundreds of drug criminals in the US and abroad.

EDUCATION & TRAINING

"Executive Leadership Institute," University of Florida, Miami, Florida: 2005
"Innovative Leadership Program," University of Virginia, Charlottesville, Virginia: 2004
"Executive Development Seminar," U.S. Office of Personnel Management, Washington, DC: 2000
"Leadership Management Assessment Program," U.S. Office of Personnel Management, Washington, DC: 1995

Bachelor of Science in Criminal Justice – John Jay College of Criminal Justice, New York, NY: 1985

21

Specialty Area: Practice Limited to Executives
Writer: Kathy Warwick

MICHAEL O. SHEA

246 Oakland Drive
West Chester, NY 12976
MShea6614@comcast.net
H: 914-858-0964
C: 914-662-6614

TECHNOLOGY EXECUTIVE – INTERNATIONAL OPERATIONS

Defining and driving strategic vision while bringing strong leadership to challenging situations.

Decisive leader able to use sound judgment to overcome complex business challenges within international and domestic environments. Key contributor to business and financial planning with ability to move companies forward.

Visionary thinker with global perspective and ability to make tough decisions that bring about positive results – clearly conveying company position to directors, employees, customers, government officials, and investors.

Results-oriented executive with reputation for no-nonsense attitude that gets the job done. Unparalleled talent hiring and managing smart, committed team players in nontraditional global environments.

- Conceived and executed startup strategy, raised private funding, hired key managers, secured international licenses, captured market share, and sold company to an internationally recognized industry leader – GTI.
- Broke longstanding industry monopoly to implement first U.S competitor in Guatemala – GTI.
- Gained 45% market share within 24 months, achieving profitability in first year of operation – Comtel.
- Managed $500M revenue responsibility, spanning 100+ worldwide markets. Focused on developing regions of Central/South America, Mexico, Caribbean, Africa, Middle East, South Asia, and Russia – RLW.

EXECUTIVE SKILLS

- Leadership & Organization Development
- International Business Management
- Geographic Management Diversity
- Cost Reduction Strategy
- Initial Capitalization & Subsequent Sales
- Startup Business Planning & Execution
- International Licensing and Regulations
- P&L Management
- Complex Contract Negotiations
- Revenue Stream & Market Share Strategy

PERFORMANCE HIGHLIGHTS

Leadership

Played lead role in managing the capital program, dramatically changing organization culture, improving efficiencies 18% per year, growing customer base 625%, and driving $19 billion protocol transformation – GTI.

Financial Planning

Raised $45M to establish the largest private-sector investment ever made in Haiti – Comtel. Raised $20M to become first cellular company to introduce competition to Guatemalan telecommunications marketplace – GTI.

Cost Reduction

Saved company $100M annually (50% of total expense category). Entered an out-of-control spending situation and implemented improved processes that had it cleaned up in 1 year – RLW.

Startup Operations

Managed startup and initial operation of two very successful companies in third-world countries, acquiring 25% market share in one year for TWT and 45% market share in two years for Comtel.

Global Operations

Negotiated international contracts and agreements in over 80 countries, working and lobbying with high-ranking government officials (Presidents/Prime Ministers) to break through barriers and obtain operating licenses – GTI.

CAREER DEVELOPMENT

GLOBAL TELECOM INTERNATIONAL (GTI) – New York, NY / Guatemala 2001–Present
Privately held wireless carrier providing nationwide service in the Republic of Guyana, South America.
PRESIDENT AND EXECUTIVE BOARD MEMBER

Recruited to lead privately held wireless company through startup stages with intention of sale in less than five years. Spearheaded pre-operational business plan development, license acquisitions, technology strategy, vendor selection, contract negotiations, network construction, and organization building. Held full P&L responsibility.

Managed geographically diverse organization with employees in Guatemala, NY, NJ, Washington DC, and LA. Reported directly to Board of Directors.

- Acquired 25% market share in first 12 months of GSM mobile operations.
- Grew Guyana subsidiary from zero to 120 employees and $20M invested in only 18 months.
- Raised $250M credit facility, 20-member due diligence team, and local investor groups to submit bid to purchase Bahamian government-owned phone company.
- Obtained licenses in Grenada, Guatemala, and Venezuela, implementing Guatemala before selling company.
- Attracted well-respected international competitor to purchase the company and maintain 119 employees.
- Negotiated contract with government/Prime Minister to improve investor confidence in Guatemala project. Secured various tax concessions and a 3-year moratorium on issuance of additional cellular licenses.

COMTEL – New York, NY / Haiti 1997–2001
Privately held CDMA mobile/cellular and wireless local-loop carrier in country of 8 million people.
PRESIDENT AND BOARD MEMBER

Brought on to break through barriers and lead first cellular carrier in Haiti. Managed all aspects of company and P&L during first two years of operation, with emphasis on technology strategy, supplier selection and management, contract negotiations, network construction, financing, regulatory compliance, interconnection negotiations, and marketing strategy. Raised $45M from private sector. Reported directly to Chairman and Board.

- Made huge social/economic impact in Haiti, bringing essential communication services to struggling country, often donating service to relief organizations, schools, and hospitals.
- Grew company from zero to 200+ employees and $50 million invested.

RLW INTERNATIONAL – New York, NY / Philadelphia, PA 1985–1997
Largest provider of communication services in the U.S., with expanding operations throughout South America.
VICE PRESIDENT / EXECUTIVE DIRECTOR – INTERNATIONAL SERVICES (NY), 1993–1997

Promoted to lead sales in 120 worldwide markets – managing offices in 33 countries – selling to large private and government owned carrier accounts. Negotiated international contracts, established product distribution agreements, interconnected with emerging carriers, and opened over 30 new markets.

Rapidly climbed corporate ladder during high-growth years, accumulating a wealth of experience in sales, engineering, and operations.

- Managed through complex, changing market conditions and deregulation to establish #1 market-share position.
- Rescued adversarial relationship with largest client (Telmex Mexico) after newly formed subsidiary of RLW began competing with client. Eventually grew the account.

(continued)

(continued)

MICHAEL O. SHEA **PAGE 3 OF 3**

CAREER DEVELOPMENT, Continued

DIRECTOR – INTERNATIONAL NETWORK ENGINEERING (Philadelphia), 1989–1993

Charged with producing cost reduction while leading functions such as long-range capacity planning, technology selection/design/configuration, short-term capacity provisioning/implementation, and performance management. Gained experience negotiating network interconnections with foreign operating companies.

- Increased network capacity more than 1000% during four-year period.

OPERATIONS AND ENGINEERING MANAGEMENT (NY), 1985–1989

Held management positions in Operations and Engineering – managing long-term planning groups to day-to-day, 24x7 operating organizations.

BOARD MEMBER EXPERIENCE

GLOBAL TELECOM INTERNATIONAL, 2002–Present
Executive Board Member for full-service monopoly carrier of Guatemala.

COMTEL, SA, 1997–2001
Executive Board Member for full-service competitive carrier in Haiti.

COSTA RICA TELECOM LIMITED (CRT), 1995–1997
Represented RLW ownership in CRT, a full-service monopoly carrier of Costa Rica. Served in unique environment of having private investors and the Costa Rica government as shareholders.

EDUCATION & CERTIFICATIONS

MASSACHUSETTS INSTITUTE OF TECHNOLOGY – M. S. Management

UNIVERSITY OF COLORADO – B.S. Business Administration – Concentration in Finance and Economics

PUBLICATIONS & SPEAKING ENGAGEMENTS

TECHNOLOGY INDUSTRY PUBLICATIONS – Articles on technology and operations, 2006, 2005

INTERNATIONAL TECHNOLOGY CONFERENCES – General and Panel Presenter, 2007, 2005, 2004

HITEC – FUTURE OF TECHNOLOGY – Specialty Participant, 2006, 2005

CTAM, *The Future of Broadband* – Panel Speaker, 2001, 2000

BUSINESS & COMMUNITY ACTIVITIES

Fund-Raiser Chairperson, American Heart Association ~ Fundraising Captain, Junior Achievement
Treasurer and Chairperson, Budget and Finance Committee, National Kidney Foundation
Treasurer, Business of Art Center ~ Advisory Board Member, Massachusetts Institute of Technology
Company Media Representation ~ Rotary of West Chester, Treasurer

22

Specialty Area: Practice Limited to Executives
Writer: Louise Kursmark

MICHAEL T. ADAMS

Email: Michael@MichaelAdams.com
Web Portfolio: www.MichaelAdams.com
Home: 415-741-0861 • *Cell:* 415-207-6519
29-A Reeds Wharf, San Francisco, CA 94105

CHIEF EXECUTIVE OFFICER

Multinational Fortune 500 Companies • Public & Private Global Enterprises

Accomplished executive with a flawless record of improving profits, building brands, and creating shareholder value:

- **Vyva:** Transformation to #1 market share, highest profitability and equity valuation in its marketplace, and largest US-owned brand portfolio.
- **Sands, Inc.:** Reversal of 4-year slide to 114% increase in stock value.
- **Frye Company:** Best sales and profit in company history.
- **Dynagoods:** Increase in sales and profits 3X, stock price from $8 to $85.

- **Value Creation**
- **Brand & Portfolio Building**
- **High-Growth Phase Management**
- **Turnarounds: Financial & Operational Restructuring**
- **Mergers & Acquisitions**

EXPERIENCE AND ACCOMPLISHMENTS

Vyva International — Oakland, CA, 2000–Present
$300M multi-brand, multi-channel, global optical and jewelry company
CHAIRMAN, PRESIDENT, AND CEO

Built the largest, most profitable company in its marketplace. Transformed unprofitable, illiquid, debt-defaulted company into a thriving corporation with world-recognized brands and the highest equity valuation of all companies in its sector. Developed an exceptional management team and a company-wide culture of performance excellence.

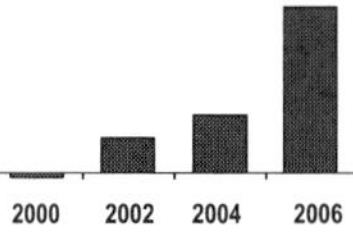

Profit Performance

Brand Building

- Created the largest US-owned optical brand portfolio by focusing growth strategy on high-value brands, divesting non-core businesses, and driving strategic acquisitions.
- Developed VyView to the top-selling sunglass brand, recognized among Top 100 Best Known Brands and Top 10 Accessories Brands by *Women's Wear Daily.*
- Achieved #1 market position for multiple product lines:
  - Sunglasses—improved from #3 to #1 with a 32% share.
  - Reading glasses—dominated the market with 47% share, #1 and #2 brands (VyVision and CoolVu).
- Licensed Levi's, Body Glove, Champion, other high-value brands to position Vyva for sustainable growth.
- Revitalized the "Vyva Viewers" advertising campaign, ranked in Top 100 Advertising Campaigns by *Advertising Age.* Brought on new celebrity endorsers Shania Twain and Nick Lachey.

Strategic Growth

- Successfully entered new markets (prescription frames, premium sunglasses) and built to 5% of sales by year 2.
- Turned around international division from earnings loss to the most profitable business in the company. Increased sales 15% and profits 33% annually and earned the leading market share in key countries.
- Transformed jewelry business from revenue and profit declines to double-digit revenue growth and profitability.
- Successfully acquired and integrated 2 companies, including 4 brands, in one year.

Financial and Operational Improvements

- Built the strongest capital structure in the industry. Completed all acquisitions without equity infusion.
- Built award-winning supply chain system, achieving 98% order accuracy and 99% on-time performance.

Sands, Inc. — Chicago, IL, 1996–1999
$600M Fortune 500 multi-brand company (NYSE)
EXECUTIVE VICE PRESIDENT

Brought on board to drive across-the-board performance improvements following 16 straight quarters of declining sales and profits. Provided vision and leadership to develop and execute successful turnaround and growth strategy.

(continued)

(continued)

MICHAEL T. ADAMS *Home:* 415-741-0861 • *Cell:* 415-207-6519 • Michael@MichaelAdams.com

EXECUTIVE VICE PRESIDENT, Sands, Inc., continued

Growth & Profit Performance

- Doubled stock value from $7 to $15 per share.
- Increased sales and profits each quarter in 4 straight years.

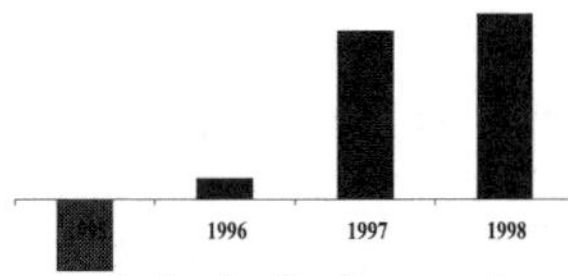

Earnings-Per-Share Improvement

Strategic Brand Building

- Defined core expertise as footwear brand management and increased brand portfolio from 3 to 7 brands; added powerful marketing value by licensing such brands as Tommy Hilfiger and Levi's.
- Restored vibrancy and vitality to 3 legacy brands. Improved products, revamped advertising, raised prices, and drove up profits.

Frye Company Los Angeles, CA, 1995–1996
$125M footwear and apparel manufacturer (OTC)
CHIEF OPERATING OFFICER (1995–1996)
MEMBER, BOARD OF DIRECTORS (1994–1996)

Recruited from Board for interim leadership role, achieved highest sales and profit in company history. Streamlined operations, improved profitability, and implemented operational systems and computer-based supply/demand matching that delivered the right products to the right places on time.

- Cut product costs 40% by increasing overseas production.
- Predicted and counteracted retail downturn—prevented losses by canceling 20% of factory orders, reducing expenses 12%, and eliminating $3M in excess inventory.

Dynagoods, Inc. Atlanta, GA, 1990–1995
$500M footwear and apparel wholesale and retail company
SENIOR VICE PRESIDENT

Planned and executed brand and operating strategy that resulted in Dynagoods' highest growth years. Repositioned brand to premium channels and price points. Built company-owned retail store chain. Initiated apparel business and positioned the brand overseas.

- Increased stock price from $8 to $85 by growing sales and profits 3X.
- Fourth best-performing stock on NYSE; recognized as most successful financial turnaround by Wall Street.
- Improved ROE from 9.8% to 21.5%.

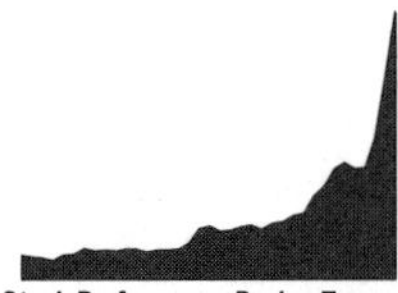
Stock Performance During Tenure

Experience Prior to 1990

- Southern Department Stores, Inc.: Vice President and Treasurer
- Adair, Inc.: Chief Financial Officer / General Manager, Altamare Division
- Sanfils, Inc.: Vice President and Treasurer / President, San Enterprises, Inc. (division)
- GM Finance Corporation: General Manager
- General Motors: Financial Analyst

EDUCATION / HONORS / PROFESSIONAL DISTINCTIONS

MBA, Graduate School of Business, Stanford University, Stanford, CA
BA Economics, Emory University, Atlanta, GA
Board of Directors, Adair, Inc.
Author, *Financial Strategies for Privately Held Companies* (Jossey-Bass, 1995)

23

Specialty Area: Military Transition
Writer: George Dutch

Patrick Rolston, MA

Home phone: 614-942-7242
Email: prolston@frederick.ca

TRAINING PROGRAM EVALUATOR

Specializing in the Evaluation of Systems Approach to Training (SAT)

Performance-driven professional offering 25+ years of advancement as a Training & Education specialist, including 10 years as a supervisor of up to 20 SAT specialists and staff in the Canadian Forces. Extensive experience with evaluation strategies, tools, and techniques. Subject matter expertise in Leadership and Development.

Relevant professional proficiencies:

- ✓ Expert knowledge of adult learning principles and training technologies for effective staff development.
- ✓ Extensive experience with evaluating and purchasing commercial-off-the-shelf (COTS) training packages.
- ✓ Significant contract management experience related to evaluation, project documentation, business case development, project initiation, documentation review, and contract supervision.
- ✓ Proven success in test measurement and evaluation procedures and strategies, including the application of statistical measurement to instructional programs.
- ✓ Commendations for team building and working with others; in particular, for helping managers to assume a new mindset on how to use day-to-day work experiences as participant learning experiences in accordance with development plans.

Strong competencies in:

Needs Assessment	Validation Plans & Reports	Computer-Assisted Training
Training Systems Analysis	Continuous Learning	Contract Negotiations
Design & Development	Training Models & Policies	Contract Supervision
Conduct & Evaluation	Human Performance Analysis	Presentations

Secret Security Clearance

NOTABLE STRENGTHS AND CAREER ACHIEVEMENTS

- **SNSC Competency Development System Pilot Study.** Prepared a Project Directive to explore approaches for development of current and newly appointed managers and development of competencies in staff aspiring to management positions. The Directive included details on how such a developmental approach could be implemented within the SNSC.
- **Manager Development.** Initiated three major programs for managers at SNSC: 360 degree evaluations with competencies; a coaching framework to assist managers in accessing the expertise of professional coaches; and a pilot Management Development Program led by managers to foster strengths of subordinates.
- **Needs Assessment.** Led a needs assessment for Post Traumatic Stress Disorder in the Canadian Forces, the first time that psychological disorders were recognized as a consequence of war zone service requiring accountability and treatment.
- **Leadership.** Promoted, coordinated, and implemented the application of SAT to the development of the Canadian Forces Individual Training & Education System (CFITES).

See* Addendum *for Training Achievements with Canadian Forces

(continued)

(continued)

Patrick Rolston, MA

page 2

CAREER HIGHLIGHTS

STANDARD NUCLEAR SAFETY COMMISSION (SNSC) 1999–present
(Federal government regulator for use of nuclear substances in Canada by licensees)

- **Training Specialist**, Programs and Learning Division, Oct 02–Present
  Research, implement, and evaluate performance improvement tools and techniques, including visioning, strategic thinking, business management, people management, adaptability, communication, stress reduction, and technical excellence.
  - Designed and implemented a Competency Development System to support leadership development as one of the six strategic objectives of the Commission.
  - Designed leadership material (self-assessment against competencies) that was used in annual management retreat.
  - Developed HR information sessions for first-line managers.

CANADIAN FORCES 1971–1999

- Staff Officer Training Support, Chief of Maritime Staff detachment, Halifax, NS
- Staff Officer Training Development, Maritime Command Headquarters, Halifax, NS
- Staff Officer Technology, Maritime Command Headquarters, Halifax, NS
- Staff Officer Technology, Canadian Forces Fleet School, Halifax, NS
- Chief Standards Officer at Combat Engineering Division, Canadian Forces Fleet School
- Personnel & Training Officer, Canadian Submarine Acquisition Project
- Staff Officer – Special Projects, Directorate of Individual Training
- Bridge Watchkeeping Officer & Assistant Weapons Officer, HMCS Huron
- Commanding Officer of YAG 312, Small Boats Unit, Esquimalt, BC
- Executive Staff Officer, National Defence College, Kingston, ON

EDUCATION

- M.A., Organizational Leadership & Training, Royal Roads University, Victoria, BC (2000)
  - Thesis topic: Adult Web-based Learning & Criteria for Success, published in *Training Magazine,* Issue 4, 2003, pp. 57–65.
- B.Ed., Queens University, Kingston, ON (1976)
- B.A., Physical & Health Education, Queens University, Kingston, ON (1975)

Relevant military training:
Officer Professional Development Program
Middle-Management Development Course
French Language Training

Advanced leadership courses and certifications:
Introduction to Professional Coaching, Integral Coaching Canada (2005)
Integrated Logistic Support Course, Montreal (1987)
Logistic Support Analysis Course, Ottawa (1989)

24

Specialty Area: Military Transition
Writer: Audrey Field

Sheldon Marrow

22 Stanton Blvd, Barrie, Ontario ▪ A1B 2C3
(h) 705.555.1234 ▪ (w) 705.555.5678 ext 1234 ▪ (e) info@resumeresources.ca

ELECTRONIC TECHNICIAN
Ready to support the operational readiness of a safety- and quality-focused environment.

Extensively qualified and resourceful electronics expert offering 20 years of maintenance and troubleshooting of several complex systems in world-class aerospace environments. Acknowledged throughout career as a reliable, proactive problem solver. Known for pinpointing critical factors in snags that have long-eluded others. Undaunted by stressful, time-pressing and unpredictable situations. Diplomatic communication capabilities easily pivot between people of diverse cultures, backgrounds, and technical and professional levels. Ready to support a civilian operation in July of 2007. **Strengths include:**

✓ Digital Systems & Fundamentals
✓ Preventive & Corrective Maintenance
✓ Navigation, Communication & Compass Systems
✓ Electrical Control Systems Removal & Installations
✓ Performance & Diagnostic Testing
✓ Technical Inspection & Quality Assurance
✓ Power Supplies
✓ Health, Safety & Procedural Adherence
✓ Calibration Functions
✓ Blueprints & Schematics Familiarization

EXPERIENCE NARRATIVE: Department of National Defence *(1987–Present)*

CFB BORDEN, ONTARIO, 2005 TO PRESENT

AVIONICS SYSTEMS TECHNICIAN

Handle wide scope of administrative details, such as aircraft forms, statistical data, maintenance logs, and internal memos. Exceptionally productive, taking over what was formerly considered two Avionics roles. Use Health and Usage Monitoring Systems (HUMS) to download cockpit voice and flight data. Accountable for all night-vision goggles and David Clark headsets and some battery charging. Requested to fulfill the section's Fire Warden duties: record fire prevention training, inspect equipment, and report safety hazards.

- Exercise natural team-building and mentoring qualities. Guide four rookie technicians both in the avionics lab and on the floor, emphasizing safety and procedural adherence while training for the full scope of job functions. Frequently requested to fill in for shop supervisor during times of absence.
- Reorganized and labeled the test equipment lockers for a more streamlined work-flow environment.
- Incorporated flowcharts for AF9000 Test Equipment Maintenance Management Information System (TEMMIS) procedures. Continued by relaying critical input towards the streamlining of the TEMMIS database and calibration due dates.
- In keeping with the AF9000 standards, review, evaluate, and update section Standard Operating Procedures (SOPs) every three months.
- Carry out performance tests, preventive/corrective maintenance, and calibration of aircraft communication, intercom, search radar, fire control radar, acoustic sensing, infrared radar, electronic warfare, navigation, compass, and flight control systems and their associated components.
- Communicate directly with incoming shift crews for flawless handover and to share the status of work in progress.

CFB COLD LAKE, ALBERTA, 2001 TO 2005

AVIONICS SYSTEMS TECHNICIAN

Served as first-line crew for the CF-18 Hornet. Dealt with systems for navigation, flight director communication, and flight controls, as well as tactical radar, ground power, and generators. Held accountable for all trades daily inspections and servicing. Performed servicing tasks such as marshalling, parking, towing, starting, refueling, cleaning, and de-icing.

Continued ⇨

(continued)

(continued)

Sheldon Marrow

EXPERIENCE NARRATIVE Continued...

- Participated on the Base Defence Force. On stand-by for Base emergency response situations.
- Earned positive performance evaluation comments, such as: *"All maintenance and supervisory actions were carried out to the highest standard...staunchly dedicated to unit success by regularly volunteering his time to assist coworkers in the completion of duties... proper procedures were carried out on all assigned tasks."*
- Assigned to support the Dissimilar Air Combat Training (DACT) operation to Alaska. Worked 16-hour days. Proactively tackled minor snags, responded swiftly to rectify an inertial navigation unit challenge, and assisted other trades to avoid schedule slippage.

CFB TRENTON, ONTARIO, 1989 TO 2001

AVIONICS SYSTEMS TECHNICIAN

Launched career as a second-line maintenance and service technician for the Boeing 707 and the CC-130 Hercules. Honed ability to install, maintain, and inspect aviation and aircraft electrical systems, tools, and test equipment. From the first year on the job, leveraged the advanced capacity to quickly analyze and isolate malfunctions within the equipment operating systems.

TRADES TRAINING

After completing basic military training, underwent rigorous trades training, setting the stage for service excellence for the balance of time served within the Forces.

EDUCATION & SPECIALIZED TRAINING

Currently taking **ELECTROMECHANICAL TECHNICIAN** course at *George Brown College*

✓ CH-146 Forward Looking Infra Red
✓ CF-188 Wire Bundle Connector Repair
✓ CF-188 Nitehawk FLIR
✓ CF-188 FLIR On-aircraft
✓ CF-188 Servicing
✓ Fibre Optic Devices
✓ CC-130 AUP Conversation Training
✓ 526 Avionics CC-130 On-type Conversion
✓ 526 Avionics Initial Occupation Conversion
✓ High Reliability Soldering
✓ CRS Technician RDR – IE Maintenance
✓ Base Defence Force Duties
✓ AN/APS 505 1st & 2nd Line Maintenance
✓ CRS Tech AN/APN 59E Maintenance
✓ VHF AM Radio Systems
✓ AMT Jet Passenger

✓ Comm, Radar Systems Technician
✓ CF-188 Electrical Systems On-aircraft Maintenance
✓ CF-188 Advanced Flight Controls On-aircraft Maintenance
✓ Night Vision Imaging Systems Maintenance
✓ Performance Oriented Electronics Training Modulation
✓ HF SOB Radio AN/ARC 505 Maintenance
✓ AN/APX 77/77A 1st & 2nd Line Maintenance
✓ AN/ARC – 511 1st & 2nd Line Maintenance
✓ CF-188 Modernization Avionics Maintenance
✓ CH-146 Avionics Systems On-aircraft Maintenance
✓ CF Avionics Systems On-aircraft Maintenance

TECHNOLOGY

Aircraft Maintenance Records – ADAM, Word, PowerPoint, Email, and Internet Research.

Reliable ▪ Determined ▪ Experienced

25

Specialty Area: Military Transition
Writer: Debra O'Reilly

JONATHAN PROULX

1717 Elm Avenue, Arboria, VA 23003 ♦
H: 703.122.1717 ♦ C: 703.002.9101 ♦
proulx_j@usb.com ♦

AIRCRAFT TEST & EVALUATION / SYSTEMS ENGINEERING / PROGRAM MANAGEMENT

LEADERSHIP: ***20+ years of operational excellence, coupled with:***

- Expertise in management of flight test & systems engineering for highly sophisticated, mission-critical aircraft.
- Consistent rapid delivery of time-sensitive projects/programs with high customer-satisfaction ratings.
- Proficiency in the employment of weapons systems in all mission environments; 1900+ flight hours in both fleet and test aircraft.
- Top-level Acquisition Career Field Certifications: *Test and Evaluation; Systems, Planning, Research, Development and Engineering* (SPRDE).
- Top Secret Security Clearance/SCI eligible. Graduate, United States Naval Academy.

Core competencies:
Program Management ... Human Resource Management ... Operations Planning ... Command and Control ... Acquisition ... Budget Management ... Team-building ... Test and Evaluation ... Joint Battlegroup Tactics ... Communications (all levels)

Technologies:
Tactical data links ... radio communications ... networks ... active and passive sensor systems simulations ... information processing ... software ... combat identification systems

HIGHLIGHTS OF EXPERIENCE AND ACCOMPLISHMENTS

UNITED STATES NAVY 1982–2007
Assistant Program Manager for Projects (2004–2007)

As **Integrated Test Team Leader,** directed a composite department of 100+ military, civil-service and contract employees in hardware and software testing for five aircraft and $300 million inventory. Managed $50+ million operations budget. Oversight included creation and evaluation of specifications, development of test plans, and writing/distribution of test reports for science and technology, system functionality, and airworthiness testing.

Highlights:

- Managed all test projects on the most complex aircraft. Team executed 100+ ground/flight test plans, accruing 1,200 flight hours and 13,000+ ground test hours. Staff performed nearly 2000 maintenance actions, 10,000+ labor hours, and more than 450 aircraft configuration changes in support of ongoing military operations.
- Led composite team to *Test Team of the Quarter* three times in less than three years.
- Successfully gained buy-in for new-facility construction to replace outdated rental structures. Projected construction cost will save taxpayers $10+ million over planned rental fees within the next five years.
- Earned top-tier Acquisition Career Field Certification in Test and Evaluation.

Assistant Program Manager for Systems Engineering (2001–2003)

Oversaw all development and in-service engineering efforts for fleet of 75 aircraft. Supervised several engineering teams in providing safe, mission-critical assets to Fleet Commanders. Responded to myriad engineering challenges in both in-service and new-production aircraft.

(continued)

(continued)

H: 703.122.1717 ♦ C: 703.002.9101 ♦ proulx_j@usb.com

Highlights:

- Post-9/11, successfully fielded new aircraft configuration to fleet, from evaluation of specs, through all ground and flight tests, to post-release technical instructions. Challenged to spearhead urgent fixes to numerous engineering defects to meet critical operational commitments safely. Coordinated with federal and civilian entities, resolving defects well ahead of schedule and enabling the concurrent deployment of 6 squadrons during Operation Iraqi Freedom.
- Led team in rapid implementation of 1000+ changes to Aircrew Operator's Manual. Team completed (normally) 9-month project in 6 weeks.
- Achieved Level 3 Acquisition Career Field Certification in Systems, Planning, Research, Development and Engineering (SPRDE).

Department Head (1999–2001)

As **Operations Officer,** orchestrated operations (20 months) for a 145-person squadron. Led squadron in achieving 1300 flight hours and 79 support missions while enforcing the No Fly Zone over Iraq.

As **Maintenance Officer** (six months), despite crippling parts shortages, led Maintenance Department to supply two fully mission-capable aircraft to meet critical operational commitments on schedule.

Naval Flight Officer (NFO) Instructor (1996–1999)

In addition to NFO instruction, served as Aviation Department Head School Coordinator. Taught a variety of tactical and mission systems courses as well as providing mentorship.

AFFILIATIONS

Boy Scout Leader
United States Naval Academy Alumni Association
Association of Naval Aviation

EDUCATION

Naval Postgraduate School
Master of Science: System Technologies

United States Naval Academy
Bachelor of Science

26

Specialty Area: Military Transition
Writer: Diane Hudson Burns

JAMES Z. SMITH

2670 Thunder Hill Road
Richmond, VA 21076

011-49-(0)-28793-4980
jameszsmith@aol.com

PROFILE

PROJECT MANAGEMENT · BUSINESS STRATEGY · OPERATIONAL MANAGEMENT
~ International & Domestic · Sales Development · Government & Commercial ~

Official Liaison · Foreign Relations/Affairs · Policy Formulation · Financial Advisor · Budget Administration Foreign Sales & Leases · International Acquisitions · Logistical Operations · Supply Chain

Top-performing logistics and project manager with over 20 years of experience in matrixed military and contractor environments including fast-paced, high-stress global assignments. Managed, planned, acquired, and directed the coordination of internal and external logistics-support functions and formulated program goals, work plans, and strategic vision for logistics operations.

Act with full commitment authority when negotiating International Exchange matters. Meet with high-ranking officials from over 30 countries. Discuss Exercises, Logistics, Security Issues, and specific Foreign Military Training Exchanges. Analyze, evaluate, recommend, and implement procedural efficiencies.

Represent the U.S. at international workshops and conferences worldwide. Polished and poised public speaker and negotiator. Prepare and deliver reports and strong presentations. Articulate sound influence into the decision-making of the multinational environment regarding sales and acquisitions.

Analyze project requests from foreign countries or U.S. sources to determine validity, qualifications, ability to support contractual requirements, political implications, and adherence to policies. Provide superior customer service and customer support. Coordinate and provide timely feedback regarding requests. Analyze and solve daily work problems and maintain accurate project requests, invoice reconciliation, contract, and budget information. Unsurpassed knowledge in obtaining funding for programs/projects.

PROFESSIONAL EXPERIENCE

United States Army, Secret Clearance *(Selected Achievements)* **1993 to present**

Chief Officer, Foreign Military Relations & Training Advisor, Germany **2002 to present**
** Develop and promulgate policy for Foreign Military Training and Education Programs, Security Assistance Programs, and Foreign Military Sales/Leases. Interface and coordinate activities with U.S. and NATO forces and U.S. embassies worldwide to implement unique initiatives/projects. Superior analytical ability.*

Scope of Operations

- Consistently successful in assessing situations/processes and meeting customer defined requirements and business specifications—delivering projects on time and within budget—providing top quality results. Sold and leased major equipment to foreign countries. Coordinated requests, reviewed cases, presented equipment for sale and started initial negotiations. Planned and scheduled project timelines and milestones.
- Actualize long-term product strategies for international, government and commercial markets. Expertly utilize resources and always exceed profitability and return-on investment objectives. Assemble and motivate cohesive working teams. Build consensus and mobilize resources.
- Precise, strategic planner. Resolve conflicts. Follow projects through complete lifecycle. Manage work in progress, anticipate, quantify, and effectively minimize project risk.
- Successfully obtained resources for deploying personnel and for visits by foreign officers. Expertly prepared and processed orders. Meticulously handled an annual budget of $9 million. Interfaced with the comptroller, processed purchase requests, orders, and other funding documents.

(continued)

(continued)

James Z. Smith **Page 2**

Highlights

- Manage and oversee the Joint Contact Team Program. Singularly responsible for establishing the best military sales program in Army-Europe.
- Infallibly managed a budget of over $35 million for three simultaneous programs.
- Selected to design the FY06 training program for three major exercises involving over 20 nations.
- Designed, wrote, and produced a Training and Procedures Manual, streamlining operations.
- Led a U.S. contingent at a NATO exercise planning conference in an Eastern European country. Worked directly with Conventional Forces Inspections (CFE) with the U.S. Embassy in the Ukraine and escorted various Russian delegations within Germany.
- Flawlessly handled logistical arrangements for visiting dignitaries and delegations: scheduled transportation, billeting, receptions, security, and training facilities. Enforced special protocol. Obtained resource support.

Supply Officer, Germany ***1998 to 2003***

- Directed daily operations and supply administration, and coordinated priorities for a team of 57 technicians, logisticians, and supply personnel working at eleven separate sites, as a one-stop shop for a variety of military equipment, maintaining an Authorized Stockage Level (ASL) of repair parts with an inventory valued at more than $27 million.
- Advisor to the Logistics Division Chief, Contracting Officer, and Maintenance Branch Head for all aspects of logistical matters to support customers. Delivered briefings orally and in writing detailing contractor performance and status.
- Designed an internal analysis schedule, which improved processes and resulted in a "no findings" rating during two separate third-party Logistical Readiness Inspections.

Safety Supervisor, Germany ***1995 to 1987***

- Directed the Safety Operation Response Center and Airspace Management for all incoming aircraft into training areas. Coordinated with firing ranges and training area managers; scheduled use of land and resources. Acted as a 911 Emergency Response Center for all personnel in the field. Coordinated Air Medical Evacuation and Ground ambulance requests. Taught or coordinated all safety courses prior to use of any training area. Additionally, supervised all Game Wardens in the training area.

Instructor Trainer, Germany ***1993 to 1995***

- Served as an instructor/trainer at the Army's premiere Leadership Academy. Awarded Instructor of the Year.

EDUCATION & RELEVANT MILITARY TRAINING

MBA, University of Maryland, 2005
BA in Business, University of Maryland, 2000
NATO Arms Control Course, Defense Institute of Security Assistance, 2006
Six Sigma, 2005 / Management Human Resources Training, 2005 / Simplified Acquisitions Procedures (SAP), Defense Acquisition University, 2004 / Acquisitions Fundamentals, Defense Acquisition University, 2002
Industrial Property Management, 2002
Advanced Officers Course, 10 weeks, 1994 (Executive Leadership & Management)

OTHER

Fluency in Spanish and German · Conversational abilities in Russian
Word, PowerPoint, Excel, Internet, Database Management
Meritorious Service Medal
Director of the Special Olympics, Maryland, 1999

27

Specialty Area: Return-to-Work
Writer: Kimberly Schneiderman

PHYLLIS CARSON

11 West 89th Street, Apt 1 ▪ New York, New York 10024 ▪ 212.555.1212 ▪ phyllis.carson@email.com

Relocation Consultant and Real Estate Agent

RELOCATION ▪ PROJECT MANAGEMENT ▪ SALES

5 years with **Nash Donavan** as ***Coordinator of Relocation Programs*** in Philadelphia, working as 3rd-party liaison between clients and transferees. Communicated transfer benefits, turnaround estimates, policies, procedures, and options. Clients: *Ford, IBM, Mobil,* and *General Motors.*

- Worked with 250+ executives and middle managers moving across U.S. and Canada.
- Arranged appraiser and title company assessments of property and researched mortgages, taxes, and market appraisals; reported information back to client for bid proposals.
- Communicated company bids on homes to transferees; administered equity adjustments until move completion and assisted homeowners with independent property sale.
- Partnered with real estate agents to quickly market and sell acquired properties for clients.

Over 1 year with **Ferris & Logan** as ***Relocation Consultant.*** Researched and created database of desired markets, including target townships, amenities, school systems, tax assessments, and statistics.

Orchestrated several ***personal*** international moves between London, Belgium, and Hong Kong. Most recently, relocated permanently to New York City.

- Managed all sea and air shipments of furniture and belongings for family of six.
- Led housing and school searches, ensuring moves to neighborhoods with excellent education systems.
- Handled pre-arrival set up of utilities and managed move notifications to schools, utilities, and families.

ORGANIZATION ▪ LEADERSHIP ▪ COMMUNITY SERVICE

2 years with **Hong Kong World School** in Hong Kong as ***Intramural Director*** of Boys Basketball Program. Recruited coaches, scheduled practices and games, and coordinated annual championship tournament with 14 teams of 130 middle school boys.

2 years with **U.S. Club** in Hong Kong as ***Chairperson*** for Annual Cotillion. Led parent committee, hired dance instructors, and coordinated events for 150 junior high school girls.

Led **U.S. Women's Club** in Belgium as ***Vice President*** for 2 years. Directed and managed fundraisers, vendor agreements, monthly member events, recruitment and welcome committees, and clubhouse renovation.

Several years as volunteer with hospitals and New York's homeless organizations.

EDUCATION ▪ TRAINING ▪ SKILLS

Licensed in July 2006, ***New York State Real Estate Sales***, **New York University Real Estate Institute**
Coursework: *License Law and Regulations, Estates and Interests, Financing, Land Use Regulations, Valuation, Construction and Fair Housing Law*

Member, ***Real Estate Board of New York***

Real Estate Institute, Temple University (50 credits)**; Marketing**, **St. Joseph's University** (50 credits)
Coursework: *Residential Sales, Appraisal, Real Estate Management, Real Estate Law and Construction*

Proficient using MS Word, Excel, and Outlook.

28

Specialty Area: Career Change
Writer: Lynn Eischen

Harriet J. Taylor

2115 State Street, Sacramento, California 93420 ~ (209) 123-4567 ~ harriet35@yahoo.com

Sales management professional desires opportunity in
PHARMACEUTICAL SALES

Value I Bring to Merck & Co.

Creative Sales Management—Established start-up business and grew sales from zero to $750K annually with steady growth and introduction of new locations during last thirteen years.

Business-to-Business Sales—Personally solicited Valley business professionals and established long-term commercial accounts with Physician Eye Care Specialists, Donald Smoot, M.D., Northern California Heart Center, California Medical Foundation, Center for Disease Specialists, Sacramento Rehabilitation Hospital, Sacred Heart Medical Center, and Sacramento Regional Medical Center *(partial listing)*.

Marketing Strategist—Envisioned strategies to increase profits and improve image of existing retail franchise. Improvements captured interest of franchiser who in turn repurchased outlet and utilized new concept in all stores.

Former Bodily Injury Adjuster—Evaluated medical records and conferred with physicians to determine extent of claimants' injuries. Substantial knowledge of medical terminology and ICD coding.

Event Planner/Coordinator—Developed professional relationships with corporate clients and individuals that resulted in additional income stream from planning and coordinating events for as many as 800 guests.

Attributes—Poised, determined, and well organized with persuasive communication skills.

Experience

HARRIET'S CREATIONS AND MORE, SACRAMENTO, CALIFORNIA **1992–PRESENT**

SALES MANAGER / PRINCIPAL

Developed concept to incorporate flowers, botanicals, and related accessories to enhance individual lifestyles that resulted in opening of high-end retail business in 1992. Second location was added within four years in one of Sacramento's premier shopping centers. In 2002 built new store with greater square footage and closed previous locations.

- Grew business from zero to profitable enterprise grossing $750K annually.
- Solicited new business and negotiated contracts to provide floral/plant and special event services for major clients—Saint Luke's Medical Center, Sacred Heart Hospital, and Jensen's Fruits and Nuts.
- Member of Merchant Association Board, 1999–2001.
- Recipient of "Best Florist in Sacramento" award, 2006.
- Nominated for Small Business Woman of the Year award, 2004.

WORLD'S BEST COOKIES, SACRAMENTO, CALIFORNIA **2002–2003**

PRINCIPAL / INDEPENDENT CONTRACTOR

Purchased cookie franchise adjacent to existing floral enterprise with plan to merge edible and botanical gift markets. Redesigned store's concept and improved operations, attracting attention of World's Best. Corporation initiated repurchase of retail store and subsequently contracted to standardize operations at all World's Best retail units.

- Instrumental in reducing corporation's overhead by closing factory and negotiating contract with third-party food manufacturer to produce raw product at substantial cost savings.

ALLSTATE INSURANCE, SACRAMENTO, CALIFORNIA **1991–1994**

BODILY INJURY CLAIMS ADJUSTER

- Discussed claimant's injuries with physicians and reviewed/interpreted medical records to determine extent of injury and legitimacy of insurance claims.
- Acquired substantial training and experience in medical terminology, medical records, and ICD coding.

Education

BACHELOR OF SCIENCE DEGREE IN PLANT SCIENCE — CUM LAUDE **1990**
California State University, Sacramento

29

Specialty Area: Career Change
Writer: Ilona Vanderwoude

STEPHANIE MCCALL

Page 1 of 2

8 Monahan Avenue · Staten Island, NY 10308 · Home: 718.209.1299 · Cell: 646.692.2298

FOCUS AND QUALIFICATIONS

FOCUS: Career in college or university environment teaching graduate and undergraduate-level students. Qualified to teach Criminal Justice, Political Science, Urban Affairs, History, and Public Administration.

QUALIFICATIONS: NYPD Sergeant with experience teaching graduate-level Criminal Justice and Public Administration courses at Baruch College, New York. Exemplary 20-year NYPD record, earning multiple awards. Talented instructor with New York State Police Instructor Certification (MOI) and a 10-year record of cross-level police instruction. Recognized by NYPD and educational institutions for outstanding academic performance, instruction skills, and community contributions. Extensive exposure to multicultural environments. Bilingual (English-German) with conversational skills in Spanish.

EDUCATION, TRAINING & CERTIFICATION

- MASTER OF ARTS DEGREE – 2002
  Major: Political Science
  Baruch College – New York, NY
  Graduated magna cum laude; G.P.A.: 3.90
  Recipient of Herbert Bienstock Research Award
- BACHELOR OF SCIENCE DEGREE – 1995
  Major: **History**
  The College of Staten Island – Staten Island, NY
  Graduated magna cum laude – G.P.A.: 3.89
- CERTIFIED SIMMUNITION TRAINING AND SAFETY SUPERVISOR – 2001
  Simmunition Division SNC Technologies, Inc.
  New York, NY
- CERTIFIED VERBAL JUDO INSTRUCTOR – 1995
  Verbal Judo Institute – New York, NY
- METHOD OF INSTRUCTION – 1992
  Division of Criminal Justice – New York State

PROFESSIONAL EXPERIENCE

TEACHING/INSTRUCTING

Solid 10-years' experience instructing recruits, in-service Police Officers, Sergeants, Lieutenants, and Captains. Selected in 2000 by Professor of Criminal Justice and Public Administration at Baruch College to serve as substitute lecturer while working toward Master's degree. Average class size comprised 20 to 35 graduate and undergraduate students. Authored lesson plans, selected textbook readings, and assigned and graded homework. Received highly positive student feedback regarding methodology, professionalism, and personality.

- Authoring lesson plans for INTAC (In Service Tactical Training Unit)—scenario-based training in a "live-fire" environment to reinforce proper tactics and firearms restraint to minimize escalation of incidents.
  Result: Sharp decline in shooting incidents since program's inception in 1996.
- Instructing NYPD Counter-Terrorism Program for INTAC Unit, teaching up to 30 people at once.
- Transforming inexperienced recruits into street-ready Police Officers as Police Science Instructor, preparing recruits for NYPD career through familiarization with police administration and legal procedures.
- Using outstanding classroom management skills and interactive, animated teaching style, generating high level of student enthusiasm.
- Applying advanced communication and foreign language skills to effectively interact with cross-cultural college students and international communities in New York City.

Continued..

(continued)

(continued)

STEPHANIE MCCALL

Page 2 of 2

LAW ENFORCEMENT

Broad and successful background as Sergeant and Police Instructor. Challenged to patrol and supervise high-crime precincts, relying heavily on superior listening, communication, and negotiation skills to thwart potentially harmful incidents. Strongly committed to well-being of all parties involved.

- Special training in suicide awareness and OSHA and hazmat regulations.
- Consistent performance reviews ranking 4.5 to 5 out of 5 for excellence and professionalism.

CHRONOLOGY

Baruch College, New York, NY — 2000 to 2001
Substitute Lecturer in Criminal Justice and Public Administration

New York Police Department (NYPD) — 1983 to 2003

- INTAC Supervisor – In Service Tactical Training Unit, Brooklyn/Queens — 1996 to Present
- Borough-based training – Uniformed in Service, Brooklyn — 1994
- Recruit Instructor Police Science – Police Academy, Manhattan — 1992 to 1994
- Sergeant; Patrol Supervisor and Desk Sergeant – Queens — 1989 to 1992
- Police Officer – Brooklyn North — 1983 to 1989

AWARDS AND HONORS

- **Herbert Bienstock Research Award** – Baruch College, New York, NY – 2000
- **Education Achievement Citation** – NYPD, NY – 2002 and 1995
  Awarded for successfully balancing full-time work and six years of education.
- **Perfect Attendance Recognition Certificate** – NYPD, NY – 2001
- **Greenpoint Community Service Award** – Greenpoint, NY – 1989
  Awarded by community in recognition of effective volunteer youth efforts.
- **Commended for investigatory skills leading to homicide confession** – NYPD, NY – 1988

30

Specialty Area: New Graduates
Writer: Laura Labovich

SOPHIA L. MEYERS

15993 Mayfair Court
West Bloomfield, MI 48323

(248) 222-8520
sophialmeyers@aol.com

Talented young professional with skills and training in:
NEUROBIOLOGY AND BIOCHEMISTRY RESEARCH

Highly-accomplished, quick learner with an impressive **hands-on knowledge base** encompassing the entire spectrum of **neurobiological research** and special expertise in Organic, Inorganic, Analytical, Solutions, Instrumental Analysis, and Physical Chemistry. Regarded by peers and mentors as an overachiever who is **committed to excellence in this field,** as demonstrated by **outstanding academic achievement.** Demonstrate thorough and detailed research capabilities. *Experience and academic preparation include:*

- Molecular Theory
- Quantum Mechanical Modeling
- Mathematical Modeling
- Particle Location and Density
- DNA Analysis and Separation
- Reagent Preparations
- EDTA Titration Process
- Electron Neutron Diffraction
- Electrophoretic Techniques
- Thermodynamic Principles
- Ethology
- Blood Typing
- Diffusion Principles
- X-Ray Diffraction
- GCMS/MS

EDUCATION

Bachelor of Science in Biology and Biochemistry
Michigan State University, East Lansing MI ~ Graduated with the Highest Honors ~ 2006

RELEVANT EXPERIENCE & EMPLOYMENT

Scheduling Coordinator ~ Sterling Radiology Consultants, Sterling VA ~ 5/2006 to present
Neuroscience Intern ~ Michigan State University, East Lansing MI ~ 8/2005 to 5/2006
Medication Care Manager ~ Sunrise Assisted Living, East Lansing MI ~ 2/2003 to 7/2006

- ***Clinical Trials:*** Administered a significant drug trial and established a dosage response curve for the identification of invertebrate behavior using neuromodulators.
- ***Medication Management:*** Completed state requirements training to confidently, legally, and safely administer patients' medication and effectively document their immediate reaction. Managed staff of 10 and ordered and controlled the administration of all narcotics.
- ***Ethology:*** Performed pet-care behavioral science medical procedures, including the administration of both local and general anesthesia, catheters, iv and injectables. Confidently handle x-rays and assess behavior modifications due to hormones, neuroreceptors, and neurotransmitters.
- ***Quality Assurance and Statistical Analysis:*** Delivered 3+ year in-depth reagent preparation and reaction writing capstone project culminating in and solidifying expertise in testing chemicals to determine molarity of any solution.
- ***Spectroscopy:*** Trained in Chemical Detection Methods including UV detection, chromotrography, and polarity, as well as finding unknown chemicals by running samples using search criteria.
- ***Gamete Shedding/Invitro Fertilization:*** Oversaw a developmental biology project devoted to the invitro vertilization of insects, rats, and invertebrates, whereby deliberate injection led to gamete shedding, fertilization of eggs in petry, and ultimately the reintroduction of eggs into animals.

PRESENTATIONS & CONFERENCES

Presented Topic: "Octopomine vs. Serotonin as a Neuromodulator and Neurotransmitter"
Society for Neuroscience National Conference, 2005, and West Virginia Academy of Science, 2006

MEMBERSHIPS, CERTIFICATIONS & AFFILIATIONS

Society of Neuroscience ~ American Chemical Society for Analytical Inorganic and Organic Chemistry
Sigma Phi Epsilon Fraternity ~ National Honor Society ~ MENSA ~Who's Who Listed

31

Specialty Area: Entrepreneurial
Writer: Louise Kursmark

SANDRA O'NEAL

760-294-7705 phone/fax • sponeal@yahoo.com
18534 Via Ascenso, Rancho Santa Fe, CA 92067

SENIOR EXECUTIVE: SERVICE INDUSTRIES

Revenue Growth • Service Excellence • Lean Operations

Entrepreneurial and growth-focused executive, twice building regional services businesses to millions of dollars in revenue and market leadership.

- **Top performance** in Sears partnership, growing the relationship to #1 in service and #2 in national sales volume among 370 contractors across the country.
- **Proven skills** as a team builder and motivational leader able to inspire staff to excellence.
- **Hands-on management experience** in all facets of the business, with notable contributions as a sales leader and finance manager, able to build lean organizations and capture emerging business opportunities.
- **Service orientation** and ability to make integrity and customer service prime differentiators in the market.

EXPERIENCE AND ACHIEVEMENTS

LA BREA MECHANICAL SERVICES, INC. Encinitas, CA, 2001–Present

President

Launched full-service repair and installation company, growing into a major service arm of Sears retail organizations in 3 U.S. regions. Defined vision/strategy emphasizing integrity and service as competitive differentiators. Grew the business from start-up to $6MM revenue, 38 staff, in 5 years.

In 2006, recruited a new, highly talented executive team (CEO, CFO, CIO) to ignite massive growth (to $200MM by 2008) and position the company for spin-off.

- **Growth:** Built a strongly ethical business foundation with exceptional pricing, quality, and workmanship; achieved lean operations through ROI-focused expense control; and delivered steady revenue growth:

	2002	2003	2004	2005	2006	2007 (proj.)
Revenue	**$1.6MM**	**$2.1MM**	**$2.5MM**	**$4.4MM**	**$6MM**	**$25MM**

- **Strategic business:** Became a prominent and valued Sears partner:
  - #2 in sales volume among 370 nationwide
  - #1 in quality service rating
  - Top 10% in attach rate—driven through partnering and relationship-building with store staff and managers
- **Expansion:** At the request of Sears executives, took over new regions nationally to improve sales, service, and the Sears brand value in those markets:
  - Washington State, June 2005
  - Phoenix, October 2005
- **Service orientation:**
  - Personally requested to provide intensive customer-service training to Sears' West Coast call center.
  - Introduced compensation plan innovative for the industry, paying service technicians salary rather than commission to drive customer-first philosophy.

SANDRA O'NEAL 760-294-7705 phone/fax • sponeal@yahoo.com

O'NEAL INSTALLATION SERVICES Encinitas, CA, 1984–2001

President, 1992–2001

Assumed ownership of the business, inheriting steep financial challenges and driving a turnaround to more than triple revenues.

- **Growth:** Increased revenues from $1.6MM in 1984 to $5MM in 2001.
- **Diversification:** Launched home-improvement subsidiary and grew to $2.7MM gross revenue in 3 years.
- **Strategic business:** Managed and grew Sears business from start-up to $2MM annual revenues.

Additional Roles & Performance Highlights, 1984–1992

Learned the business from the ground up, advancing to new areas of responsibility to gain expertise and tackle significant business challenges.

- **Finance Manager:** Identified accounting discrepancies and assumed responsibility for the company's financial operations—A/R, A/P, payroll, worker's comp, liability, and vehicle maintenance as well as oversight of 8 administrative staff and 30 field technicians.
  - Overhauled processes, upgraded technology, and eliminated source of significant financial loss.
  - Developed proprietary system for tracking daily cash flow to the penny.
- **Operations Manager:** Oversaw field service and fleet of company-owned vehicles. Continuously sought opportunities to cut costs, improve efficiency, and increase service.
  - Saved $60K annually by redesigning service flow and assigning dedicated truck/driver for appliance pick-ups.
- **Sales Manager:** Developed new business and managed major accounts including regional appliance dealers, Lowe's, Sears, and Home Depot.
  - Recognized market opportunity with the arrival of Lowe's in the San Diego market; cold-called to develop first Lowe's business and grew to the company's #1 account.

Active volunteer in the San Diego community.
References provided upon request.

32

Specialty Area: Consulting
Writer: Sandra Lim

AMBER TSE

#323 – 78 Lansdowne Avenue, Toronto, Ontario, M3P 8D2 • Tel: (416) 436-8889 • E-mail:a_tse@yahoo.ca

PAYROLL / HR / FINANCE IMPLEMENTATION CONSULTANT

"Your efforts and consistent successes are sincerely valued... The [Professional Services] functional team [has] had a wonderful year, and [is] building an excellent reputation in our business... You have represented Ceridian and Ceridian Professional Services extremely well."

Director of Professional Services, Ceridian Canada Ltd.

Solutions-oriented leader and team builder – experienced in analyzing and streamlining clients' business processes by working closely with clients, programmers, and product management to provide customized Payroll / HR / Finance solutions. Exceed client expectations through effective project management from concept to completion, complemented by ongoing client relationship management. Manage up to 8 professionals throughout project lifecycle, promoting a team environment. Liaise with development teams and product management and clearly communicate deliverables to project team members. *Expertise includes:*

Project Management	***Communications***	***Technical & Analytical Skills***
Business Process Reviews & Documentation	Client Relationship Management	Systems Testing & Troubleshooting
Customized Solutions Development	On-Site Support & Training	Ad Hoc Solutions
Systems Implementation	Sales Presentations	Process Analysis

Possess high-level knowledge of PeopleSoft through implementation of payroll systems interfacing with PeopleSoft. Proficient in MS Word, Excel, Access, Visio, Project, SQL 2000.

PROFESSIONAL QUALIFICATIONS

Candidate, ***Certification in Project Management***
Ryerson Polytechnic University

Green Belt Six Sigma Certified *2003*

Bachelor of Commerce in Information Technology *2003*
Ryerson Polytechnic University
Relevant Courses: ERP Systems, Gathering User Requirements for Systems Development, Process Analysis & Design, Concepts in Supply Chain Management, Project Management, Organizational Change

Honours: Dean's Honours List, 1997—2002
Recipient of *the Faculty of Business Award for Excellence, 1998*
Recipient of the *Daedalian Systems Group Award* for highest cumulative GPA, 1998
Member, *Golden Key National Honour Society* recognizing academic excellence

Honours Bachelor of Science *1997*
University of Toronto
Major: Psychology & Human Biology
Relevant Courses: Statistics, Foundations in Learning / Personality Theory

EXPERIENCE

Ceridian Canada Ltd., Toronto, Ontario *2000 – Present*
Professional Services Functional Consultant (2001 – Present)

Present sales demonstrations and provide in-depth product knowledge to both internal and external customers. Conduct Business Process Reviews to streamline HR / Payroll / Finance processes, including facilitating group meetings with users and senior management to gather and document data, identify functional gaps, and document detailed business requirements. Provide updates on project deliverables to clients, manage resources, and execute implementation including system testing, troubleshooting, and final release.

Achievements:

- Generated $200,000 in revenue for 2007, including retaining 3 clients that would have otherwise been lost due to customer dissatisfaction (this would have represented an annual loss of $130,000 in revenue).

AMBER TSE

Page 2 of 2

EXPERIENCE *(continued)*

Ceridian Canada Ltd.

Achievements:

- Integrated HR / Payroll / Time & Attendance systems for one of the largest government social housing providers in Ontario.
- Contribute to enhancement of Ceridian Professional Services' consulting methodologies by improving Business Process Reviews – created a summary tool to highlight issues for executives that was so successful it was subsequently built into the software Ceridian uses to document client processes.
- Received positive client feedback on skillful handling of data-gathering interviews, building client trust and pinpointing right questions to ask.
- Recognized for product expertise and problem-solving skills; often called upon to work with Product Management to offer ad hoc solutions to larger clients and support National Sales and Service teams regarding product knowledge.

Implementation Specialist (2000 – 2001)

Implemented HRIS systems for various clients by gathering requirements around data mapping and customizing HRIS systems to clients' business needs. Migrated clients from legacy systems onto new systems, and provided on-site support and training.

Achievements:

- Implemented over 30 HRIS systems for various client organizations.
- Contributed expertise to sales pitch, assisting National Sales and Service teams to secure client accounts.

Scotiabank, Toronto, Ontario *1999 – 2000*
Project Officer

Standardized and increased efficiency of back-office operations for offices nationwide.

Projects:

- Centralized database for processing of foreign exchange transactions, managing a team of 3 employees to implement new system and check data integrity. Designed and documented new foreign-exchange transaction processes for end users.
- Initiated and developed a centralized MS Access database for customer contact data.

"...thanks so much for all your extra time and hard work to ensure we met our extremely tight timeline. Without you... we couldn't have done it!!... Special thanks for your expertise, long hours, and dedication to this project. It's nice working with people who care so much about their [customers'] needs."

Supervisor of Payroll and Benefits
Multi-Site Government Organization

"I just wanted you to know that we had a very successful week with Amber. She [possesses] a wealth of knowledge and personality and made it comfortable for everyone to be open and work through this process."

Manager, Human Resource Systems and Benefits
North American Multi-Site Manufacturing Organization

33

Specialty Area: Consulting
Writer: Erin Kennedy

JONAS COFFIN

INTELLIGENCE CONSULTANT | PROJECT MANAGER | PROGRAM MANAGER

Business Leader & Intelligence Expert with a track record of achievements in program and project management and communication analysis—driving value for companies through a balance of counter-intelligence collection and production mixed with project lifecycle savvy. Consummate professional with unmatched expertise in cultivating and nurturing relationships with departments, staff, and key decision-makers. Forward-thinker able to view the "big picture" while executing the minute details of strategy, analysis, and business that drive the end result. Hold a Top Secret/SCI Security Clearance with Full Lifestyle Polygraph (Dec. 01). Fluent in English and Spanish. Additional qualifications in:

- Fiscal Management & Budgeting
- Mission-Critical Projects Management
- Program Planning & Development
- Intelligence Analysis & Consultation
- Leadership Training & Development
- PMI Certified & MBA degreed

PROFESSIONAL EXPERIENCE

EYESPY NETWORKING, INC., New York, NY — 2006 to Present
Senior Consultant
Brought on board to enhance company's intelligence analysis business through networking and development of new leads within the intelligence community. Joined company-wide recruitment process by identifying and interviewing ideal candidates. Assisted with asset management and marketing.

Project Leadership

- Developed comprehensive company descriptions ("white papers") to provide solutions and process improvement initiatives for customer organizations.
- Monitored and governed a $200,000 data-quality project with a government client to enhance client needs; gained extension of existing contract.

WORLDVIEW LINKING CORPORATION, NEW YORK, NY — 2003 to 2006
Senior Intelligence Expert, Advanced Analysis Lab
Supported all aspects of complex systems analysis for advanced analysis lab. Collaborated with other product-line analysts to evaluate and recommend the need for new analytic technologies while ensuring analytic needs were met.

Program Management

- Key participant in landing a $1.1 million contract that contained proposed efforts for staffing requirements, statement of work, and risk mitigation.
- Grew a classified program by generating an additional $235,000 and receiving a contract extension of six months, resulting in increased client satisfaction.
- Planned, implemented and controlled more than 2500 hours of overall requirements including customer objectives, existing systems literature, analysis, preprocesses, staffing, budget, contracting employee evaluations, and information for automated entity extraction methodologies to support computational modeling efforts.

LINGUAL INFORMATION SYSTEM TECHNOLOGIES, INC., Fort Meade, MD — 2001 to 2002
Intelligence Language Analyst, Regional Targets Office
Hired on a contractual basis to plan and execute more than 2000 hours of analysis, research, and translation of foreign language materials on complex and diverse issues.

1827 Nantucket Way | Upstate, NY 77687 | 212-877-8755/212-206-3265 (c) | coffinj@msn.com

Project Lifecycle Management

- Coordinated all aspects of network management production during system development project lifecycle. Analyzed, defined, measured, developed, and implemented a working way to track and report on specific classified targets. Implemented new ways to track and analyze target, increasing efficiency in the customer office while fostering communication with other offices due to an interest in what the team was taking on.
- Drafted English-language reports for distribution to national-level policy makers and consumers throughout the U.S. Intelligence Community.
- Single-handedly coordinated all aspects of Satellite Network Collection Management production project including developing, tracking and reporting.
- Assisted in the analysis and instruction of Digital Network Intelligence.

UNITED STATES AIR FORCE, Fort Custer, TX 1995 to 2001

Linguist Translator, Dominant Chronicle (1998 to 2001)

Promoted to manage a 10-member multi-service linguistic team responsible for the translation of high-priority foreign language documents. Ensured the accurate reporting, translation, and storage of complex documents in the project database.

Analysis & Leadership

- Hand-picked by superiors to be one of the lead Quality Control Non-Commissioned Officers (NCOs); inspected over 4,200 translations while serving in this position.
- Logged 900 hours of translation of 6,000 intelligence summaries.
- Provided crucial support to Department of Defense decision-makers and multiple national-level consumers through translation of classified documents customized to assist entities such as DIA and NSA in becoming familiar with the target.

Cryptologic Linguist Specialist, 987th Intelligence Group (1995 to 1998)

Accelerated the flow of critical information and educated officials at the same time. Concurrently served as linguist/translator/reporter involving technical, collection management, conventional, metadata analysis, and reporting objectives.

Communicator & Consultant

- Briefed FBI, DIA, and NSA officials on various counter-narcotic surveillance targets.
- Utilized foreign language skills daily, primarily through collection, transcription, and analysis of foreign language materials.

EDUCATION | CERTIFICATIONS | AFFILIATION

MBA, Global Management, NEW YORK UNIVERSITY, NY—2005
BS, Liberal Studies, JONESTOWN UNIVERSITY, NY—2003

Project Management Professional Certification (PMP)—2006
Certificate of Completion, SAS Base Programming—2006
Certificate of Completion (7/9/5 DLPT), **Advanced Spanish Crypto-logic Course**—1999

Member, PMI Manhattan Chapter, Project Management Institute

1827 Nantucket Way | Upstate, NY 77687 | 212-877-8755/212-206-3265 (c) | coffinj@msn.com

34

Specialty Area: Consulting
Writer: Donna Farrise

JOHN R. DELROSARIO, RPA-C

701 Park Avenue • Setauket, New York 11771 • (631) 563-7209
johnrdelrosario@yahoo.com

PROFILE

Professional Forensic Investigator / Physician Assistant seeking to transition background and experience into a new consulting venue for television/film. Successfully combine literary consultant experience and published crime-scene authoring. Natural ability to communicate professionally with individuals of all levels. Organized, detailed-oriented, and efficient administrative abilities.

TRANSITIONAL SKILLS

- Investigated approximately 500 deaths a year, over 23-year career as Forensic Investigator, including homicides, suicides, accidental deaths, undetermined deaths, and deaths from natural causes.
- Supervised crime scene for Medical Examiner's Office; pronounced death, physical examination of the deceased, scene investigation, accident reconstruction, identification and preservation of evidence.
- Advised detectives, crime scene technicians, and morgue drivers.
- Obtained biological exemplars for evidentiary purpose at direction of police agencies, courts, or their authorized agents.
- Identified and established evidentiary value of items, i.e., samples for toxicological analysis; documented evidence and directed removal while safeguarding quality and chain of evidence.
- Testified in court. Assisted in prosecutions in over 1,000 DWIs cases.
- Conducted formal lectures, educational programs, and conferences in forensic medicine for physicians, NYSSPA, and staffs.
- Provided regulatory reporting to OSHA, Long Island Police Departments, F.B.I., New York State Health Department, Center for Disease Control, and Consumer Product Safety.
- Participated in research of Huntington's Disease.

PROFESSIONAL EXPERIENCE

MEDICAL EXAMINER'S OFFICE • Riverhead, NY **10/78 to 10/01**
Forensic Investigator

Conducted independent and confidential investigations of deaths. Interviewed witnesses, recorded detailed observations of scenes, took photographs, collected evidence, reviewed physician and hospital records. Obtained factual history and recorded events with emphasis on manner and circumstances of death. Prepared and submitted detailed reports.

- *Co-founder and creator of the "Forensic Investigator" role in 1978 – replacing 20 P/T police surgeons and deputy medical examiner positions.*
- *Senior Forensic Investigator for Suffolk County Medical Examiner's Office investigating TWA Flight 800 disaster.*
- *Assisted in implementing new Medical Examiner's facility, 1988.*

STONY BROOK HOSPITAL • Stony Brook, NY **10/91 to 7/93**
Hospice Nurse On-Call – P/T

Provided patient care and comfort and administered medications to 40–50 ill and dying patients. Interacted with family members and loved ones to educate them on patient status and care.

Prior to 1978, served as a Physician Assistant and EMT/ORT at several surgical and medical practice centers: Huntington Surgical Group, New York Group, Good Samaritan Memorial Hospital, and Massachusetts Memorial Hospital.

JOHN R. DELROSARIO, RPA-C

- Page Two -

EDUCATION

Regents College, NY,
Associate of Applied Science in Nursing, 1990

New York University, New York, NY
Bachelor of Science in Health Science Technology, 1974

State University of New York at Stony Brook School of Allied Health, Stony Brook, NY
Physician Associate, 1973

LITERARY CONSULTANT

Technical Adviser to Tom Philbin on Precinct Siberia Crime Novels for Fawcett Publishing: Precinct Siberia / Undercover / A Matter of Degree / Cop Killer / Jamaica Kill / Death Sentence / Street Killer
Antiquarian Book Dealer – Flitcraft Books

PUBLICATIONS

American Journal of Forensic Pathology:
"Open Revolver Cylinder at The Suicide Death Scene," (Pending)
Wrote stories for Physician Assistant Update Magazine

CERTIFICATIONS / LICENSES

Certification by The National Commission of Physician Assistants (NCCPA) – #981744
New York State Licensed Registered Nurse – #426200
Registered Physician Associate – #000149

MEMBERSHIPS / ASSOCIATIONS

Pioneering Member of Physician Assistants Profession
Founding Member of New York State Society of Physician Assistants
Original Member of The American Academy of Physician Assistants
Attended First Physician Assistant Program at the State University of New York at Stony Brook

Life Member of The First Marine Division Association

TASK FORCE SERVICE

Emergency Medical Service (EMS) Council of Suffolk County

MILITARY SERVICE

U.S. Navy, 1965–1971
2nd Battalion – 1st Marines
1st Marine Division – Vietnam

35

Specialty Area: Education
Writer: Freddie Cheek

ROBERTA L. SHORE

456 Cooper Road, #7, Buffalo, New York 14211 • 716-555-1212 • robertashore@yahoo.com

EDUCATION PROFESSIONAL

Literacy Specialist • Reading Resource Instructor • Elementary Educator

Talented and dedicated teacher and reading specialist with experience using accepted educational techniques to accommodate diverse learning styles. Skilled at planning and presenting lessons for remediation, academic growth, and advanced instruction in self-contained and team-teaching classrooms. Develop individualized, outcome-based lessons and accurately assess student progress with the flexibility to adjust lessons to meet students' needs. Solid and highly successful experience with Reading First Program. Adept at delivering in-service training to teaching staff. Prepare accurate and timely State Education reports.

EDUCATION AND CREDENTIALS

Master of Science in Education, 5/2007
BUFFALO STATE COLLEGE – Buffalo, New York
GPA: 3.95/4.0

Bachelor of Arts in Communications, 5/2001
STATE UNIVERSITY COLLEGE AT BROCKPORT – Brockport, New York
GPA: 3.7/4.0 • Graduated with Highest Distinction

New York State Certified Literacy Specialist, Birth–6

New York State Certification in Childhood Education, 1–6

Professional development training: Phonetic Awareness with DIBELS ~ Rubric Writing
Curriculum Writing Workshops ~ Earobics Computer / Audio Literacy
SRA Direct Instruction ~ Voyager Passport ~ New York State Standards

PROFESSIONAL EXPERIENCE

STEPHENSON ACADEMY – Buffalo, New York 2007–Present
Reading First Instructor / Coordinator

- Oversee the full and ongoing implementation of Reading First Program in all grade levels.
- Mentor and collaborate with Reading First teachers to implement instructional strategies and achieve desired outcomes.
- Provide classroom support to professional staff; model lessons; and assist with Palm and laptop technology usage.
- Order supplies, maintain inventory control, distribute materials, and oversee budget.
- Team with administrators to schedule and facilitate professional development training; train teachers using New York State Reading Academy.
- Update and maintain binders, including School Data Notebook, Grade Level and Literacy Leadership Team Notebook, and Coach Log Book.
- Hold monthly data meetings, attend meetings with principal and Reading First supervisor, and participate in grade-level meetings; attend Reading First conference.
- Ensure valid and reliable application of screening, diagnostic, and monitoring instructional assessment tools.
- Review and analyze diagnostic and progress data, as well as individual and grade-level results.

GETZVILLE PUBLIC SCHOOLS – Amherst, New York 2004–2006
Grade 1 Teacher

- Participated in all aspects of classroom instruction and management, in inclusion classroom, creating and presenting lesson plans for single lessons and units of instruction in mathematics, science, reading, and language arts.
- Utilized knowledge of learning styles, teaching methods, guided reading techniques, positive engagement techniques, and phonetics instruction.
- Presented Reading First lessons designed to increase oral reading fluency, enhance students' phonetic awareness, increase children's vocabulary and word attack skills, and encourage creativity and self-expression.

...continued...

ROBERTA L. SHORE • Page 2

- Integrated the six traits of writing in teaching the entire process from brainstorming to graphic organizers, rough draft, editing process, and final piece with the addition of oral language practice.
- Designed extremely well prepared lesson plans that promoted reading appreciation, enhanced writing skills, and encouraged participation; developed for each unit of instruction: objectives, differentiation, rubrics, rationales, related standards, and associated media and visual aids.
- Worked with both homogeneous and heterogeneous reading groups, based on DIBELS scores and classroom observation, creating literacy centers that incorporated a wide range of creative activities and learning tools; developed math centers with areas of differentiated instruction.
- Evaluated and tracked student progress and accomplishments, building self-esteem through rewards and encouragement; fostered home-school communications to update parents and encourage family support and participation.
- Used programs from Success For All, Harcourt Reading Roots, DIBELS, Edison & Reading First, and Scott Foresman to present lessons that addressed New York State Learning Standards.
- Coordinated with Special Education instructors to prepare Behavior Improvement Plans and assist students with Family and Student Support Team process; participated in CSE meetings to write IEPs.
- Utilized skills in Microsoft Office, the Internet, and wireless generation Palm Pilot for reading assessment.

Selected Achievements:

- Selected as sole classroom teacher from school to attend Reading First National Conference in New Orleans, LA.
- Chosen by Instructional Leadership Team as Peer Coach to assist new and developing teaching staff.
- Created sticker and color-coded behavior chart to help students monitor their progress and work toward improving their conduct and performance.
- Working with at-risk students in blended class, consistently raised percentage of DIBELS scores against benchmarks and guided majority of students to meet or exceed (almost 50%) math standards.

PLANK ROAD ELEMENTARY SCHOOL – Falls Island, New York — Spring 2004

Grade 3 Student Teacher

Collaborated with 5th grade teachers in creating and presenting individualized spelling tests given by 5th grade students to 3rd grade classes. Created and presented unit on poetry. Designed and utilized learning centers to complement geometry unit. Worked in team-teaching situation.

PREPARE ACADEMY – Buffalo, New York — Spring 2004

Grade 5 Student Teacher

Provided differentiated instruction in inclusion classroom. Created and implemented a unit on electricity with supportive learning centers and bulletin boards. Implemented Black History Month project in conjunction with *Philadelphia Tribune*, including directing class play.

BUFFALO CITY SCHOOLS – Buffalo, New York — 2001–2004

Substitute Teacher

With little or no advance preparation, taught lessons to students in English language arts, mathematics, science, and social studies classes. Quickly gained rapport and control in presenting assigned materials.

ADDITIONAL EXPERIENCE

BROOKS COMMUNITY CENTER – Buffalo, New York — 2003–2005

Lead Tutor, Youth Development Program

Assisted 25 at-risk SES students increase their reading levels as part of Reading and Homework Intervention Program. Provided supplemental education services through Read 180 Program. Utilized team planning to scaffold at-risk students in homework completion. Helped students achieve increased scores on DRS and Read 180 assessments.

STARBUCKS – Buffalo, New York — 1999–2004

Retail Service Manager

Supervised up to 15 servers in providing the highest quality product and customer service.

36

Specialty Area: Education
Writer: Tracy M. Parish

Savannah Wright

1423 Richmond Dr. • Bradford, IL 61001 • Home: (505) 555-6893 • swright@email.com

◆ ELEMENTARY ADMINISTRATOR ◆

Motto: "I believe in leading by example."

VISION STATEMENT

To continually improve the quality of student education by providing a positive learning environment through the encouragement of classroom ownership, the integration of solid reading programs, and the championing of direct parental involvement.

- **Classroom Ownership** stresses the importance of morals and significantly reduces disciplinary problems, providing a thriving learning environment at school.
- **Reading Encouragement** instills a love of learning that will be used throughout a lifetime to obtain knowledge at all levels.
- **Direct Parental Involvement** produces extremely successful learning results and builds a positive home/school connection.

Dedicated and highly motivated Educational Administrative Professional with a proven track record for implementing successful programs that produce lasting results. Experienced in writing and submitting government grants to obtain additional funding. Active in supporting and encouraging teachers through continuing education, staff development, and leadership roles. Knowledgeable of current trends in education and capable of motivating staff to try new, creative techniques in continually improving teaching skills. Polished public speaker and instructor who relates effectively to people of diverse levels and backgrounds.

EDUCATIONAL BACKGROUND

MSE, Educational Administration (K–8), DRAKE UNIVERSITY – Des Moines, IA (1997)
Principal Endorsement ◆ Evaluator One License ◆ Coaching Endorsement

BS, Elementary Education (K–6), SIMPSON COLLEGE – Indianola, IA (1986)
Endorsement 10 ◆ Approvals, 81– Mentally Handicapped, 91 ◆ Reading Endorsement

Academic Highlights: Selected for "Who's Who Among Students in American Universities and Colleges" ◆ Recipient of the school's annual Student Athlete Award ◆ Dean's List

PROFESSIONAL EXPERIENCE

MADISON COMMUNITY SCHOOLS – Madison, IL
Progressed through the following positions:

Elementary Administrator (1998 to Present)
District Reading / Language Arts and TAG Coordinator (1998 to Present)
Direct all aspects of educational programs and activities for two separate elementary school facilities consisting of approximately 400 students. Directly supervise and mentor 35 staff members and evaluate all teachers. Manage business, building maintenance, behavioral / disciplinary problems, parent / teacher relations, staffing schedules, and various daily activities.

- Successful in securing over $50,000 in grants used for new technology, literature, playground equipment, and building improvements.
- Spearheaded a successful "Character Counts" program, resulting in a drastic drop in disciplinary referrals from154 to 37 annually, after just one full year of implementation.
- Introduced a monthly Parent Advisory Committee to foster a positive home-school partnership.
- Changed procedures to support inclusion for special-needs students with excellent results.

Administrative Staff Member / Practicum Experience (1996); **Elementary Teacher** (1986 to 1998)

◆ References and Supplemental Information Available Upon Request ◆

37

Specialty Area: Healthcare
Writer: Angela P. Zimmer

CATHERINE MARY SOPRANO, R.N., B.S.N.

250 Meday Drive
Toms River, New Jersey 08755

Telephone: (732) 281-6581
E-Mail: nursecathy74581@aol.com

PROFESSIONAL PROFILE

Highly skilled and knowledgeable Nurse Educator with 13 years' experience instructing L.P.N.s in medical centers, hospitals, and nursing homes—long-term care, healthcare centers, and school classroom environments. Self-directed, enthusiastic educator with a passionate commitment to student development and the learning process as a whole. Demonstrated leadership, training, and presentation skills, having dealt with a diversity of professionals, student nurses, and staff members. Qualifications include diverse background in patient care treating adults, adolescents, children, and the elderly.

Areas of Classroom and Clinical Teaching

- **Anatomy & Physiology**
- **Fundamentals of Nursing**
- **Obstetrics**
- **Pharmacology**
- **Nutrition**
- **Pediatrics**
- **Medical/Surgical**
- **Psychiatry**
- **Geriatrics**

CAREER CHRONOLOGY

Contributing Writer & Reviewer	Lippinstein, Wilkinson and Waters, Philadelphia, PA	2002–Present
LPN Instructor	Ocean County Vocational Technical School, Freehold, NJ	1995–Present
Nurse Educator	Ocean Medical Center, Toms River, NJ	Current
Nurse Educator	Community Medical Center, Brick, NJ	Current
Nurse Educator	Kimbal Medical Center, Lakewood, NJ	Current
Nurse Educator	Manchester Manor Nursing Home, Manchester, NJ	Current
Nurse Educator	Claremont Care Center, Point Pleasant, NJ	Current
Nurse Educator	Whiting Health Care Center, Whiting, NJ	Current
Nurse Educator	Leisure Chateau Care Center, Lakewood, NJ	Current
Staff Charge Nurse	Riverview Medical Center, Red Bank, NJ	1980–1987

PROFESSIONAL NURSING EDUCATOR EXPERIENCE

Ocean County Vocational Technical School, Freehold, NJ – *LPN Instructor*
Teach and educate student nurses in both classroom and clinical settings in various therapeutic areas and in medical procedures encompassing Anatomy and Physiology, Pharmacology, Medical/Surgical, Nutrition, Psychiatry, Obstetrics, Pediatrics, Geriatrics, the administration of medication, and fundamentals of nursing in a laboratory environment.

- Utilize Internet and nursing library in researching state-of-the-art, up-to-date procedures and technology, as well as current literature to complement learning activities.
- Develop, create, and write lesson plans, curricula, and instructions.
- Aid in the selection and design of textbooks and learning tools.
- Counsel and advise students on a variety of issues, encompassing job recommendations and interview coaching.
- Motivate students through positive reinforcement and increased self-esteem.

Continued on Page 2

(continued)

(continued)

CATHERINE MARY SOPRANO, R.N., B.S.N. **Page 2**

PROFESSIONAL NURSING EXPERIENCE

Riverview Medical Center, Red Bank, NJ – *Staff and Charge Nurse*
As Charge Nurse, provided leadership and supervision of nurses, including ancillary personnel, providing tracheotomy, colostomy, ventilator, oxygen, wound, surgical drain, gastrostomy, ureterostomy, and chest-tube care. Oversaw medication administration, IV initiation and maintenance, foley catheter insertion, as well as head-to-toe and neurological assessments.

- Assessed, planned, implemented, and evaluated patients on a 26-bed unit.
- Direct responsibility for safety, evaluation, goal setting, and patient care through high-quality standards.
- Educated newly diagnosed patients in diabetic, ostomy, and post-operative care.
- Supervised and directed daily monitoring of respiratory diseases; managed oxygen use and pulse oximetry.
- Managed and coordinated between patients, family, physicians, and interdisciplinary modalities to ensure continuity of care.
- Oriented new nurses and acted as resource person and preceptor.

VOLUNTEER RELATED WORK EXPERIENCE

Nurse – American Red Cross – Obtained blood from donors during blood drives

EDUCATION, CERTIFICATIONS and LICENSES

Education:
Seton Hall University, South Orange, NJ: B.S.N., 1993 – GPA 3.9
- Internships included Visiting Nurse Service of Central Jersey and Ocean County Board of Health—tuberculosis and children's clinics.

Brookdale Community College, Lincroft, NJ: A.A.S. in Nursing, 1983

Certifications:
IV and PICC Line | TPN and CPR | Charge Nurse

License:
New Jersey Board of Nursing Licensed

PUBLICATIONS

Contributing writer and reviewer of textbooks:
- *Pathophysiology Made Incredibly Easy* – Publication pending January 2008
- *Care of the Surgical Patient, 5th edition* – Publication pending January 2008
- *NYCLEX-PN Questions and Answers Made Incredibly Easy* – 2006
- *NYCLEX-PN Review Made Incredibly Easy* – 2006
- *Best Practices: Evidenced Based Nursing Procedures* – 2006
- *LPN Expert Guides: Fluids and Electrolytes* – 2006
- *Elder Care Strategies, Expert Care Plans for the Older Adult* – 2004

All books published by Lippinstein, Wilkinson, and Waters.

38

Specialty Area: Hospitality and Entertainment
Writer: Susan Geary

Johnny Slash

2022 South Corona Street • Denver, CO 80210-4123 • (303) 765-5488 • johnnydj@hireme.com

Award-winning Morning Radio Air Personality with major market experience, high ratings, and a loyal listening audience

Summary of Qualifications

- More than 15 years' experience as a Country Music Air Personality.
- Consistently achieve high Arbitron Ratings with Adults 25–54.
- Well-known Denver native with positive name recognition.
- Earned numerous industry and philanthropic awards.
- Tuned in to local news and celebrity gossip.
- Highly involved in community and charitable events.
- Solid knowledge of the music industry, including trivia, history, artists, and song titles.
- Strong work ethic, reliable, with clean sense of humor.

"He's become one of the most-listened-to personalities on the air by rejecting the usual snickering tag-team byplay in favor of a format that blends good conversation with humor that dares to be smart." – *Westword Best of Denver Issue, May 2006*

Career Achievements

Friend In Need – Service to America Award • 2005
Best Major Market Morning Team – Country Music Association • 2003
Best Major Market Morning Show – Colorado Broadcasters Association • 2001 • 2002 • 2006
Denver's Best Morning Wakeup – Westword Best of Denver Issue • 2002 • 2004 • 2007
Colorado's Top Morning Show Personality – Achievement in Radio (AIR) Award • 2001 • 2004
Radio Personality of the Year – Billboard Magazine • 1999

Professional Experience

98.5 KYGO/Today's Best Country – Denver, CO **2000–Present**
Air Personality *for the Mile High City's #1 rated morning show known as the Coffee Club.*

- Increased ratings (Arbitron 25–54) by 21% within first 18 months on the air, surpassing all other station day parts in Time Spent Listening (TSL) and audience cume.
- Helped generate more than $3.4 million in station partnerships, endorsements, and advertising sales revenue during tenure.
- Emceed KRMA-TV's charity auction, the Jerry Lewis MDA telethon, and the Boys and Girls Club annual fundraisers.
- Developed and implemented *World's Longest Remote Broadcast,* remaining on the air for 98.5 hours and realizing goal of 2000 donations benefiting Toys for Tots.
- Earned *Employee of the Quarter* four times since 2001.

(continued)

(continued)

Johnny Slash   johnnydj@hireme.com   Page 2

Professional Experience (continued)

102.5 KNIX/Arizona's Best Country – Phoenix, AZ **1994–2000**
Afternoon Drive Time Announcer / Production Director *for Buck Owens' award-winning country music radio station.*

- Collaborated with engineers to improve digital production facility, upgrading 16-track analog board to fully computerized 24-track recording studio.
- Suggested new music spins, resulting in numerous #1 hits and breakout artists.
- Improved relationships with record reps and recording artists, resulting in exclusive on-air interviews and sold-out concert promotions.
- Worked closely with sales department to secure a multimillion-dollar contract with the Arizona Diamondbacks Baseball Team.

93 KAFF Country – Flagstaff, AZ **1991–1993**
Air Personality *for Northern Arizona's top-rated country music station.*

- Combined personality with phones, topical bits, and extensive knowledge of music.
- Recorded commercials for broadcast, utilizing state-of-the-art digital studios.
- Represented station during promotional appearances.
- Selected as the commercial voice of Babbitt's Department Store Chain.

Professional Development

Morning Show Boot Camp, presented by TalentMasters • 1997–2006
Personality Radio, presented by Dan O'Day • 2002

Community Involvement

Volunteer, Boys and Girls Club of Denver • 1997–Present
Member, Colorado Broadcasters Association • 1999–Present
Volunteer, Jerry Lewis/MDA Annual Telethon • 1998–2000
Auction Announcer, KRMA-TV (PBS) Annual Auction • 1999–Present

Computer & Technical Skills

DAD • SIS • RCS • Scott Studios • ProTools • Prophet • Selector • Session 8 • Audicy • VoxPro • NexGen • Cool Edit • Macintosh • Microsoft Windows 95/98/ME/NT/2000/XP • MS Word • Netscape • Outlook • Explorer • HTML • Adobe PhotoShop • PowerPoint • Quicken

Education

NORTHERN ARIZONA UNIVERSITY – Flagstaff
Bachelor of Science in Broadcasting with an emphasis on Announcing and Performing

39

Specialty Area: Hospitality and Entertainment
Writer: Jill Grindle

DAVID L. WINSTON
50 Old Village Lane ★ Suffield, CT 06078 ★ 860.668.0111

EXECUTIVE CHEF

Award-winning, self-taught culinary professional with over 15 years of experience in establishments that include a world-class resort and several upscale restaurants. Unique blend of creative flair and passion for food, strong business sense, and engaging interpersonal skills. Strong record of streamlining operations and improving service while preserving the highest levels of quality. Natural ability to create enthusiastic, productive working environments with customer-oriented professionals. Highly skilled at performing financial analysis, troubleshooting operations, and recommending effective cost controls.

HIGHLIGHTS

- ★ Worked with noted chefs such as Thomas Keller of *French Laundry* and *Per Se*, Mario Batali of *Babbo*, Ming Tsai of *Blue Ginger*, and Masayoshi Takayama of *Masa* at charity events. Interned with Edward Leonard, CMC of *Westchester Country Club*.
- ★ Nominee for Best Northeast Regional Chef Award from the James Beard Foundation in 2005, and also named Best Rising Chef in 2000.
- ★ Earned Distinguished Restaurant of North America Award from DiRona in 2003, *Max's of Manchester*, Avon, CT.
- ★ Appeared on TV shows including *Phantom Gourmet*, *Lidia's Italian Table*, and *Cooking Live*.
- ★ Written up in magazines such as *Gourmet*, *Food and Wine*, and *Bon Appetit*, with recipes published in cookbooks such as *Joy of Cooking*.

PROFESSIONAL EXPERIENCE

POMEGRANATES, Avon, CT — 2004–2007
Upscale restaurants with full banquet facilities offering gourmet international cuisine

Executive Chef – Managed a staff of up to 44. Oversaw all kitchen and food operations for 2 restaurants, and assisted in managing others in corporation, including opening a new facility. Negotiated with vendors on food supplies of up to $4.8M annually. Spearheaded purchase of commercial vehicle for catering and transport of perishable goods. Personally traveled to Boston weekly to select fresh produce and fish. Developed wine list and menu. Supervised catering for events accommodating up to 400 people. Conducted budgeting, marketing, and financial/cost analyses.

- ★ Earned *Best Fine Dining in Farmington Valley Award.*
- ★ Achieved optimum food service operating costs for the corporation at a critical juncture:
  - Kept restaurant food costs at **25.5%** versus industry standard of **32%–34%,** and owner goal of **30%.**
  - Maintained whole staff labor costs at **26%** versus industry standard of **30%.**
- ★ Streamlined all kitchen operations and set up a commissary unit for 5 restaurants that provided the necessary structure for the corporation to run as profitably as possible and fueled its future growth.

MAX'S OF MANCHESTER, Hartford, CT — 2000–2004
Three-star fine dining restaurant with eclectic international cuisine

Executive Chef – Managed daily operations with a staff of 25. Trained new hires and retrained existing staff on food presentation techniques and wine decanting. Revitalized internship program for students from local schools, colleges, and universities. Managed dessert production. Oversaw purchasing, menu development, and wine selections. Attended weekly management meetings and conducted monthly staff meetings.

- ★ Nominated *Best Chef: Connecticut* from the James Beard Foundation, 2002–2004.
- ★ Leveled food services expenses across 4 categories while preserving quality and service:
  - Maintained restaurant food costs at **32%,** compared to industry standard of **34–36%.**
  - Controlled restaurant labor costs at **17%** in line with industry standard of **17%–20%.**
- ★ Featured in numerous local newspapers and in both *Gourmet* and *Bon Appetit* on multiple topics including seasonal menus, restaurant critique surveys, and charity events.

(continued)

(continued)

DAVID L. WINSTON **Page 2 of 2**

ELENA'S ON THE GREEN, Westchester, NY 1998–2000
Upscale Italian-American restaurant with $3.5 million in annual revenues

Executive Chef – Provided hands-on expertise in areas that included menu planning, cost-control and analysis, staffing, budgeting, and marketing. Supervised entire restaurant staff of 22.

- ★ Earned Best Upscale Restaurant in Westchester County Award in 2000.
- ★ Controlled food and operating expenses while enhancing food quality and improving kitchen techniques:
  - Maintained restaurant food costs at **33%**, in line with industry standard of **32%–34%.**
  - Cut kitchen labor costs to **10.5%,** far surpassing industry standard of **17%–18%**
- ★ Won recognition for several eclectic entrees, with recipes published in local cookbooks.

WHITE DIAMOND BEACH & TENNIS RESORT, Sanibel, FL 1995–1997
Five-star diamond luxury resort ranked as #3 tennis resort in the US and #2 in the world

Executive Sous-Chef/Assistant Pastry Chef – Under direction of executive chef, managed kitchen staff of up to 60 and functions that included scheduling, menu planning, and purchasing for a resort with 5 different restaurants and $10M in yearly revenues. Assisted pastry chef with delicate pastry preparation, baking, cake decorating, and menu planning for PattiGeorges and Michael's on East, affiliated restaurants.

- ★ Received Florida Wine Spectator Award for 1995–1997.
- ★ Instrumental in keeping expenses in check while preserving reputation for excellence and quality:
  - Lowered banquet food costs to **29.75%,** below industry standard of **32%.**
  - Kept restaurant food costs at **33.5%**, in line with industry standard of **34-36**%.
  - Evened out banquet labor costs to **4.5%**, in line with industry standard of **4%–6%.**
  - Held kitchen labor costs at **17.25%** versus industry standard of **17%–20%.**

CAFÉ MADELAINE'S/ MADELAINE'S RESTAURANT, Providence RI 1991–1995
Family-style Italian-American restaurant with $1.75million in annual revenues

Sous-Chef/Line Cook – Helped owner with preparation of all foods, assisting chef/owner with ordering, organization of kitchen staff, and menu planning. Augmented culinary skills and gained hands-on business experience to advance professional career in culinary arts and hospitality. Assisted in planning, development, and construction of a new restaurant.

PROFESSIONAL DEVELOPMENT & ADDITIONAL SKILLS

Certified Food Safety Manager (CFSM)

Fluent in French and Spanish, conversant in Italian

Computer proficiencies include: MS Word, Excel, Outlook Express, ACT, Key Gourmet, and Eventmaster

VOLUNTEER & COMMUNITY SERVICE

Avid participant in charitable events that include Taste of the Nation – *Share Our Strength,* March of Dimes - *Chefs for Healthy Babies*, Dana Farber Cancer Institute – *Jimmy Fund,* Habitat for Humanity, Ronald McDonald House, and many others.

40

Specialty Area: Manufacturing
Writer: Tanya Taylor

SHIRLEY A. EDWARDS

Innovative Quality Assurance Manager

LEADERSHIP PROFILE

Dedicated Quality Assurance Professional with nearly 10 years of successful career progression in quality optimization and operations management. Proven performer who transitions easily from vision and strategy to implementation and follow through. Focused on adhering to organizational missions and philosophy while positively impacting bottom line and daily performance. Recipient of multiple company awards for superior leadership, technical expertise, and innovative contributions.

• Quality Control • Product Development • Vendor Relations •
• Technical Analysis • Internal Auditing • Project Management •
• Performance Testing • Budget Planning • Process Improvement •
• Problem Resolution • Cost Control • Team Building v

KEY PERFORMANCE INDICATORS

- Spearheaded ISO9001 certification project; certification granted on first attempt.
- Stabilized vendor relations, smoothing product flow; increased revenue by 7%.
- Implemented process refinement, improving discard rate from 18% to 2%.
- Instituted team concept work philosophy, doubling staff performance efficiency.
- Elevated total product quality by 10% through strict adherence to methodologies.
- Increased customer satisfaction by 20% by implementing timely delivery process.
- Authored standard operating procedures manual for 100% training consistency.
- Conducted plant visits and tours for customers, elevating company credibility.
- Initiated installation of computerized audit stations, reducing test time by 24%.
- Interfaced with senior managers, attaining highest profits in 5 years.

Shirley A. Edwards

H. (416) 519-7775 ❖ shirleyedwards@aol.com ❖ C. (416) 647-7775
❖ 415 Willowdale Avenue Unit 807 ❖ Toronto ON M2N 5B4 ❖

(continued)

(continued)

SHIRLEY A. EDWARDS

Page 2

CAREER DIGEST

ABC METALS, Concord ON **1998–Present**
North American manufacturer of thermoplastic injection-moulded components and assemblies specifically for the automotive industry offering 30 leading product lines. Annual revenues in excess of $180 million. A division of the worldwide Fortune 200 Company, ABC Tool Works.

Quality Control Supervisor 2005–Present
Promoted to direct and lead a 23-person team of Technicians and Assemblers responsible for quality assurance and acceptance testing for the various lines of products. Act as a hands-on leader and mentor to staff while maintaining positive relationships with vendors and customers.
Career Advancement:

- Identified as the leading successor for the Quality Control Manager role.

Quality Technician 2000–2005
Appointed to perform a variety of inspection-related duties and testing on incoming materials and outgoing products to ensure compliance with quality assurance system requirements. Analyzed and compiled data for the preparation of statistical reports.
Career Advancement:

- Promoted to Quality Control Supervisor through outstanding performance.

Machine Operator 1998–2000
Hired to operate and maintain conventional, special-purpose, and injection-moulding machinery. Responsible for setting up all machines to produce quality products.
Career Advancement:

- Appointed as Quality Technician. Recognized for dedication and taking iniative.

EDUCATION

Certificate - *Certified ISO 9001 Auditor,* *York University* 2006

- Achieved honourable standing while working on a full-time basis.

Certificate - *Business and Commerce,* *Durham School of Business* 2000

- Awarded Durham Leaders Bursary for outstanding academic achievement.

COMPUTER SKILLS

Expert computer proficiency in MS Office programs and quality control systems.

Shirley A. Edwards

H. (416) 519-7775 ❖ shirleyedwards@aol.com ❖ C. (416) 647-7775
❖ 415 Willowdale Avenue Unit 807 ❖ Toronto ON M2N 5B4 ❖

41

Specialty Area: Manufacturing
Writer: Tom Albano

RICHARD MILLINGTON

1717 Culver Court
Dublin, OH 43071

Cell: (614) 515-2222
milling@hotmail.com

MANUFACTURING EXECUTIVE

OPERATIONS • PRODUCTION PLANNING • ENGINEERING • LOGISTICS

Results-oriented manufacturing professional with an extensive track record of delivering visible improvements in productivity and cost control within high-volume manufacturing facilities. Expertise in implementing lean manufacturing methodologies to turn around under-productive work processes, reduce costs, and drive sustainable "big-picture" change. Demonstrate strong leadership qualities in developing high-performance teams that are self-managed, accountable, quality-oriented, and highly productive. Extensive knowledge of plastics bonding and packaging equipment.

CORE LEADERSHIP QUALIFICATIONS

- Team Leadership & Development
- Budgeting & Cost Control
- P&L Management
- Workflow Optimization
- Operations Start-Up
- Process Reengineering
- Lean Manufacturing
- Self-Managing Work Teams
- Regulatory Compliance
- On-Time Delivery / Distribution
- Operations Management
- New Product Development
- Quality Assurance
- Automated Process Controls
- Project Management

PROFESSIONAL EXPERIENCE

ACE PRODUCTS, INC. Clinton, MA — August 1995 to May 2007

OPERATIONS MANAGER – Mexico City, Mexico *(10/00-03/07)*
Selected by company President to orchestrate the start-up of this new contract manufacturing facility that replaced two existing manufacturing operations, producing medical devices, located in the US and Europe. Fully accountable for the production, maintenance, and engineering departments with direct management responsibility for 3 department heads and 8 engineers with a total complement of 420 employees.

- Served as planning team lead, directing all phases of start-up operation from construction to obtaining product approvals, covering regulatory requirements related to ISO9002 and QSR.
- Coordinated the seamless transfer of equipment and products from facilities in the US and Europe that entailed the full-cycle process from validation to market approval. Completed the transfer and installation of all equipment in accordance with established company goals and guidelines.
- Recruited and trained all manpower resources for the production, maintenance, and engineering departments.
- Created high performance team-based system by setting clear direction and focusing on key objectives.
- Maintained full accountability for the maintenance of all manufacturing equipment, spare parts, and supplies.

PRODUCTION SITE MANAGER – Newark, NJ *(08/95-10/00)*
Charged with P&L management, strategic planning, staffing, and operations of this 24 x 7 automated production facility, with annual revenues of $30 million, that manufactured medical devices for Burlington Pharmaceuticals. Maintained full responsibility for new product introduction / validation as well as the transfer of equipment and products from remote locations. Supervised 25 production and maintenance personnel including 8 engineers.

- Implemented automated procedures for packaging process that reduced direct labor headcount by 31% and resulted in a cost savings of $280,000.
- Secured certified supplier status with Burlington, reducing the delivery time for products distributed to the US and European markets by 50%.
- Maintained full accountability for the maintenance of the facility and all manufacturing equipment.
- Filled in as acting plant manager at sister plant during management transition over 10-week period.

(continued)

(continued)

RICHARD MILLINGTON **RESUME PAGE TWO**

PROFESSIONAL EXPERIENCE
(Continued)

MEDICAL PRODUCTS CORPORATION, Cleveland, OH April 1990 to April 1995

PROCESS & PRODUCT ENGINEERING MANAGER – Guadalajara, Mexico

Managed Industrial Engineering Department of 6 engineers responsible for the introduction and approval of new products for this medical device manufacturing facility with more than 900 employees and annual sales of $200 million. Fully accountable for plant validation processes, products, and equipment.

- Implemented best practices in managing I.E. department to achieve savings at 5% over SVOP.
- Utilized lean manufacturing methodologies to develop and implement new standards for material workflow and production that reduced AOQL for finished products from 9% to 1% within 3-year period.
- Orchestrated the transfer of a large number of products from the European facility to Mexico, resulting in a cost savings of approximately $12MM.
- Collaborated with Corporate Product Development Group to implement product design changes to meet corporate cost and quality goals.
- Reduced size of packaging for all products that resulted in an immediate savings of over $320k.
- Revamped management structure by introducing new Group Leader positions that reduced number of production supervisors by 60% while significantly improving workflow efficiency.

GEORGIA PACIFIC CORP., Bowling Green, KY March 1987 to March 1990

PLANT MANAGER

Directed the daily operations of this high-performance paper-plate manufacturing facility with 174 employees. Managed five direct reports in the areas of Finance, Human Resources, Technical Support, Operations, and Planning and Logistics.

- Turned around under-performing plant by implementing continuous improvements in safety, quality, production, and cost savings to the level where it became the most profitable of the 9 Georgia Pacific manufacturing facilities in the nation.
- Guided plant through complete management change and restructuring, filling key positions with inside people that included a Human Resource Manager, Operations Manager, and Plant Technical Manager.
- Applied consistent performance management to achieved maximum machine uptime and continuity of schedule, driving reliability rate to 99%.
- Significantly enhanced productivity over original specifications by improving individual machine output by 10% and increasing the number of machines by 16%.

EDUCATION

Master of Science in Industrial Engineering
Worcester Polytechnic Institute

Bachelor of Science in Industrial Engineering
Stevens Institute of Technology, Hoboken, NJ

42

Specialty Area: Not-for-Profit and Association Management
Writer: Janice Worthington

SENTA WEIL

3841 McCarley Drive
Columbus, OH 43230-1120
www.sentaweiloutreach.com
Cell: 614-476-4023
sentaweil@outreach.com

ASSOCIATION MANAGEMENT ♦ COMMUNITY AFFAIRS ♦ PUBLIC RELATIONS

Recognized **Public Relations Consultant, Community Activist, Political Campaign Manager, Publisher/Editor, College Professor,** and **Fundraiser.** Visionary leader blending **people skills**, program development, and project management abilities with achievements in **communications** and **consensus building**. Superb strategist adept at managing execution and strategy simultaneously.

AREAS OF EXPERTISE

- General Management
- Relationship Building
- Staff Development
- Project Development
- Customer Service
- Sales & Marketing
- Employee Relations
- Needs Assessment
- Strategic Planning & Initiatives
- Communication & Client Management
- Troubleshooting & Problem Solving
- Policies & Procedure Development
- Public Relations & Media Relations
- Program Development & Implementation
- Contract Review & Recommendations
- Staff Training & Development
- Productivity Improvement
- Startups & Turnarounds
- Creative & Strategic Selling
- Project Planning & Analysis
- Recruiting & Staffing
- Budgeting & Expense Reports
- Project Risk Analysis
- Performance Evaluations

CAREER HIGHLIGHTS

- Directed the advertising, sales, marketing, news staff, and circulation of three statewide newspapers with a combined circulation of 400,000 and represented the newspapers at local and state civic and social events.
- First African-American female assistant administrator/head of operations of City of Columbus Refuse Collection Division overseeing over 600 personnel, 23 supervisors, and 6 managers at 4 locations in greater Columbus area.
- Recipient of over 85 awards from private, public, and nonprofit institutions including Governor of Ohio, Columbus City Council, United Way, the Ohio Civil Rights Commission, and Ohio House of Representatives.
- Taught undergraduate and graduate business courses at Franklin University, University of Phoenix Online, DeVry Institute of Technology, Cardean University Online, and Kaplan University.
- Wrote speeches, composed scripts, created campaign literature, and provided strategic consulting services to campaigns of both Democratic and Republican candidates.
- Served as a panelist for the United States Commission on Civil Rights Affirmative Action and contributed to local and Federal affirmative action legislation.

RECENT EXPERIENCE CHRONICLE

VOLUNTEERS OF AMERICA ... Columbus, OH — January 2000 to June 2005

National, nonprofit organization providing local human service programs and opportunities for individual and community involvement; from rural America to inner-city neighborhoods, organization provides outreach programs dealing with today's most pressing social needs. **www.voa.org**

President and Chief Executive Officer

Provided comprehensive oversight for administrative/support and program functions comprising finance, human resources, internal and external communications, fund development, and property and asset management; primary responsibility included direct and indirect contributions to revenue and profit growth of organization via implementation of planned giving and major gifts programs, cultivation of donor relationships, identification of new business ventures, and determination of new funding opportunities with local, state, and federal funding sources. Primary contact for national office, subsidiaries, and affiliates.

(continued)

(continued)

Senta Weil

Page 2 of 2

Administered $10 million annual budget employed to forecast revenue and expenses for ensuing fiscal year; prepared and monitored budget while simultaneously incorporating periodic adjustments to ensure projections. **Developed, communicated, and implemented operations and management strategy (including relative programs to execute strategy);** accountable for operations consistent with national charter and strategic plan. Analyzed and assessed operational and financial performance with outcomes and recommendations provided for Board of Trustees.

Recruited and collaborated with board members; built and managed relationships with donors, media, business, and legislative leaders; and worked in concert with community organizations as well as local, state, and federal agencies to facilitate strategic vision and direction; promoted positive community relations through active involvement in community affairs.

- **Income performance included:** Increase of major gifts/planned giving 9% of budget resulting in 111% growth; increase of thrift stores/auto donation 79% of budget resulting in 18% growth; increase in government grants 12% of budget resulting in 62% growth.
- **Launched 2001 opening of Logan (Hocking County) center, expanding services to 150 unduplicated recipients;** services provided children and adults access to technology in addition to tools for success through literacy, GED, education, and employability services. *Initiative part of mission to expand organization throughout 37-county service area.*
- **Saved $50,000 annually via development of performance goals for key management staff;** goals, established annually and evaluated quarterly, were measurable and used in staff evaluations.
- **Lowered costs $100,000 annually by removing collection boxes for donated goods (drop boxes), resulting in reduction in trash bills.**

COMMUNITY ACTION AGENCY OF SOUTH CENTRAL MISSOURI ... Branson, MO 1992 to 1999

Non-profit organization dedicated to promoting economic and social opportunities to assist citizens of Barris, Branch, Calhoun, and St. Joseph counties. Organization assisted more than 15,400 children, seniors, and low-income individuals via 300 staff and operating budget eclipsing $7 million. **www.caascat.org**

Chief Executive Officer

Spearheaded implementation of strategic plans and policies developed by Board of Directors; scope of role steered daily operations including budget forecasting and controls, strategic planning and implementation, human resources management (direct reports included 11 administrative and support program staff), and administration of financial and physical resources.

- **During tenure, grant revenue performed at 99% of budget resulting in 87% growth with contributions revenue performing at 1% of budget resulting in 25% growth;** within first year of assuming position, reduced entire **$500,000** operating deficit and maintained positive fund balance throughout tenure.
- **Elevated services provided to recipients via relationship building and strong collaboration with other human service providers and private organizations in development of community-based strategies;** collaborated with grass-roots organizations providing skills empowering citizens to develop youth programs within local communities, including training, advocacy skills, grant writing and technical assistance.
- **Coordinated expansion of Head Start program (targets prevention and early intervention objectives for children aged three to five) to improve accommodation of more eligible at-risk children.**
- **Improved overall performance with implementation of performance matrices for all programs and services;** matrices enabled management to periodically and quantitatively evaluate and report impact of programs on customer base. Ultimately resulted in increased local, state, and federal funding.

EDUCATION

CAPITAL UNIVERSITY – Bexley, OH
MBA (1982)

SOUTHERN UNIVERSITY – Baton Rouge, LA
BA, Political Science/Government (1973)

43

Specialty Area: Not-for-Profit and Association Management
Writer: Deanne Arnath

JACK SMITHERS

4406 Lonesome Dove Trail ▪ Fort Worth, Texas 76119 ▪ 817.763.7089 ▪ jsmithers@aol.com

SUMMARY OF QUALIFICATIONS

Over eight years of leadership experience in the cattle industry as an elected officer. Positively impacted associations' membership growth, retention, and participation. Effective communicator and team builder with planning, organizational, and negotiation strengths as well as the ability to lead, reach consensus, establish goals, and attain results. MS in Leadership Education and BS in Animal Science. Available for travel and relocation.

PROFESSIONAL EXPERIENCE AND ACCOMPLISHMENTS

LEADERSHIP

- Elected as President of the MSU Block & Bridle Club to lead committee chair elections, recruit new members, hold informal and formal initiations, direct participation in local, state, and national events, solicit event sponsors, organize fundraising events, and coordinate club's involvement in community service activities. Succeeded with the largest pledge class in club's recent history.
- Selected by the Nebraska Beef Council to lead start-to-finish coordination of the 2004 Nebraska Youth Beef Leadership Symposium in collaboration with NU's Department of Animal Science and Department of Agricultural Leadership. Scope of involvement included budget management, site selection, coordination of attendees and presentors, and travel/accommodations planning. Garnered praise from symposium participants.
- Demonstrated success in feedyard management, including animal health, animal nutrition, pen management, and personnel management with Pinal Feeding Company—one of the largest cattle feeding operations in the southwest with over 150,000 head of cattle.

SALES AND COMMUNICATIONS

- Successfully executed strategy for launch of Range and Pasture products into Tennessee market for top-tier agricultural company, Dow AgroSciences. Developed extensive contact list of local dealers and retailers for full-time sales representative. Effectively responded to new customer inquiries regarding product use.
- Researched and authored papers on "An Analysis of the NCBA's Response to the BSE Crisis in 2004"—a search of the relevant literature on the topic of crisis, crisis management approaches, and the Bovine Spongiform Encephalopathy crisis, and "My Vision of the US Beef Cattle Industry in 2025."

PUBLIC POLICY

- Worked closely with National Cattlemen's Beef Association Center for Public Policy staff to research policy issues, organize issues and strategic communications, and write policy briefs, fact sheets, talking points, and other documents related to cattle-industry policy. Attended hearings at federal agencies, meetings on Capitol Hill, and NCBA Summer Conference. Supported assembly of the NCBA policy book.
- Served as expert and technical consultant for U.S. Customs & Border Protection in the areas of inspection, intelligence, analysis, examination, and law enforcement activities related to the importation of agricultural/ commercial commodities and conveyances at port of entry.

PROFESSIONAL WORK HISTORY

U.S. CUSTOMS & BORDER PROTECTION, *DFW, Texas* — 2006–Present
Agricultural Specialist

SMITHERS FARMS, *Shubuta, Mississippi* — 2004–2006
Assistant Ranch Manger

NEBRASKA BEEF COUNCIL, *Lincoln, Nebraska* — 2003–2004
Project Coordinator

(continued)

(continued)

JACK SMITHERS

4406 Lonesome Dove Trail ▪ Fort Worth, Texas 76119 ▪ 817.763.7089 ▪ jsmithers@aol.com

PINAL FEEDING COMPANY, *Maricopa, Arizona* 2001–2002
Management Trainee

DOW AGROSCIENCES, *Nashville, Tennessee* 2001
Range & Pasture Intern

NATIONAL CATTLEMEN'S BEEF ASSOCIATION, *Washington DC* 2000
Public Policy Intern

EDUCATION AND SPECIALIZED TRAINING

UNIVERSITY OF NEBRASKA – LINCOLN, *Lincoln, Nebraska* 2004
MS, Leadership Education with Minor in Business Management (GPA 3.76)
Critical coursework included the following:

- *Environmental Leadership*
- *Leadership in Organizations*
- *Supervisory Leadership*
- *Organizational Behavior*
- *Advanced Teaching Strategies*
- *Human Resource Planning*
- *Environmental Law*
- *Statistical Methods*

MISSISSIPPI STATE UNIVERSITY, *Starkville, Mississippi* 2000
BS, Animal Science
Critical coursework included the following:

- *Agricultural Marketing*
- *Advanced Livestock Evaluation*
- *Livestock Nutritional Requirements*
- *Livestock Management Practices*
- *Animal Breeding*
- *Beef Cattle Science*
- *Forages / Pasture*
- *Meat Processing*

JONES COUNTY JUNIOR COLLEGE, *Ellisville, Mississippi* 1997
AA, Animal Science

AWARDS AND SPECIAL RECOGNITION

Collegiate Livestock Leaders Institute Award
Graduate Assistantship Award
Graduate Tuition Fellowship Award
Mississippi Cattlemen's Association Scholarship

PROFESSIONAL MEMBERSHIPS AND ACTIVITIES

Current Member, National Cattlemen's Beef Association
Lifetime Member, Mississippi Cattlemen's Association
Past President, Mississippi Junior Cattlemen's Association
Past President, MSU Block & Bridle Club
Former Vice President, Society for Agricultural Leadership
Former Board of Directors, Collegiate Cattlemen's Club

44

Specialty Area: Not-for-Profit and Association Management
Writer: Judith Vince

Carrie M. Bradley

1895 Charles Avenue
Parlton, NJ 07983

cmbradley@ggmail.net

Cell: 908-805-7682
Home: 908-949-4156

PROFESSIONAL PROFILE

Detail-oriented, organized, high-energy, compassionate, and diplomatic professional with strong management and multi-tasking skills. Exceptional public relations ability. Customer focused. Skilled communicator and public speaker. PC knowledgeable.

QUALIFICATIONS SUMMARY

Federal and private fund and program management, evidence-based program administration, outcomes measurement, Geriatric and Women's Health program development, health promotion and wellness program coordination, curriculum development, community and state agency liaison, community outreach, caseload management, grant writing, newsletter editor, facility ambassador, program marketing, quality improvement processes, resource management, budgeting, cost containment, policies and procedures, planning, change management, public and private partnering, project management.

SELECTED ACCOMPLISHMENTS

- Served on the State of NJ HealthEASE Advisory Board from 2002–2007, piloting the program in Ocean County. As a result of favorable satisfaction surveys, the County Office of Senior Services awarded an additional $5,000 in grant funding to carry the program into 2008. Due to the success of the program, received an invitation to speak at the NJ State HealthEASE conference in October 2005.

- As the Director of the Center for Women's Health, successfully ran a $250,000 grant-funded program entitled BONES (Basic Osteoporosis Nutrition Education & Screening) from 2003–2007. As a result of the success of the program, received a three-year appointment to ICO (Interagency Council on Osteoporosis) from Commissioner of Health, Dr. Frank Loeb, in May 2006.

- Instrumental in securing the award of a mini grant from the State of NJ to Arlington Medical Center for the Center for Women's Health in 2005. This grant was issued for the continuation of the Healthy Bones program to be offered in six counties. Selected by the State of NJ to be one of three trainers for the Healthy Bones program.

- Served on the NJ State Commission on Aging Health Promotion Subcommittee from 2003–2007. Most recently assigned to a workgroup charged with developing a new program to be entitled "Blueprint for Healthy Aging."

- As the 2006 Program Director for the Annual Women's Health Day Fair for Arlington Medical Center, set a new record high for number of attendees at the event—600.

CAREER HIGHLIGHTS

Saint Augustus Health Care System **1991 to 2007**

Arlington Medical Center, Capetown, New Jersey (4/02–2/07)
Director, Regency House - A Center for Senior Health, and The Center for Women's Health
Directed the administrative and operational activities. Identified new grant opportunities. Composed RFPs. Developed and managed grant-funded programs for health promotion and wellness including lectures, seminars, support groups, screenings, and health fairs at multiple sites.

(continued)

(continued)

Carrie M. Bradley Page 2

Riley Medical Center, Ridge Lake, New Jersey (7/97–4/02)
Arlington Medical Center, Capetown, New Jersey (7/97–4/02)
Director Care Coordination/Senior Outreach
Administrative and operational responsibility for the Care Coordination department and the Senior Outreach M.O.R.E. (Multicultural Outreach and Resources for the Elderly) project. Development of outcomes measurement tools and protocols. Chairperson for system-wide Care Coordination sub-committees.

Arlington Medical Center, Capetown, New Jersey (6/95–7/97)
Manager, Regency House – A Center for Senior Health
Managed staff and day-to-day operations for a 35,000 member program. Hosted monthly radio show.

Arlington Medical Center, Capetown, New Jersey (3/91–6/95)
Case Manager – Care Coordination Department
Provided fee-for-service geriatric home care management. Conducted in-home needs assessment including evaluation of social supports, ADLs and IADLs. Developed and implemented treatment plans. Monitored continuity of care.

Farmington Senior Care Center, Ridge Lake, NJ **1990 to 1991**
Assistant Administrator/Admissions Director
Assisted with facility planning, operations management, and fiscal responsibilities.

Longview Nursing Home, Ridge Lake, NJ **1988 to 1990**
Social Worker
Resident advocate assuring that emotional, physical, and social needs were met.

ACADEMIC QUALIFICATIONS

Roger Williams University, Bristol, RI
Master of Social Work – Administration, Policy, and Planning

Quinnipiac College, Hartford, CT
Bachelor of Science – Program Distinction Social Work, Gerontology Certificate

Parlton County College, Parlton, NJ
Associate in Science – Community Services Technician, Minor in Gerontology

Rutgers University School of Social Work, New Brunswick, NJ
Certificate – Human Services Management Program

Licensed Social Worker – State of NJ License # 89AT92987

AFFILIATIONS

NJ Commission on Aging Health Promotion Subcommittee
Advisory Board Member for the NJ State Department of Health & Senior Services, HealthEASE
ICO (Interagency Council on Osteoporosis)
Ridge County Office of Senior Services Wellness Coalition
Interfaith Volunteer Caregivers of Southern NJ
Easterley Court University Social Work Advisory Board
Geriatric Health Alliance
National Association of Social Workers

45

Specialty Area: Public Sector/Government
Writer: Don Orlando

Mark Kliner
26 2nd Avenue Old Kinderhook, New York 12100 mk1000@yahoo.com 518.555.5555

WHAT I CAN OFFER **TOPLINE** AS YOUR NEWEST **PROTECTIVE SECURITY ADVISOR**

❑ **Leadership** that people naturally accept as their own good ideas ❑ **Managing risk** better and faster than our adversaries ❑ **Building coalitions** between stakeholders that share our critical interests ❑ **Bringing in exceptional results** under trying conditions ❑ **Thinking**, nearly instinctively, **like our customers—and our adversaries**

RECENT WORK HISTORY WITH EXAMPLES OF PROBLEMS SOLVED

❑ *Hired away by COO to serve as* Business Continuity Advisor and **Business Security Manager,** Trans Asia Petroleum Indonesia Oct 03 - Mar 07

Trans Asia is one of the world's largest energy companies.

THE CONTEXT

Asked to build and lead security operations in one of the **most volatile environments on the globe**. Coordinated security for more than 4,000 people and billions of dollars in investment including more than 300 off- and on-shore facilities; ground, air, and sea transportation assets; and an office campus. Revolts, insurrections, tribal warfare, and terrorism were common. Served as direct reporting official for a national business security manager, Liquid Natural Gas Project Security Manager, an offshore operations chief, and an in-house intelligence and anti-fraud consultant.

THE RESULTS

Quickly found, and countered, inflated contractor service agreements in the security system I inherited. Enforced new performance standards. ***Payoffs:*** Documented **savings exceeded $132M**. Cut consultant costs in half. Won the Annual Award for Security Excellence—one of only two such awards given that year throughout our worldwide company.

Got control of security at 34 airports from Jakarta International Airport to unimproved jungle air strips. Recruited a top expert in aviation security—when such expertise was very hard to find. Established alliances with companies that used the same facilities we did. ***Payoffs:*** Much better security for our people and cargo with **25 percent lower operating costs**.

Persuaded management to replace inefficient employees by proving labor cost savings. Built and maintained a network of "honest brokers" to find, attract, recruit, and retain the best people in key security positions. ***Payoffs:*** The security managers I recruited soon started to pass on their work ethic and knowledge to the rest of our security staff. **Performance rose and stayed high**.

Revamped old, jargon-filled, cumbersome contingency policy. Quickly assigned specific responsibilities, then tested portions of the plans. ***Payoffs:* Earned confidence** of staff members and their families. Number of **urgent calls fell 50 percent**. Productivity rose because virtually all families agreed to stay during unsettled times—down from the nearly 50 percent that usually left on short notice.

Used a team of diverse investigators to limit attacks and sabotage incidents affecting our assets. Found and **stopped a black market** that forced us to buy back equipment stolen from us. ***Payoffs:*** Once I rationalized procurement contracts, competition among our vendors increased, quality went up, costs went down.

*More indicators of performance **Topline** can use …*

(continued)

(continued)

Mark Kliner **Protective Security Advisor** 518.555.5555

Thinned the ranks of 600 undertrained, poorly paid, and badly led guards. Built relationships with other companies that employed local guards. Researched the law to avoid unpleasant confrontations. Then sold my plan to limit expensive overtime. Tied salary to performance. ***Payoffs:*** **Saved $2.1M** in contract labor costs over 3 years. Our guards were better trained and led than ever before.

Built a **first-of-its-kind, national community security operation**. My teams traveled to dozens of remote villages selling the idea of giving people power to control their own security. We started with those who had little skill, few ways to communicate with their neighbors, and a long history of inter-tribal warfare. ***Payoffs:*** Made remarkable progress in 16 months. Took special care to respect human rights and the environment so **NGOs helped us build good will**.

- Military Attaché for Defense Programs, US Embassy, Jakarta, Indonesia Oct 99 - Oct 03

THE CONTEXT

Recruited by the defense attaché to run security assistance operations offered to the Indonesian armed forces.

THE RESULTS

Helped turn around deteriorating military-to-military relations: military sales and international training were at record lows. Found the very best in Indonesia's armed forces and set up useful contacts for these future leaders. ***Payoffs:*** Planted fundamental ideas that make military organizations predictable. Most important: we **maintained contacts** with key government officials—the very people who played key roles as we ramped up anti-terrorist efforts after the Bali bombings of 2002.

- Chief of Army and Training Divisions, US Embassy, Jakarta, Indonesia Jan 96 - Oct 99

THE RESULTS

Ran this program so well it was "bullet proof" when unfounded allegations launched a GAO investigation. Our records were so complete, our **compliance so well documented** that auditors couldn't find a single discrepancy during their entire extended visit. ***Payoffs:*** Less than one month after the visit, GAO cleared us completely.

- Politico-Military Advisor to the Joint Staff, The Pentagon, Washington, DC Jan 94 - Dec 96

THE CONTEXT

Helped develop U. S. policy for Southeast Asia. Represented the Chairman of the Joint Chiefs of Staff in interagency policy-setting meetings with representatives from across the executive branch of government.

THE RESULTS

Got up to speed fast when new President ordered an in-depth policy review of military-to-military relations—just 60 days after I started this job. Uncovered which of 40 action officers would be my strongest allies to preserve our military relations with Indonesia—even as some powerful figures pushed to end all such activities. ***Payoffs:*** **Fielded tough questions from** the senior leadership up to and including **the White House**. The main thrust of my compromise proposal was adopted; threatening legislation never appeared

Mark Kliner **Protective Security Advisor** 518.555.5555

EDUCATION & PROFESSIONAL DEVELOPMENT

- ❑ MA, **Political Science**, North Carolina State University, Raleigh, North Carolina 88
  *Selected from the top ten percent of hundreds of Army officers to receive a **full scholarship**. **Completed** this **two year course in just 14 months**.*
- ❑ BA, **Political Science**, The Citadel, Charleston, South Carolina 78
  *Chosen from 4,000 applicants as 1 of 40 to receive a **full scholarship**.*
- o **Senior Security Managers' Course,** Group 4 FALK (a leading private security firm Sep 05
  This two-week course covered technological trends in physical security with special emphasis on dealing with contractors.
- o Foreign Military Sales Management Course, US Army, three months 95
  Covered the application of acquisition policies in foreign military sales.
- o Foreign Officers' Area Course, JFK Center for Special Warfare, six months 92
  The main thrust of this course was a comprehensive political, economic, and cultural review to analyze information regarding terrorist threats.

PROFESSIONAL RECOGNITION

- o **Annual Award for Security Excellence**, Trans Asia Petroleum 06
  One of only two organizations in this worldwide company to be recognized for an exceptional security program that saved our company nearly $87M in the first year alone. In addition our anti-fraud efforts saved and recovered an additional $24M.
- o Commended by the **White House** for supporting the President during Asia-Pacific Conference 97
- o Decorated for my work in the **White House-sponsored Comprehensive Security Review** 95

LANGUAGE CAPABILITIES

- ❑ Read, write, speak, and **think in fluent Malay** and Indonesian.

IT SKILLS

- o Expert in proprietary **personnel, training, travel, contracting, and budget management** software suite, **Getting Security Right, a proprietary security-incident software that uses diagnostic tools to develop threat trends,** Word, and advanced Internet search protocols
- o Capable with Excel and PowerPoint

PROFESSIONAL AFFILIATIONS

- o Member, American Society for Industrial Security (ASIS) International Since 01
  ASIS International, with more than 33,000 members, is the preeminent international organization for professionals responsible for security, including managers and directors of security.

46

Specialty Area: Retail
Writer: Louise Kursmark

HERMAN RICHARD hrichard@gmail.com • Mobile (82) 74 99 0091

Olympic Park Boulevard 75, #47B
Seoul 10110, South Korea

GLOBAL EXECUTIVE: RETAIL OPERATIONS

Managing Director • Chief Operating Officer • Business Unit Leader

High-performance change driver, repeatedly accelerating profit growth and delivering business transformation for multinational retail organizations. True leader able to build cross-cultural consensus and motivate individuals and teams to embrace change and strive for ambitious goals. Strategic thinker who rapidly analyzes complex operations, zeroes in on the most effective improvement opportunities, and executes initiatives across dispersed organizations to achieve rapid and sustainable results.

Global citizen, multilingual (French, English, German, Portuguese, Mandarin) and comfortable in diverse cultures.

Performance Highlights

- Turned around declining profitability to 30% EBIT growth and created business model that was adopted nationwide. *(Carrefour South Korea)*
- Built Carrefour's Macao operation from the ground up to 5 stores and repeated #1 sales performance. *(Carrefour Macao)*
- Developed blueprints for integrating retail operations into their unique local areas—building community goodwill, creating team-based culture, and encouraging diversity while boosting same-store sales and profitability *(Carrefour Switzerland, Macao, South Korea)*
- Build the fastest-growing sales agency in the country. *(AXA Switzerland)*

PROFESSIONAL EXPERIENCE

Carrefour

CARREFOUR **Europe and Asia, 1998–Present**
World's second-largest retailer, with $88B annual sales and 12,000+ stores in 30 countries.

Regional Director, Carrefour South Korea South Korea, 2006–Present

Drove performance turnaround—cutting costs, reducing waste, increasing productivity—to achieve record profitability and create operational model for entire organization. Assumed executive leadership of $275M region (8 stores, 3000 staff) with steadily eroding profit performance. Analyzed entire operation and developed aggressive improvement plan touching on all areas of labor and operations. Led change across the region, strengthening communication and implementing cross-functional work groups to build teamwork and reduce fear; succeeded in instilling customer focus and building a high-performance organization.

- Increased EBIT 30% in 2006 and 31% in 2007, delivering $4.6M additional profit to the company—the only region in the country to meet (and exceed) profit targets both years. Region has since become a pilot to boost EBIT country-wide.
- Launched a "total satisfaction program" that develops and motivates teams to deliver exceptional customer service. Designed systematic processes, surveys, training programs, and tools to evaluate performance.
- Slashed administrative costs 52% through business process improvement and back-office reengineering. Initiative has since been deployed country-wide.
- Cut average inventory days by 14%, more than 5% below country average.
- Created company standards and benchmarks for cost-cutting action in low-performing areas.

Manager, Carrefour Macao Macao, 2001–2006

Launched Carrefour into Macao and built the #1 sales performers in the region. Arrived in Macao alone with the challenge to oversee construction, ensure on-time start-up, recruit staff, and establish all HR, finance, and operational systems as the template for an expanding regional organization. Directly managed $30M, 400-employee store while creating and executing expansion and start-up strategy for the entire South Asia Region.

HERMAN RICHARD hrichard@gmail.com • Mobile (82) 74 99 0091

Manager, Carrefour Macao, continued

- Overcame resistance to introduction of foreign retailer into traditional Chinese neighborhood; gained trust and established positive reputation in the community.
- Used novel recruiting methods and team-building strategies to create a team of top-performing managers who fueled Macao growth from 1 to 5 stores in 5 years.
- Managed 100% local team with no English speakers; learned basic Portuguese and Mandarin Chinese to improve communications and establish credibility and trust.
- Built entire corporate organization (HR, recruitment, sales and marketing, business processes, accounting and finance) for South Asia Region; became a blueprint deployed for the entire operation in Asia-Pacific.
- After 1 year, analyzed and adjusted product mix and store layout to better meet customer expectations. Store became #1 in South Asia and first Carrefour store in the country to reach sales and net income targets.
- Led aggressive expansion, creating launch strategy for 4 new stores and hiring/training 200 managers and 1600 employees in 9 months. Directly managed opening of store that quickly became #1 in Macao.
- Delivered $15.9M/year savings by driving a business process reengineering initiative across the region.

Store Manager, Carrefour Bahn Canton Switzerland, 1998–2001

Led struggling store from breakeven to surging profitability while improving community and labor relations. Assumed leadership of undersized 25-year-old store with limited growth potential, located in an economically challenged area. Created and executed strategic plan to cut labor costs, eliminate waste, and boost store space and sales. Maneuvered adroitly in a difficult union environment.

- Drove up EBIT from break-even to $1.53M in 2000, on track to achieve $1.8M in 2001.
- Increased same-store sales 6.7% year-over-year.
- Successfully positioned the store as an asset to its community and gained rare unanimous approval for expansion from local authorities.
- Built an assertive diversity program promoting staff advancement and outreach to the community.
- Ousted antagonistic union from 4 of 5 board seats by introducing a new union program and transitioning core group of employees to the new union.

AXA **Switzerland, 1995–1998**
$84B global insurance and financial management company

Deputy Regional Sales Manager 1996–1998

Transformed faltering sales region to the fastest-growing in the country. Accepted turnaround assignment to lead a $120M region with sales staff of 250. Analyzed entire operation and defined comprehensive restructuring to drive sales growth, cut costs, and improve customer service. Solicited input from staff and clearly defined expectations to create a new, high-performance culture.

- Ranked #1 in sales growth for first quarter 1998. Reduced operating costs 40% in 18 months.
- Replaced traditional salary plan with incentive and commission sales structure.
- Introduced new marketing tools and directed staff efforts toward relationship-building with key accounts.
- Launched an ambitious year-long training program to boost sales skills.

Sales Associate 1995–1996

Built sales agency from the ground up to $200,000 sales in one year.

EDUCATION

Master of Business Administration (MBA), 1994 – New York University, New York, NY
Bachelor of Arts in European Business (BAEB), 1986 – University of Geneva/University of London (joint program)

INDEX

L

M

N

S

T–U